P9-DXH-766

New Directions in European Historiography

New Directions
in European Historiography

BY GEORG G. IGGERS

With a Contribution by Norman Baker

Wesleyan University Press
MIDDLETOWN, CONNECTICUT

Library of Congress Cataloging in Publication Data

Iggers, Georg G., 1926–
    New directions in European historiography.

    Bibliography: p.
        1. Historiography–History. 2. Historians–Europe.
I. Baker, Norman, 1936–   , joint author. II. Title.
D13.I35   940′.07′2   75–12665
ISBN 0–8195–4084–6

Manufactured in the United States of America
First edition

Contents

Acknowledgements

THE PAST SEVERAL decades, but particularly the last ten to fifteen years, have seen a marked reorientation of historical studies both here and in Europe. Under the impact of the modern social sciences and of changing social and political realities, the methodological procedures, foci of interest, and explanatory conceptions which had guided a large segment of professional historical studies since the nineteenth century appeared increasingly inadequate to younger generations of historians. The following essays are not intended as a comprehensive assessment of present-day historical scholarship. They seek, however, to examine several of the more important directions in which European historians have gone in search of new paradigms for a history conceived as a historical social science.

Early versions of these essays were given as lectures at various universities and institutes in West Germany, France, and Poland during my sabbatical leave 1971–72. Each essay underwent repeated revision as a result of the discussions which followed these lectures as well as of the critical comments of colleagues to whom I sent parts of the manuscript during these past two years. I am thus indebted to a large number of persons for their advice and support. Professor Ernst Schulin invited me to present a very early formulation of the problems of these essays to his seminar at the Technische Universität in West Berlin; Professors K. F. Werner (German Historical Institute,

Paris), Manfred Schlenke (Mannheim), K.-G. Faber (Saarbrücken), Theodor Schieder (Cologne), and Werner Conze (Heidelberg) enabled me to submit early versions of the first chapter to the criticisms of their students and colleagues; Professor J. Kocka invited me to present the essay on the *Annales* at Münster; M. Jean Glénisson (École Pratique des Hautes Études, Sixième Section), Professors Jerzy Topolski (Poznán) and Imanuel Geiss (then at Hamburg) asked me to discuss drafts of what became the third chapter on recent West German historiography. I am grateful to M. Glénisson and John Day for introducing me to members of the *Annales* circle, to Professor Topolski for arranging conversations with Polish colleagues, and to Dr. Angelo Ara (Parma) for arranging such conversations in Italy. Dr. A. F. Grabski (Łodź and Warsaw) was particularly helpful in providing me with an introduction to the history of historiography in Poland.

Professors Richard Vann, George Nadel, and Harold Parker read early versions of the entire manuscript; Rudolf Vierhaus and Ernst Hinrichs, versions of the first three chapters. I found very useful the comments I received on early versions of the first chapter from Karl-Georg Faber, Manfred Schlenke, Jörn Rüsen, Hermann Wein, Dieter Groh, Fritz Ringer, Robert Pois, Jack Roth, and my colleagues Bert Hall and David Hollinger. John Day, Martin Siegel, William Keylor, Elizabeth Genovese, Dietrich Gerhard, Harry Paul, Ernst Schulin, Hans Albert, Robert Mandrou, and Karl-Georg Faber read versions of the chapter on the *Annales;* Jürgen Kocka, Imanuel Geiss, John Moses, and Horst Dippel read early versions of the third chapter on German historiography; Leo Loubere, the chapter on Marxist historiography. My colleague Norman Baker contributed the section on British social history in Chapter IV. I am very grateful for the cordiality with which I was received in Göttingen where I spent the major part of my sabbatical year, to Professor Rudolf Vierhaus of the Max-Planck-Institut für Geschichte, to Rudolf von Thadden of the Historische Seminar of the university and to Wilhelm Abel of the Institut für Wirtschafts-und Sozialgeschichte of the university for giving me not only free access to the libraries of their institutes but also continued opportunities for discussion. I found particularly stimulating the colloquium in the summer of 1972 in Professor Abel's institute on problems of methodology and the informal Thursday evening discussions of Professor Hermann Wein and his students, which several times provided me with a forum for my own work.

I gratefully acknowledge a Senior Fellowship from the National Endowment for the Humanities for the academic year 1971–72 as well as two grants-in-aid from the Research Foundation of the State University of New York, the second of which enabled me to return to Europe once more during the summer of 1974 to talk with historians in Great Britain, West Germany, the German Democratic Republic, and Poland while making final revisions in the manuscript. I very much appreciate the assistance which I have steadily received in my work at the Niedersächsische Staats- und Universitätsbibliothek in Göttingen and at Lockwood Library of the State University of New York at Buffalo.

Throughout this study I have benefitted from my wife's suggestions, advice, and encouragement.

Georg G. Iggers
Buffalo, New York
October 1974

New Directions in European Historiography

I

The Crisis of
the Conventional Conception
of Scientific History

I

IN LOOKING over the literature on historical thought of the past fifty or even hundred years, we are struck by the sharp divergence in the assessment of the historiographical situation among philosophers and practicing historians. Since before Nietzsche's essay on "The Use and Abuse of History" doubts have increasingly been expressed not only regarding the utility of history to life but regarding the possibility of a science of history, doubts which in recent years have led Claude Lévi-Strauss and Michel Foucault[1] to raise the very question whether man has a history. The challenge to the scientific character of history was most recently expressed in Hayden White's search for a metahistorical basis of historical thought in linguistic protocol and poetic imagination, which denies a meaningful distinction between proper history and philosophy of history and reduces the choice of one over the other to "ultimately aesthetic or moral rather than epistemological grounds."[2] Yet this hypercritical attitude regarding the scientific character of history, shared not only by early twentieth-century vitalists, post-mid-twentieth-century structuralists, but also by logical positivists like Karl Popper, runs counter to the increasing scientization of historical studies which has markedly intensified in the past two decades. It may be, as Hayden White suggests, that "the demand for the scientization of history represents only the statement of preference for a specific modality of historical conceptualization,"[3] yet it is a preference which has had increasing fascination for historians of very different orientations.

Indeed, the old models of historical science, which dominated historical scholarship in the nineteenth and well into the twentieth century, have in recent decades been increasingly regarded as inadequate. So have certain assumptions underlying the older scholarship regarding the possibility of objectivity in historical knowledge, the insistence on value freedom in historical inquiry, and the belief in the continuity of historical development. While the rupture with traditional practices and assumptions has led historical thought to frequent skepticism regarding the possibility of historical science, practicing historians have sought to place history on foundations more in accord with contemporary conceptions of science, particularly of the human sciences, and thus to overcome the inadequacies of a conception of historical science which reflects the intellectual interests and social realities of an earlier period.

In dealing with those historians who have viewed history as a science in the broader continental meaning of the term, as a discipline guided by rigorous methodological assumptions, we have admittedly narrowed the scope of this book to a small fragment of historical writing and historical thought. History has been written for very different purposes and in very different ways, so that the borderline between history and myth, history and poetry, history and ideology has often been a fluid one. Moreover, the days when historians could confidently write that "history is a science, no less and no more"[4] are long past. To speak of history as a science is subject to controversy in the English-speaking world where the term has come to be so closely linked to the model of the natural sciences. There has been less question for French or German scholars that history is a science (*science, Wissenschaft*), even if distinct from the exact sciences. It is certainly correct, as historians from Leopold von Ranke to J. H. Hexter have maintained, that the subject matter and the methods of history differ fundamentally from those of the natural sciences, that "history, as it is practiced, is a rule-bound discipline with rules and a rhetoric different from those of scientific explanation, i.e., of explanations in the natural sciences."[5] Yet what joins historians to scholars or scientists in other disciplines is the recognition that whatever the difference in the methods of inquiry and the rules of explanation in history and other sciences may be, these methods and rules do not in the last analysis rest on personal hunches — whatever role these may play in the process of scientific thought — but are governed by inter-subjectively acceptable rules of inquiry. That history is not only a science but also an art has been generally recognized even by such advocates of a "scientific" history as Ranke.[6] But however important the literary, aesthetic, and rhetorical considerations may be in historical presentation, there has been broad consensus among historians and philosophers, since Aristotle,[7] that history is nonetheless in fundamental ways different from poetry or fiction. The historian's task remains to reconstruct and interpret an actual past.

The history of historical scholarship has until now not taken sufficiently into account the extent to which historians since at least the Renaissance have regarded history as science (*Wissenschaft*) in the broader continental sense of the term. The history of historiography has generally been written as a history of men, books, or ideas. At its best, as in the works of Fueter, Gooch, Butterfield, and Kon,[8] it has sought to place the historians within the broader context of the history of ideas or of scholarship. However, until recently it has only seldom approached the history of historical studies as an ongoing discipline within its social and institutional context. The following essays seek to make a contribution to such a study of the discipline of history in the nineteenth and twentieth centuries. The essays remain fragmentary. Moreover, they are written in the awareness that history is only in part a science, that other aspects such as rhetorical considerations enter into even the most strenuous attempts to introduce methodological and conceptual rigor into historical study. They are further guided by the awareness that the history of history can never be understood in terms of the internal development of the discipline but that it reflects the social, political, and institutional context within which history is written.

It has become increasingly difficult to write the history of a science with confidence, even more so that of a discipline as little characterized by consensus on methods or agreement on interpretations as history. The conviction is gone with which eighteenth-century and nineteenth-century thinkers, from Turgot and Condorcet to Auguste Comte, John Stuart Mill, and J. B. Bury, assumed that the very structure of reality guaranteed a constant progress in scientific knowledge pointing in the direction of a unified theory in each of the major areas of knowledge. The conception of the objectivity of nature which still directed much of nineteenth-century science was displaced in scientific thought from Kant to modern logical positivists. There is broad agreement today among philosophers of science that "scientific hypotheses and theories are not derived from observed facts, but invented to account for them."[9] This, of course, by no means excludes the possibility of criteria for the validation of scientific theory. Nevertheless, a broad and very diverse segment of thought from Oswald Spengler to Gaston Bachelard and T. S. Kuhn has emphasized that extra-scientific factors enter and co-determine the questions which scientists ask and the theories by which they seek to understand or explain events. Spengler thus argued that every science, including mathematics, is an expression of the prime symbols of a specific culture.[10] Bachelard and Foucault stressed that science in each age was marked by an *episteme,* not unlike Kuhn's "paradigm," a way of seeing and organizing a body of knowledge, and that the history of science was marked not by the transformation of scientific theory as the result of the cumulation of knowledge but by sudden epistemological breaks (*"coupures épistémologiques"*), which marked fundamental reorientations in the scientific outlook of an age.[11] The history of science was thus characterized not by continuity but by sharp discontinuities. A similar point regarding the time boundness and cultural relativity of all histories has been made by historical theorists from Theodor Lessing,[12] who held that all history was myth, to Karl Popper[13] and Claude Lévi-Strauss,[14] who from very different perspectives argued that history had no object and that every history possessed validity only for the age and the culture within which it was written.

Seen from this perspective, the history of science — or the history of historical studies — appears to lack any meaningful direction. It is marked by a sequence of world views through which reality is seen, views each of equal dignity, none able to command greater authority for a coherent conceptual perception. Yet neither Kuhn nor Bachelard is quite willing to concede this — nor are we in respect to historical studies. For Kuhn, not unlike Bachelard, the history of science is marked by "revolutionary" changes in "paradigms" by which the whole manner in which a generation of scientists sees its work is radically altered and new coherent traditions of scientific research come into being. Like Bachelard, Kuhn wishes to dispense with such concepts as "truth" and "reality." Yet at the same time he, too, wishes to avoid the charge that he is "making of science a subjective and irrational enterprise." Although a change in "paradigm" never just results from "an increment to what is known," it occurs in a real historical situation, at a point of profound professional insecurity, when the older approaches no longer suffice to solve convincingly the problems which the scientific community has posed for itself. The revision of paradigms does not occur merely as a result of anomalies in the data but because of a deeper crisis which involves a change in "world view" inseparable from a broader crisis of social reality. For Kuhn, in the final analysis, scientific truth is resolved into the consensus of the scientific community. But this community is a very special community of "experts bound together by rigorously defined questions and highly technical methods."[15] This, as David Hollinger has pointed out, assumes a transition from a "transcendent objectivity," retaining the conception of a "fixed permanent scientific truth," to a "socially grounded objectivity,"[16] which nevertheless constitutes an objective factor not entirely reducible to the consensus of the scientific community but contributing to the consensus of this community in its search for the solution of the problems which it has posed. To be certain, every scientific revolution involves "losses as well as gains," losses because the new orientation ceases to be able to deal with certain problems which fall outside its perspective.[17] Nevertheless, Kuhn feels compelled to recognize that despite "losses" to the individual scientific communities which occur as a result of changes in paradigm, "the nature of such communities provides a virtual guarantee that both the list of problems solved by science and the precision of individual problem-solutions will grow and grow," and that "a sort of progress will inevitably characterize the scientific enterprise so long as such an enterprise survives." This assumes an "increasingly detailed and refined understanding of nature,"[18] which wisely gives up the concept of finality, and recognizes the historical character of scientific inquiry, but by no means relinquishes a concept of reality.

It may be argued that Kuhn's conception of the history of the sciences is of little relevance to the history of historical scholarship, that history is not a "science," or, if so, a science in a very different sense. The latter is undoubtedly the case. But there is no question that "the discipline of history is at least an academically organized branch of inquiry"[19] and has been for the past two centuries. To be sure, a good deal of history has been written outside this organized discipline and has not always followed its rules. History, moreover, in its modes of expression, has even within the academy preserved much greater freedom than other disciplines devoted more to explanation, and in matters of style and form has been subject to the criticisms of the educated readers, not merely to those of the guild of colleagues. The community of historians, in its commitment to verisimilitude and understanding, has admittedly been much more loosely constituted than ordinary scientific communities, subdivided within itself, yet not without certain shared assumptions about what constitutes rational discussion. Within their discipline historians have been committed not merely to telling a story about the past but to telling "the most likely story that can be sustained by the relevant existing evidence," to what J. H. Hexter has called the "reality rule"; and while this reality is meaningless unless approached by a conceptual scheme, it nevertheless introduces a point of reference which makes meaningful "the common commitment of physicists and historians to exploring, understanding, and rendering the best possible account of reality," which for the historian is "the reality of what happened in the past."[20]

The commitment to a reality principle makes possible a dialogue seeking increasing understanding of the past. Relatively soon a "negative" consensus won ground among historians on what is inadmissible in historical scholarship. Particularly since the professionalization of historical studies, but even before, there has been general agreement on the rules of evidence, rules which have been used less to establish with finality what has happened than to determine what could not have happened. This consensus has given historians an element of common language and logic which, as we shall see, has made possible within limits a continuous dialogue across ideological lines.

There is a difference, however, between history as a learned enterprise, as it was practiced by erudites since the Renaissance, and history as a discipline, not only conscious of its methodological procedures, as to an extent historical erudition was too, but seeking to go beyond antiquarian interest in the noteworthy details of the past to the broader reconstruction of aspects of past reality on the basis of convincing evidence. Yet obviously the "negative" consensus, we described above, did not suffice for the writing of a history which seeks to grasp meaningful connections among events and structures. Such a history required a broader theoretical framework which made interpretation possible. For history to make the transition from erudition to a discipline which considered itself a science (*Wissenschaft*), it was necessary that the critical use of evidence find its place within broader models of historical inquiry which provided the conceptual framework by means of which the questions to be posed could be approached. These models were deeply rooted in the interests, viewpoints, and intellectual concerns of the scholarly communities which employed them. Thus on the basis of a consensus of what constitutes evidence, very different histories could be written, different not only in their interpretation of a common topic, but different in their fundamental assumptions, approaches, and style. This, it has been argued, makes any sort of development in historical conceptions impossible. The history of history is marked by radical discontinuities. Every history, it is argued, is valid only for the creed, party, class, nation, or age from which it originates.

It can thus be argued that every tradition of historical scholarship reflects the conditions under which it emerged and developed, that the Rankean "scientific" model of historical inquiry, with its narrow concentration on a political history separated from its broader social setting, its narrow concern with the foreign affairs of the great European states, its heavy reliance on documents of state to the neglect of other sources, represented not only a step back from the aspiration of German Enlightenment historians to write a cosmopolitan social history of politics but reflected the political, social, and intellectual limitations of the early nineteenth-century Prussian university at which this model of inquiry emerged. This is undoubtedly true. Yet it would be a fallacy to argue that the origins of an idea obviate its cognitive significance. For the very fact that history is so intimately linked to its historical context also introduces a source of historical insight, however perspectivistic. The Rankean model appeared at a point when the claim of the eighteenth-century German Enlightenment historians to scientific status no longer sounded true in the setting of early nineteenth-century Germany. The changing nature of the Western and non-Western world in the nineteenth and twentieth centuries, the emergence of a highly technological society with its political, social, and intellectual concomitants, the appearance of submerged classes and peoples on the political scene have all provided a real basis for the growing dissatisfaction with the paradigms of scholarly method provided by the nineteenth-century scientific school. In this sense the transforma-

tion of the discipline of history is inseparable from the history
of the society and culture of which it is a part.

But despite the deep divergences in outlook within modern historical scholarship, certain points of convergence have
emerged. Thus the scope of historical studies has widened not
only to include the non-European world but also to give serious
attention to broader segments of the population and to areas of
human behavior previously neglected. More important, a broad
agreement has appeared, shared by historians of very different
ideological perspectives, that a history centering on the conscious actions of men does not suffice, but that human behavior
must be understood within the framework of the structures
within which they occur. These structures often are hidden to
the men who make history. Modern historians have thus taken
up themes which already interested the German Enlightenment
historians whom we shall discuss below but with which the
latter were unable to deal convincingly in terms of their methodological and conceptual apparatus. In an important sense,
the "scientific" history of the nineteenth century marked a
needed retreat in the historians' ambitions even if, as we shall
see, this retreat may have been as deeply effected by ideological
as by scientific considerations. History had to be placed on a
sound methodological basis. The historians of the twentieth
century have remained committed to the critical use of evidence
upon which the nineteenth-century "scientific" school insisted;
yet at the same time they have recognized that the documents
do not tell their own story and that the historians of the nineteenth century in letting the past speak for itself were generally
insufficiently aware of the presuppositions which enabled them
to establish threads of historical development. The result has
been a strengthened recognition of the role which theories,
hypotheses, and conceptualizations occupy in historical analysis and narration. No unified social or historical science has
provided a fund of theory for historical explanation or guidelines for the selection and organization of historical data. Yet,
as these essays suggest, despite the profound differences in
perspectives and commitments which have divided historians,

the continuous questioning of positions from within and from outside the community of historical scholars, intensified by the social, political, and intellectual pressures of the times, has contributed not only to a broadening of historical perspective but to increasing methodological and conceptual rigor which has marked the human sciences generally.

2

SOMETIME in the eighteenth century there began to occur at the German universities, foremost in Göttingen, the transition from erudite scholarship to the new scientific orientation in history which combined the critical examination of evidence with the narrative reconstruction of a course of events. This transition was closely interwoven with the emergence of an organized academic discipline. Accompanying this transformation, a paradigm emerged for historians in the course of the nineteenth century as historical research became institutionalized and professionalized throughout the world. This paradigm continued to assert its influence on a broad segment of academic history until very recently. The theme of these essays is the decline of this model of historical science in the twentieth century, a decline which for professional historians did not result in a surrender of the notion of historical science but in a search for alternate models which offered greater scientificity in the sense not only of more comprehensive exploration of the past but of inter-subjectively more convincing guidelines for such exploration.

A rich tradition of historical studies existed outside the universities as well, of course, long before the eighteenth century and continued to exist throughout the nineteenth century. Yet a relatively sharp dividing line persisted until the eighteenth century between historical erudition and historical writing. On the one hand, there was the great tradition of narrative history going back to Thucydides and revived in the Italian Renaissance, a tradition represented at its best by men in public life, statesmen, generals, and philosophers who saw their function as a didactic and philosophic one and who, while they sought to tell the truth, only in a limited way applied the strict rules of source criticism developed by erudite scholarship. On the other hand, there existed a tradition of philological criticism with its origins in the Renaissance and the Reformation. As Donald Kelley and George Huppert have pointed out,[21] a sense of history was very much evident in the efforts of scholars since the Renaissance with the use of critical philological methods to establish how the past, particularly in its legal institutions, differed from the present. Yet this scholarship, lacking a sense of development, in Kelley's words failed to "combine erudition with literary merit and intelligent organization," producing in method "rather a patchwork than a paradigm."[22] Rigorous critical research took place in the Benedictine monasteries and, in the eighteenth century, increasingly at the academies.[23] But here the main concern was not the writing of history but still the edition of texts. The canons for the critical treatment of the texts had been well worked out since the Renaissance and by the time Jean Mabillon published the *De re diplomatica* in 1681 had become a well developed art. Yet the edition and analysis of texts no more constituted historical science than the mere observation of phenomena, which preceded Newtonian physics by millennia, constituted natural science. History became a "science" only at the point at which the chasm between antiquarianism and historical writing was bridged.

We are now well aware of the inadequacy of the nineteenth-century Romantic notion of the eighteenth century as an age hostile or at the least indifferent to history. The modern conception of historical science had its origin in the Enlightenment, patterning itself on Enlightenment notions of man and reality and reacting against them. The development of the modern natural sciences presented an important model for the understanding of historical studies. The institutional organization of historical studies partially followed that of the natural sciences. As in the latter, an organized community of scientists and scholars emerged in the seventeenth century, first centered around the academies, then, beginning in Germany in the eighteenth century, increasingly at the universities. In the place of the traditional universities, conceived as teaching institutions dedicated to the training of future officials and members of the professions, the new University of Göttingen, founded in 1737, emerged as a center in which research occupied an increasingly important role.[24]

Only slowly were chairs of history established separately from those of politics. Yet as in the sciences, stress was laid on technical training, in this case on the so-called auxiliary sciences (for example, diplomatics, the study of documents, paleography, numismatics, and such). But increasingly attention was given also to philology and to the new science of "statistics," which, as pursued by Gottfried Achenwall at Göttingen after 1748, sought to found history on a firm factual basis including data on population, political and administrative organization, law, commercial and industrial activity among other things. The term "statistics," as used by Achenwall, had a different meaning from that which it acquired later: statistics were not required to be presented in the form of numbers but involved the description — in quantitative or verbal terms — of the concrete institutions and characteristics of a society. In a sense, the historians trained in the late eighteenth century in Göttingen by Johann Christoph Gatterer and August Ludwig Schlözer combined the broad perspective of the philosophical historians, such as Montesquieu, Voltaire, Gibbon and Iselin, with the technical skills of the erudites and the legal scholars trained in textual exegesis and criticism. The Göttingen historians were seeking to establish an historical art able to grasp the interrelatedness of events. For although in their opinion events formed the "real subject matter of history,"[25] they did not by themselves constitute history. There was no history, Gatterer and Schlözer agreed, without a conception on the part of the historian by means of which he could organize the chaotic "mass" of materials into an integrated whole.[26] "History," Gatterer observed, "is not merely the biography of kings or the chronological listing of changes of reigns, wars and battles," as German historians had thought until the British and French taught them better in recent decades.[27] At the same time the Göttingen historians rejected any attempt to impose a philosophic scheme on history or to introduce an overly simple conception of historical objectivity. All history involved selectivity. And while they believed that there existed an objective, or "true," history, they recognized that the "position" (*Standort*) at which the historian stood and the perspective (*Gesichtspunkt*) from which he viewed history would determine what aspects of this "truth" he would see, so that a Greek, a Roman, a medieval monk, or a modern German would each arrive at a different history.[28]

From the very beginning, the Göttingen historians were keenly aware of fundamental differences in historical methods and the methods of the natural sciences. They reflected the new historicist outlook, which was deeply conscious of the element of change in human institutions, customs, and thought and which recognized the extent to which any attempt to understand human nature required an examination of the historical circumstances in which this nature manifested itself. Essentially they shared Vico's notion that "human history differs from natural history in this, that we have made the former but not the latter."[29] While all men in a sense were "creatures of one kind," Schlözer observed, "man is nothing by nature" and receives content and character only in history.[30] Natural forces, such as geography and climate, played a role in the conditioning of man, and history could not be fully divorced from natural science; but these natural forces in turn were effected by human causes. Insofar as history reflected the purposes, trends of direction, both conscious and unintended, resulting from human actions, history required methods of inquiry quite different from those of the abstract sciences. History, Gatterer recognized, had to take into account the individuality of events. It therefore required a different type of evidence than that of the natural sciences, one which seeks understanding of human relationships. Like the natural scientist, the historian had to approach his subject matter with questions by means of which he could establish "a system of events." Yet the use of hypotheses, while required for historical science, was by no means as

effective as in the natural sciences.[31] Because of the aspect of individuality in historical events, hypotheses in fact created certain
obstacles to historical understanding. Thus, as Peter Reill suggested, there became apparent in historical studies a certain
methodological dilemma, which remained persistently insoluble
for future historians, between the insistence of the historian on
elevating history to the rank of a science by seeking to introduce conceptualizations into history buttressed by empirical evidence and the recognition of the limits of conscious rational
thought, particularly of empiricism and induction, in the comprehension of meaningful human relationships which required
an element of empathy and sympathetic understanding which
resisted strict methodological procedures.[32] Nor could a rhetorical and emotive element be as strictly eliminated from historical discourse as from that of the abstract sciences.

The Göttingen historians — Gatterer, Schlözer, and, a generation later, Ludwig Heeren — sought a balance between the
analysis of social structures and the narration of events. Reflecting the Enlightenment concern with the study of human nature
in its historical context, the Göttingen historians wished to
write a history which approached the past both "synchroni-
cally," taking into account the structures of societies at a given
historical moment and comparing these, and "chronologically"
pursuing a continuous development of interconnected events
around a selected theme.[33] Like Voltaire and Iselin, they sought
to overcome a narrowly event-oriented political history and
aspired to write a broadly conceived social and cultural history
which nevertheless received its unity and continuity through
certain key social institutions, among which the state for them
occupied a central role. In a sense, this balance between political and social history, between narration and "statistics," appeared to have fitted in well with their political stance, their
attachment to an enlightened monarchy which would overcome
the remnants of a feudal social and economic order and lay the
foundation for a state guaranteeing legal equality.[34]

There was indeed something at once very modern and very
outmoded in the work of the Göttingen historians. On the

one hand, they pointed at comparative social and economic history of politics and began to ask questions which historians were going to raise again in the twentieth century. Yet on the other hand, they remained incapable of transforming the wealth of demographic, geographic, and economic data they presented into a conceptual whole, or of integrating it into their narratives. Their universal histories, like those of the polyhistorians, remained compilations of the kind they criticized. Heeren somewhat later was more successful in organizing an account of historical development around the central theme of commercial activity.[35] Nor did the Göttingen historians advance toward a history based on the critical examination of evidence. While Gatterer repeatedly warned the historian against reliance on tradition and called for a history based on primary sources,[36] he and Schlözer in fact continued to base their accounts of the ancient world on the uncritical use of Biblical and classical narration.

The emergence in the early nineteenth century at the newly established University of Berlin of the new scientific orientation of history, of which Ranke became the most influential exponent, represented an advance not only in the critical use of evidence but also in the utilization of this evidence in the construction of a coherent narrative. However, the very nature of the evidence used led to a narrowing of scope from the broadly conceived social and cultural history of the Enlightenment scholars to a history focused on political and religious events, the actions of persons of power and influence, isolated from their broader structural context, a narrowing which reflected a fundamental reorientation in the political as well as the intellectual climate. Like the Göttingen circle, the new scientific school stood in an ambiguous relationship to the Enlightenment ideal of scientific objectivity. Its historians were fully convinced that history could be elevated to the rank of a science, much more confident than the Göttingen scholars had been that definitive accounts of past events were possible which were able to overcome the perspectivity and subjectivity of the historian. Yet at the same time they drew even more sharply the line between historical method and method in the natural sciences and philosophy. While the latter sought causal explanation of recurring phenomena, the former dealt with meaningful human phenomena which required to be understood in their unique individuality.

The balance which the Göttingen school had sought to establish between the analysis of structural relations and the intuitive understanding of unique historical expressions was thus rejected by the new scientific school. Scientific certainty was possible in history. It rested, however, on the understanding of the motives and intentions of historical agents as these revealed themselves in the sources. The proper instrument for historical study was therefore hermeneutics, the art of correctly understanding the texts. Much more emphatically than the Göttingen school, the new scientific orientation insisted that the historian must reconstruct the past on the basis of primary sources. For the realm of modern history, these according to Ranke consisted of "memoirs, diaries, letters, reports from embassies, and original narratives of eyewitnesses."[37] To establish the genuineness and credibility of these sources, the new historians utilized techniques of external and internal criticism already well established by the erudites. In seeking to establish the meaning of the evidence, they built on a long tradition of the exegesis of texts established by Biblical, classical, and legal scholarship. Yet they introduced into their analyses of the texts certain holistic assumptions, which conflicted with their explicit insistence that historical scholarship should be guided by the sources alone. A model for the use of what came to be called the critical-philological method of the scientific school was contained in F. A. Wolf's famous *Prologomena to Homer* (1795) in which he sought to establish the authorship of the Homeric poems. Wolf proceeded from the assumption that a source can never be understood in terms of linguistic analysis alone but must be viewed as an historical document reflecting the spirit of a nation (*Volksgeist*), which alone is the key to the understanding of the source. In a similar manner Johann Winckelmann had sought from the remnants of classical art, Georg

Barthold Niebuhr from Roman law, to recapture the spirit of classical Greece and Rome.

The transformation of historical scholarship reflected a rapidly changing political atmosphere. The University of Berlin itself was established in 1810 in the period of Prussian Reforms under the guidance of Wilhelm von Humboldt as an institution in which narrow technical training would be replaced by an education firmly based on research. More than in other countries with a less well organized bureaucracy, the Prussian university provided the training place for a broadly educated class of civil servants, who in the absence of a politically powerful middle class occupied a position of particular influence and status. Many of the men called to the university in its early years, such as Georg Barthold Niebuhr in Roman history, Friedrich Ernst Schleiermacher in theology, Friedrich Karl von Savigny and Karl Friedrich Eichhorn in law, and in 1825 Leopold Ranke, shared certain epistemological and political assumptions. They emphasized the need of a hermeneutic, historical approach to all studies relating to man. They rejected the heritage of the French Revolution, yet opposed a feudal reaction and acknowledged their loyalty to a monarchical Prussian state, governed by an enlightened bureaucracy committed to policies favoring the development of a modern capitalistic economy without making major political concessions to the middle classes. Ranke in the pages of the *Politisch-Historische Zeitschrift,* which he edited upon the request of the Prussian government from 1832 to 1836 to defend the policies of the government against both its feudal and its liberal critics, gave expression to these views and saw the function of historical science as in part a political one. Reminiscent of Edmund Burke, he saw in history a powerful argument against revolutionary change in favor of gradual growth within established structures.

The hermeneutic method as conceived by Ranke was inseparable from certain basic philosophic assumptions. What made historical knowledge possible for Ranke, as it did for the German tradition of hermeneutics for over a century from Wilhelm von Humboldt and Friedrich Schleiermacher to J. G.

Droysen, Wilhelm Dilthey, and Friedrich Meinecke, was the notion that history was the realm of "spirit," but of spirit conceived very differently from the way it was understood in Hegel's philosophy. If Hegel had stressed the unity of world history and had seen in history a process in which spirit through continuous self-negation translated itself into increasingly rational institutions, the hermeneutic tradition, with which we are dealing here, stressed that spirit manifested itself in individualized forms. History was made up of "individualities," each possessing their internal structure and a meaning and purpose unique to them alone. Not only persons possessed the qualities of individuality but in an even more profound sense so did the great collective bodies which had grown in the course of history — states, nations, cultures, mankind. These individualities were not merely fleeting appearances but each "represented an idea rooted in actuality."[38] They could be grasped not through abstract or inductive reasoning but only through hermeneutic methods, through the interpretation of the expressions which they manifested in the world of the senses. Hence the need for the rigorous analysis of the sources as the starting point of every historical inquiry. Yet the significance of the events were "only partially visible in the world of the senses; the rest has to be added by intuition, inference, and guesswork."[39] Hence while the historian always began by concentrating on the particular manifestations of historical event, his aim, as Ranke insisted, was not to gather facts but to proceed by means of a "documentary, penetrating profound study . . . devoted to the phenomenon itself . . . to its essence and content."[40]

What prevented the dissolution of history into a fragmented cluster of individualities was the deep belief that while "history could never have the unity of a philosophical system," it nevertheless was "not without inner connection."[41] There existed a ladder of historical individualities ranging from individual persons to great collective entities, nations, epochs, mankind itself, joined in a rather Leibnitzian fashion in an ultimate harmony in which each preserved its individual integrity. This harmony was not static. Rather, great "tendencies" were at work in history which gave history a sense of continuity and direction. It was the task of the historian through immersion into the documentary evidence to recapture these great tendencies as they revealed themselves. Yet while strict methodological procedures capable of inter-subjective control existed for the critical examination of sources, the nature of historical individualities permitted no such criteria for the comprehension of historical processes. The irreducibility of historical individualities to terms other than their own inherent principles of development ruled out any causal analysis (or social or political criticism). The "forces" operating in history, Ranke wrote, "cannot be defined or put in abstract terms, but one can behold them, observe them, and develop a sympathy for their existence."[42] The only form of historical presentation was therefore the narrative. The Rankean school did not confront the problem of selection and perspectivity of which the Göttingen historians had at least been aware. It is thus not surprising that the German scientific school, despite its stress on the critical examination of documents, did not effectively contribute to a lessening of the ideological function of historical scholarship but lent itself to the increased political utilization of history in the service of nationalistic and domestic political aims.

The hermeneutic method, linked with the historicist notion that an adequate understanding of the nature of anything human is to be gained by considering it in terms of its development, was able to be applied to all spheres of human cultural activity. Nor, as the historians of Antiquity — Winckelmann, Niebuhr, Boeckh — demonstrated, did history have to restrict its sources to written documents. As Droysen suggested, there "is nothing which moves the human spirit and has found expression through the senses which is not capable of being understood."[43] If the scope of history was so narrowly reduced by Ranke and the scientific school to the actions of states and to ecclesiastical matters, this undoubtedly reflected a number of scientific as well as extra-scientific considerations.

The insistence on the critical examination of written sources excluded the scientific treatment of universal history which had been the aim of the Göttingen school. It led historians to the archives, and the opening of the archives after the 1830s gave impetus to the study of the political history of the European states. But archival material could be used in the pursuit of very different questions, as Alexis de Tocqueville's study of administrative centralization demonstrated. Ranke's concentration on diplomatic and military affairs reflected a political philosophy which viewed states as "spiritual substances," "thoughts of God,"[44] governed by inherent principles of development irreducible to external factors. The "special tendencies" of states expressed themselves primarily in the pursuit of their independence in conflict with other states which obliged them "to organize all its external resources for the purpose of self-preservation,"[45] hence the primacy of external over domestic policy's conception which served well as a justification of the Prussian bureaucratic monarchy.

From this perspective the bureaucratic state, representing the interests of the whole, stood above the conflicts of particular groups, for Ranke as it did for Hegel. To introduce an element of popular control into the political decision-making process would deflect the state from the pursuit of its great objectives. Seen in this manner, the broader realms of social history became irrelevant for the study of political history. The political realm, particularly in the crucial area of foreign affairs, followed its own inner necessities, separate from the social and economic spheres. The latter were profoundly shaped by political intervention and could only be understood within the framework of the state. The course of political events as it became apparent in the documents of state provided the thread of continuity in history. The Rankean conception of the state revealed an optimism regarding the state not dissimilar to that expressed in Hegel's philosophy of history. "It would be infinitely wrong to seek in the struggles of the historical powers only the work of brute force," Ranke observes. "In power itself a spiritual essence manifests itself."[46] "But seriously," he has Friedrich comment in the "Dialogue on Politics," "you will be able to name few significant wars for which it could not be proved that genuine moral energy achieved the final victory."[47] If Ranke called on the historian to be impartial and suspend moral judgments, the "impartiality" of the historian consisted for him in observing the objective "moral" forces which struggled for dominance on the historical scene.[48] Ranke's assertion that "every epoch is immediate in God" and "must be seen as something valid in itself"[49] must thus not be taken at its face value, for Ranke at the same time distinguished sharply between nations of interest to the historian, such as those of Europe, and those of Asia, for example India and China, whose "antiquity is legendary, but their condition is rather a matter of natural history."[50] For Ranke and indeed for most of the German historians of the tradition of "scientific" history, the direction of modern development appeared clear, the steady rise in the political and cultural significance of the great Protestant states, namely Germany and England, monarchies which yet permitted room for the economic and cultural aspirations of the middle classes, the decline of Catholicism and the Catholic world, namely France, and the final defeat of the heritage of the French Revolution.[51]

Ranke's conception of historical science in many ways remained the model for German historical scholarship well into the twentieth century. In part this undoubtedly resulted from the fact that despite the profound social and intellectual changes which took place in the course of the nineteenth century, there remained in Germany strong forces resisting these changes. The Rankean conception of historical scholarship satisfied the demand for professionalization and specialization and the striving for scientific objectivity and carried with it a perspective which centered on political elites yet recognized "the principle of movement not as revolution,"[52] but as evolution toward a modern state, providing equal protection before the law, efficient government, and pursuing policies intended to free the capitalist economy from older corporative restraints. It is true that in the period preceding German unification, the majority of Prussian-oriented liberal historians, many trained in Ranke's seminars, rejected Ranke's ideal of objectivity.[53] They merged a moderate liberalism with an intense nationalism, neither of which was shared by Ranke, who remained rooted in the vision of an older European order of conservative monarchies. Nevertheless, the basic methodological premises remained unshaken, even if increasingly divorced from their idealistic philosophic presuppositions. In many ways, the Rankean concept of the state standing above economic and social interests was maintained. If various historians had opposed Bismarck in the Prussian constitutional conflict of the early 1860s, the German historical profession after 1866 closed ranks behind Bismarck in the struggle against the socialists. In Germany the political implications of the "scientific" school were more clearly apparent than elsewhere and certainly not unrelated to the failure of parliamentarization. The hermeneutic form of historicism lent itself well to a critique of socialism, because it rejected social analysis as a legitimate function of historical inquiry in favor of a narrative chronological account.

The hermeneutic historicist approach by no means needed to exclude social history. Hermeneutic historical methods could be applied to all aspects of human activity and, as we noted, were indeed so applied, with the result that political economy, philosophy, law, literature, study of art and linguistics all became historical sciences in Germany. Droysen in his lectures on the nature of history and historical method,[54] delivered in the mid-nineteenth century, provided a basis and theory for a broad social and cultural approach to history, which he, however, did not pursue in his own historical writings. The hermeneutic approach did not require the emphasis on politics and the reliance on documents of state which characterized much of nineteenth-century historical scholarship. Within the framework of historicism an important tradition of economic and social history emerged which found its high point in the work of Gustav Schmoller and the *Acta Borussica*. But in continuing to stress the autonomy of politics and the understanding of economics primarily as a function of state policy reflecting national values, this tradition of social history resisted a sober analysis of the factors which influenced the state and often reduced economic history to administrative, legal, and constitutional history. Karl Lamprecht's attempt to introduce analytical conceptions into history in his *German History,* which began to appear in 1891, was widely suspected as giving aid and comfort to the socialist enemies, notwithstanding Lamprecht's own intensely national convictions.

The Rankean model of "scientific" history certainly did not possess a monopoly over historical research. The great burgeoning of historical studies generally in the first half of the nineteenth century was effected only to a limited degree by the German example of historical scholarship. Although archival studies received increasing emphasis in France and the École des Chartes was founded in Paris in 1821 for the professional training of archivists and librarians, the rigorous training in historical method which Ranke has offered in his seminars was lacking. The continuity with the cultural concern of Enlightenment history was still apparent in the work of François Guizot. The interest in domestic politics, the emancipation of the communes and the rise of the bourgeoisie in France, the concentration on constitutional conflicts in England reflected the different political contexts and traditions within which historical studies took place in these countries. Nevertheless by the last third of the century, when the idealistic assumptions of the scientific school had widely lost their credibility, the Rankean seminar method became the model of historical inquiry generally in the world as historical studies became increasingly professionalized and institutionalized — in France, for example, with the establishment of the École Pratique des Hautes Études in 1868, in the United States with the introduction of the Ph.D. program at Johns Hopkins in the 1870s.[55] To be sure, this trend was by no means universal and particularly in Great Britain, where the university resisted the trend to specialization and continued to see its function in the education of a broadly cultured elite, the continuity with older literary traditions remained strong. Yet the study of history, as it became a professionalized, university-centered discipline in a large part of the Western and the Westernized world, as for example in Japan, now appeared to enter a phase not entirely unlike that which Kuhn described as the stage of "normal" science in which the new generations of scholars were trained in the basic conceptions and practices of the profession with little time being devoted to questioning the basic foundations of the science. Textbooks on historical method appeared such as Ernst Bernheim's *Lehrbuch der historischen Methode* (1889)[56] and C. V. Langlois and Charles Seignobos' *Introduction aux études historiques* (1898),[57] which served well into the twentieth century as guides for the training of historians and as a model for the composition of similar texts in other languages. We must stress, however, that critical historical research did not have to wait for German models and that in France well before 1870 Alexis de Tocqueville, Numa Denys Fustel de Coulanges, and others had shown how it was possible to write history which proceeded critically on the basis of sources, yet worked with concepts and assumptions quite different from those of German historical science at the time.

What historical scholarship accepted from the German school was less its conception of history than its techniques of historical research. Its stress on facts, once divorced from the idealistic assumptions which had eroded even in Germany, fitted well into the empirical frame of mind of the late nineteenth century. The literary qualities which had constituted an integral part of the persuasive power of the great historians of the nineteenth century, not only of Jacob Burckhardt, Jules Michelet, Ernest Renan, Thomas Macaulay and Lord Acton but of Ranke and Heinrich Treitschke, receded in significance as a new generation of historians trained in the techniques of archival research tended to minimize the rhetorical qualities of historical writing.[58] Yet a total divorce between the methodology of German historical scholarship and its theoretical presuppositions remained impossible. The critical-philological method could be used for very different political purposes, as it was in France in defense of republican traditions.[59] Yet the "scientific" school outside of Germany continued to assume that political processes could be reconstructed from the verbal evidence contained in official records and presented in a narrative form, generally without recourse to an analysis of social and economic factors which entered into political decisions.

3

BY THE TURN of the century, the period of the greatest academic triumph of the scientific school, the theoretical assumptions of the school, however, came under serious criticism almost every-where in the Western world, including Germany. Almost si-multaneously Karl Lamprecht in Germany, the contributors to Henri Berr's *Revue de synthèse historique* and Emile Durk-heim's *Année sociologique* in France, Frederick Turner and such advocates of a "New History" as James Harvey Robinson and Charles Beard in the United States began to question his-torical science as it was practiced in the late nineteenth century. Historical science, these critics charged, no longer met the de-mands of modern society and contemporary science. The critics questioned the elitist presuppositions of the preindustrial and predemocratic time in which the hermeneutic approach to his-tory came into existence. A history which concentrated on the role of persons in politics, diplomacy, and military affairs had to be replaced by a comparative social and cultural history which studied the life of the masses and did not restrict itself to the actions of individuals but attempted to analyze anonymous social processes. At the same time they began to question the objectivism of the scientific school, which had assumed that the historical world revealed itself to the historian who ap-proached it with an open mind. They recognized the extent to which historical knowledge was inseparable from the questions posed by the historian and to which hypotheses consequently were as indispensable to historical as to other studies. History itself was to become a social science; the hermeneutic concern with describing a unique series of events was to be replaced in part by a more analytical approach, seeking historical explana-tions with the help of generalizations gathered from the social sciences.[60]

The intense discussion on historical method which began among historians and philosophers in the 1890s and has con-tinued until today involved more than purely scholarly consider-ations. It reflected fundamental changes in the social, political, and cultural context within which historical science had emerged in the post-Napoleonic period. The extent to which important aspects of the traditional order and outlook persisted explains in part the resistance, particularly in Germany, to the reorientation of historical studies. The intensity of the reaction in Germany to Karl Lamprecht's *German History* is in some ways surprising because Lamprecht's work was so steeped in romantic notions of morphology, national psyche, and cycles of development not entirely alien to the German tradition of historical writing. Yet his critics found in his shift of emphasis from political to social and cultural history and his search for "laws" of development an implied threat to German political and social traditions.

The challenge in Germany to the conventional history thus possessed ideological and political implications which it did not in the same way in France or the United States. Yet the philosophers and historians who came to the defense of the hermeneutic tradition of German historical science were much more deeply divided among themselves than they recognized at the time.[61] Historians and philosophers both stressed the distinction between the historical and cultural sciences, which sought understanding (*Verstehen*) of values and meanings, and the explanatory natural sciences. The historians for the most part —as did also the philosopher Wilhelm Windelband—clung to the belief in an objective historical reality which made it possible to contemplate the past without approaching it with questions and hypotheses that reflected the subjectivity of the inquirer. Others, such as Wilhelm Dilthey and Heinrich Rickert, among the philosophers, and the historian Otto Hintze,[62] now recognized—as did analytical critics of conventional "scientific" historiography outside of Germany like Henri Berr—the untenability of the notion that the past presented itself as something objectively given to the historian who contemplated the course of events as they emerged from the documents. While insisting that historical explanations rested fundamentally on meaningful wholes which defied causal analysis, Dilthey and Rickert nevertheless acknowledged that the historian, as did all cultural scientists, had to operate with principles of selection which imposed a conceptual structure on the historical subject matter. History, thus too, to a degree was an analytical science, although one which operated with concepts that brought into sharper focus the uniqueness of historical individualities. Introducing the concept of explanation into an essentially still idealistic conception of history, Max Weber pointed at what he considered the basic error of a conception which had held that the uniqueness of historical and social phenomena as expressions of meaning precluded explanation. The very element of intentionality, he stressed, made possible the calculability of social behavior. While all social science remained historical in character, as science it nevertheless required rigorous explanatory concepts, yet concepts which took into account the elements of meaning and purpose in human societies and provided hypotheses, "ideal types," to be measured against the empirical course of events, regarding the lines of development which societies might be expected to follow in the pursuit of their purposes. Thus historians and philosophers representing a broad spectrum of thought on historical method, extending from defenders of a hermeneutic approach like Dilthey and Hintze to those who like Lamprecht and Berr assigned a significant role to generalizations, began to agree that there were definite limits to narration in historical discourse.

This recognition was part of a decline of a complex of ideas which had served as the philosophical foundation for the German tradition of historical science. For at heart, despite moments of despair, the historians of the scientific school had been optimistic regarding the nature of man, the beneficial character of the established political order and the future of European culture. The voices of pessimism came interestingly from scholars who stood outside the dominant tradition of historical science and who, like Burckhardt and Huizinga, departed from a linear, developmental approach to history or, like Tocqueville and Lorenz von Stein, introduced broader social categories into their critical analysis of European historical development. Within the German tradition itself, idealistic assumptions were increasingly replaced by naturalistic and biologistic ones; while Droysen had still viewed the state as a moral community, Treitschke only a little later defined it as power (*Macht*),[63] as did the "Neo-Rankean" historians of the early twentieth century who sought to justify German navalism and colonial expansion in terms of Ranke's concept of the balance of power applied to the world scene.[64] Before the development of the twentieth century called into question the preeminence of European culture, the loss of idealistic foundations already threatened the belief in the unity and direction of history which had been basic to the historicist assumption that history is the key to the understanding of all things human, the essence of culture, and the queen of the sciences. History now led to historical relativism. Ernst Troeltsch relatively early in the new century could speak of the crisis introduced by the historicization of all norms and well before the publication of Spengler's *Decline of the West* write that the notion of the unity of human history, to which he himself still clung as a matter of faith, was nevertheless no longer intellectually compelling and that in the place of one human history there was a variety of histories incapable of understanding each other.[65]

Still, an obvious lag existed between the fundamental structural transformation of the modern world, the changes in intellectual outlook and the practices of historians within the confines of the university. The historical context in which the conventional historiography had emerged and the already very changed context in which it found world-wide acceptance with the professionalization of historical research changed beyond recognition in an age of extensive industrialization, political and social revolutions, the decline of old elites, and the loss of European world status. So did the intellectual context. But the classical model of historical studies remained firmly established in academic institutions well into the second half of the twentieth century repeating dominant themes of nineteenth-century historiography. Thus in Germany national unification, in England the triumph of parliamentary government, and in Italy the Risorgimento continued to occupy an important role in historical studies which, as before, stressed the role of personalities and of ideas in political change and emphasized the broad basis of consensus within the national community. Where a new interest was shown in social and cultural aspects of historical development, as in Trevelyan's *Social History of England,* or in the history of ideas, as in the works of Friedrich Meinecke and Benedetto Croce, this occurred within the traditional conception of national political development.

World War II appears to have been followed by a clearer caesura in European historiography than World War I. First in France and Eastern Europe after 1945, then more slowly in Great Britain, Italy, and Western Germany, the dam began to break and alternative models of historical inquiry, proceeding from different questions, began to gain influence. To an increasing degree, historical studies began to close the gap which had broadened since the turn of the century between the empirical social sciences in which theory played an increasingly important role and a relatively conventional history. Although the reorientation in historical studies has been profound, Kuhn's concept of a "scientific revolution," which Peter Reill recently employed to describe the fundamental changes in historical scholarship in Germany in the eighteenth and early nineteenth centuries, does not fit well here.[66] No new "paradigm" has emerged which within the community of historians has gained the degree of acceptance that the Rankean model, however limited its influence, had temporarily possessed in the late nineteenth and the early twentieth centuries. Rather, in the place of one "paradigm" a number of paradigms have emerged, each presenting a model of inquiry seeking greater scientificity for a community of historians and each closely interwoven with certain general notions regarding the nature of historical reality which reflect the ideological, social, and political divisions within the scholarly community. To a degree the relationship of history and the social sciences was now reversed. If in the nineteenth century, particularly in Germany, the cultural sciences were deeply affected by historicist assumptions, now historians began to apply theories and methods of the social sciences to the in-

vestigation of historical phenomena. But the diversities in social
science theory and methods had their counterpart in the eclecticism and pluralism within recent historical scholarship.

4

IT IS THUS even more difficult to bring present-day historical
studies under a common denominator than those of the nineteenth century; for the latter, despite ideological and national
dividing lines, in their stress on the nation-states and their reliance on documents of state reflected a broad consensus on what
deserved the interest of the historian. This broad agreement on
what constitutes the subject matter of history and a scholarly
approach to this subject matter has in part dissolved, as has the
homogeneity of social and educational background which
marked much of the profession in the past. Yet despite sharp
ideological divisions, certain points of contact exist among
contemporary historians, including those historians who have
consciously sought to keep alive many of the hermeneutic notions and practices of conventional historiography. Present-day
historiography has taken much more seriously than traditional
historiography the historicist motto that all that is human is of
historical interest. It has assigned a relatively greater significance
to conceptualizations in history, and while it has left macro-
history to the speculative philosophers of history or to the sociologists and anthropologists, it has nevertheless frequently sought
to apply theories of limited or medium range taken from the
social sciences — often, as we shall see, a multiplicity of such
theories — to the partial analysis of historical situations and
processes.

But very different conceptions of what constitute the aims
and methods of "history as an historical social science" have
informed modern historical scholarship, and these have reflected
the diversity of cognitive interests and ideological commitments
of modern historians. For purposes of this exposition we shall
distinguish three types of conceptions of history as a "historical
social science" which have recurred in nineteenth-century and
twentieth-century historical thought and which we shall briefly

identify as a nomological, a hermeneutic, and a dialectical (Marxist) materialist approach. This typology does not suffice to classify the rich variety of contemporary historical writing and thought. It may, however, throw some light on what the historians whom we shall discuss in the following three chapters were attempting to do. Although the relevance of well articulated theories of historical knowledge should not be overestimated, the traditions of historical writing which we have chosen to discuss in these chapters have generally been more highly aware of theoretical assumptions guiding their research than was the case with the older conventional historical scholarship.

All three of these orientations had their predecessors in the nineteenth century. The Rankean tradition with which we dealt was essentially hermeneutic. Positivist historians like T. H. Buckle and Henri Taine sought to introduce a nomological approach to the study of English civilization and literature. Marx and Engels provided examples for a history written from a dialectical, materialistic perspective. The hermeneutical tradition dominated the historical profession. The positivistic and Marxist traditions only to a limited extent succeeded in bridging the gap between their historical conceptualizations and historical evidence, and concerned themselves relatively little with the methodological problems involved in achieving this. In turn, the hermeneutic tradition ascribed a relatively minimal or even negative value to concepts and generalizations. In stressing that the uniqueness of historical phenomena defied abstractions — although in practice they were never able to avoid them — the hermeneutic historicism of the German "scientific" school differed sharply from the later hermeneutic historicism, as influenced by Dilthey, Weber, and Mannheim, with which we shall be dealing in the following section. For the latter, in recognizing that analysis and understanding of historical behavior as expressive of human meaning required the use of theory and conceptualization, moved hermeneutic historicism into closer proximity with the other two orientations we shall discuss in this section.

The nomological approach involves the attempt to reduce the line of distinction between the logic of inquiry of the historical sciences dealing with human phenomena and the natural sciences. The extreme formulation of the nomological position is contained in Hempel's famous covering law model:

> In history as anywhere else in empirical science, the explanation of a phenomenon consists in subsuming it under general empirical laws; and the criterion of its soundness is not whether it appeals to our imagination, whether it is presented in suggestive analogies, or is otherwise made to appear plausible — all this may occur in pseudo-explanations as well — but exclusively whether it rests on empirically well confirmed assumptions concerning initial conditions and general laws.[67]

In this absolute formulation, the covering-law model has, however, shown itself to be inapplicable to historical explanation, as Hempel himself came to realize. Indeed it has been noted that Hempel told historians how they should, not how they do proceed. Paul Lacombe[68] and Karl Lamprecht[69] in the 1890s in their critique of the conventional historiography of the time had argued that all sciences, including history, passed from a prescientific phase in which they employed individualizing methods and assembled facts to a scientific phase in which they sought to explain these facts in terms of generalized explanations. Attempts had been made, particularly by nineteenth-century positivists, such as Auguste Comte, Henri Taine, and Henry Thomas Buckle, to formulate a social physics, including general laws of historical development; but these attempts remained the work of speculative philosophers of history or sociologists who failed to satisfy their own demands for empirical validation.

The belief in the continuity of history as an evolutionary process became as untenable for most neo-positivists in the twentieth century as it did for other orientations of historical thought. Karl Popper thus stressed that "history has no meaning," that "there is no history of mankind, there is only an indefinite number of histories of all kinds of aspects of human life,"[70] and saw in the attempt to read direction into history and develop history into a predictive science a delusion with serious political consequences for the freedom of men. Yet in a more modest way, the belief remained alive that "speaking scientifically, the only social history is quantitative history,"[71] and that from this perspective history must seek to establish measurable "regularities and principles of order obtaining between isolable formalized elements."[72] Particularly in economic, social, and demographic history — to a lesser extent in political history, as, for example, in the study of electoral behavior — the attempt has been made to construct quantitative models to analyze certain isolable variables capable of quantification and bring them into relation with other variables, such as demographic curves and price developments in preindustrial societies. Yet such models are unsatisfactory to many historians; they fail to take into account the complexity, structure, and uniqueness of the historical situation, the context of meaning within which these measurable phenomena occur, a context which defies quantitative reduction. Walt Rostow's model of the stages of economic growth involved in industrialization has therefore been questioned by economic historians, such as Alexander Gerschenkron,[73] who have maintained that the conditions leading to industrial "takeoff" which obtained in the case of British industrialization never recurred in other economically more backward societies in which industrialization took place later within a very different constellation of political, economic, and technological factors. An attempt to abstract economic processes from their broader social and political context is contained in the studies by the New Economic Historians in the United States. Thus Robert Fogel in his *Railroads and American Economic Growth*[74] sought to analyze the railroads as a factor in American economic growth by setting up certain "hypothetico-deductive" systems by which the influence of the railroads on economic growth in America could be measured by comparing the actual course of measurable events and relationships with models in which the railroads did not exist.

A very different attempt at a nomological approach which has proved more fruitful to historical inquiry has been the attempt by many of the social historians of the French *Annales* circle to proceed from empirical, often quantifiable data, to the structural contexts within which these data receive their significance. On the surface there are certain points of similarity between the concern on the part of the historians of the *Annales* orientation and of American psychohistorians to probe the subconscious structures underlying social and cultural phenomena. But the two approaches are in fact quite different. Structuralist anthropologists and historians have indeed freely used psychoanalytical concepts. But while American psychohistory has concentrated on the biographies of individuals of historical significance, such as Luther, Gandhi, or Hitler,[75] and sought to explain these biographies in terms of childhood and adolescent identity crises governed by certain laws of psychological growth and generational conflict abstracted from a broader cultural and political context, French structural historians such as Lucien Febvre or Emmanuel Le Roy Ladurie have been much more broadly cultural and anthropological in their approach. Neo-orthodox Freudians such as Wilhelm Reich and Max Hork-heimer[76] have in fact sought to establish the link between social and cultural factors and the family; but these studies, begun in the 1930s, have had relatively little significance for American psychohistory, which has been slow in relating psychobiography convincingly to social and political history.

French structuralism in anthropology and history comes from a very different tradition of social science than does psychohistory. Although both stress the naturalistic and biological basis of all conscious life, structuralism seeks to proceed on the basis of tangible data, hard "societal" facts; in contrast, psychoanalysis views itself as a hermeneutical science seeking understanding which largely defies quantification. French structuralist anthropology has not been as hostile to the role of history as some of its critics such as Dieter Groh and Alfred Schmidt[77] have suggested. It is not coincidental that the historians of the *Annales* circle, who include practitioners of radically empirical and quantitative approaches to history, are affiliated with the *Sixième Section* of the École Pratiques des Hautes Études in Paris — about which we shall say more in the next chapter — which has also been the institutional home of structural anthropologists, linguists, psychoanalysts, and literary critics, including Claude Lévi-Strauss, Jacques Alcan and Roland Barthes, and that close professional and personal ties exist between the historians, the anthropologists, and the linguists within the *Sixième Section*. Structural anthropologists and structural historians have been joined in the investigation of the "unconscious structures" which they believe underlie all institutions and customs and give them coherence. The assumption, of course, is that such structures exist and that neither the historian nor the ethnologist may take verbal evidence at its face value but must "decode" this evidence and proceed from the recurrent phenomena, economic data, social relations, word usage, art forms, symbolism, which permit a degree of quantification, to the deeper structures concealed behind these.

As against the attempt by neo-positivists and structuralists to reduce the fundamental distinction between historical and natural phenomena, an important hermeneutic tradition of historicism has remained alive which has reiterated the autonomy of the historical world. Yet while occasional theorists such as Isaiah Berlin[78] have continued to define history as Ranke and Windelband had done, as the science dealing with the individual, this has not been a key argument against the generalizing approach of the neo-positivists or the structuralists. As we saw above, the philosophic defenders of the hermeneutic tradition of history since Rickert had recognized that while history dealt with meaningful relationships, a science of history dealing with such relationships could no more dispense with concepts than could other sciences. It was indeed the very element of meaning which, as Karl Mannheim suggested, opened up the "possibilities of precision in the combination of meaning-analysis and sociological diagnosis that in time it may be possible to compare them with the methods of the natural sciences." This method Mannheim continued, "will have, in addition, the advantage that it will not have to disregard the realm of meaning as uncontrollable, but will on the contrary make the interpretation of meaning a vehicle of precision."[79]

Yet history and the social sciences were no more able than the natural sciences to recapture a reality past or present as it "really" was or is. This reality was a chaos of events. Only from the conceptualizations with which the historian approached his subject matter did the coherence among the events become apparent.[80] In a basic way these conceptualizations, which Max Weber named "ideal types," differed from the conceptualization employed in the natural sciences. They sought not formalized relationships but "thought models created for activistic purposes in real life" which took into account the unique elements of meaning and purpose found in concrete historical settings. These models assumed that human beings individually and collectively acted in pursuit of certain purposes, that an element of calculability thus entered into all social behavior, and that it was hence possible to formulate conceptually how historical agents or groups could be expected to act ideally in pursuit of their purposes. Yet although these conceptualizations are not taken directly from empirical observations but rather represent "intellectual apperceptions" by which the historian or the social scientist seeks to penetrate and understand human actions, they nevertheless are capable of a degree of empirical validation. The function of the "ideal type" was to permit a comparison between the scientific conceptualization of a historical process and its empirically observable course. Thus despite the stress on the elements of meaning in every historical context which cannot be reduced to the formalized relationships envisaged by logical positivists or structuralists, the Weberians too are willing to use models, at times capable of a degree of quantification, in the search for broader structural contexts of change. Nor did such an approach in principle exclude the use of anthropological and psychoanalytical concepts. Yet history inspired by Weberian notions concerned itself much more strongly than that which followed neo-positivists' or structuralists' beliefs with the question of the role of collective human consciousness and intentions in effecting changes of structures through time.

The third orientation which we wish to consider here is Marx's dialectical materialist approach to history. It must be stressed, however, that in practice not all Marxist historians have been dialectical in their approach, that a good many have operated with assumptions which resemble older positivistic notions of history as a natural science. Marx himself gave grounds for the misunderstanding of his position by referring to the "tendencies" in capitalism working with "iron necessity towards inevitable results," "with the necessity of a process of nature."[81] Yet there is too much in Marx's philosophical and historical work — not least of all in his actual historical writings — which speaks against this narrowly deterministically conceived view of history. Marxist theorists since the 1920s (Lukács, Korsch, Gramsci) have increasingly pointed to a Marx who emphasized the role of conscious human activity and recognized the fundamental difference between history as an area of meaningful human action and nature, which in important aspects itself reflected human, that is, historical activity.

There is little question that for Marx and Engels the productive relations are indeed ultimately decisive in historical change. Yet the productive relations themselves bear the imprint of human consciousness. Significant for the historian from Marx's perspective is that all social phenomena and historical events must be viewed within the framework of a system of social relations undergoing constant change. This change, however, is neither automatic, determined by "laws working independently of the consciousness of men," as the East German *Philosophical Dictionary*[82] suggested, nor by pure human will, but the result of "a process in which both man and Nature participate."[83] But precisely because history is not made by "abstract-isolated-individuals" but by men who live and act in an "ensemble of social relationships,"[84] that possesses not only an internal structure but contains inherent tendencies of change, the historian can be satisfied neither with the hermeneutic search for grasping the uniqueness of historical personalities and collectivities nor with the empirical approach as practiced by the analytical historian who seeks to isolate quantifiable factors unaffected by conscious human action. For in contrast to other directions in contemporary historical thought which we have discussed, much of Marxism[85] continues to view history as a process leading to human emancipation. It carries with it the notion of history as a critical social science seeking not merely to interpret but to change the world and views itself as rooted in the concrete material and political situation making for change.

A Marxist approach to history in principle makes it possible to combine important aspects of a hermeneutic and an empirical-analytical approach. Like the latter it analyzes the structural setting within which social behavior occurs. It is capable, as Marx demonstrated in *Capital,* of formulating medium-range models of economic development, in this case that of British capitalism, which permit empirical examination. As Eric Hobsbawm observed, "the immense strength of Marx has always lain in his insistence on both the existence of social structure and its historicity, or in other words its internal dynamic of change."[86] The tremendous diversity of approaches to social science and history among Marxist scholars forbids any broad observation on Marxist scholarship. As we shall note in Chapter IV, a great deal of Marxist historical research has combined Marxist questions and social critique with rigorous empirical-analytical and text-critical methods. Difficulties arise where the attempt is made to dispense with these methods without finding an adequate, inter-subjectively controllable, alternate logic of inquiry. Yet much of Marxist historical research, particularly where it has freed itself from narrow partisan dogmatism, has struck a balance between quantitative analytical and qualitative hermeneutical methods which recognized the need for both approaches but also their limits. The insistence on the inseparability of theory and practice, of political commitment and scholarship, and the recognition of men as active factors in societal change set limits to the reduction of the past into numerical relationships. Marxist historians — such as Jürgen Kuczynski, Albert Soboul, Eric Hobsbawm, and George Rudé — have thus stressed the role of "objective" economic factors as well as that of consciousness. Marxists have thus made important contributions to a broadly socially conceived history of structural change, which has been a central concern of analytical historians as well, yet at the same time focused more sharply on the dysfunctions within the structure and on the problems of change. They have thus at times provided important correctives to an overly narrowly conceived analytical approach.

The essays which follow are not in any sense intended as a comprehensive survey of the most significant developments in recent historical writing, nor as illustrations of the theoretical orientations discussed above. They center on attempts to redefine what constitutes historical science among three groups of historians, each loosely held together by common assumptions and a common heritage and to an extent by a common institutional framework. These three approaches are not presented here as a succession to higher forms of historical understanding or science. They represent attempts, contemporary with each other, to respond to the inadequacies of conventional historiography. The first of these essays will examine the French "School of the *Annales*" as an example of an attempt to apply analytical models to historical studies without losing a sense for either the uniqueness of historical situations and developments or the structural contexts within history. The second will examine the response of historians in Germany standing within the tradition of hermeneutic history who sought to take into account the changed social and intellectual conditions which led to the crisis of the German tradition of historiography based on hermeneutic assumptions. A third will seek to analyze attempts to develop Marx's paradigms as an alternative to hermeneutic and analytical approaches. In dealing with Marxism, we shall turn our primary, but by no means exclusive, attention to Marxism in western European countries, in this case particularly France and Great Britain, where Marxist historiography developed relatively late and relatively free from a strong communist or socialist party, as a response to certain tensions in modern capitalist societies and an attempt to deal with the inadequacies of the hermeneutically or analytically oriented historiography.

These essays proceed from the assumption that a critical history of historiography is inseparable from a critical history of society and culture. Yet this criticism involves an examination of logical inadequacies and limitations of scope in historical science. These limitations themselves are historically located as are the critical tools with which the historian approaches history. In the absence of an Archimedian platform from which the historian can judge scientific truth and in view of the very historical character of scholarly cognition, the history of historical writings itself, as the continuous dialogue of historians situated in historical reality, becomes the indispensable source for a critical examination of the scientific character of history.

II

The *Annales* Tradition —
French Historians
in Search of a Science of History

I

THE NOMOLOGICAL model of inquiry in history is not new. It proceeds from a conception of science which assumes that the logic of scientific inquiry is one for the cultural as well as the natural sciences, that "in history as anywhere else in empirical science, the explanation of the phenomenon consists in subsuming it under general empirical laws."[1] If "among [historians] the strange idea prevails, that their business is merely to relate events,"[2] this is held merely to reflect the prescientific character of modern historical studies.

From Condorcet to the New Economic Historians, historians, sociologists, and philosophers have frequently voiced the demand that history seek generalizations. Some, like August Comte, Henry Thomas Buckle, or Friedrich Engels in his later years, postulated that human actions are governed by mental and physical laws which it is the task of the historian to discover. Against this call for generalizations, historians in the hermeneutic tradition have long protested, not only because they held these generalizations to be insufficiently based on empirical evidence or the critical analysis of sources and hence to represent speculative rather than scholarly thought but also because they considered the aim of the historian to be the discovery of the unique in every event, in Ranke's words, the "infinite in every existence."[3] The weakness of every philosophy of history, Ranke maintained, consisted in its attempt to subordinate the very events of history to a construct. History dealt with living men. If generalizations were forced upon history, not only "all that which is interesting about history would disappear" but "history would lose all scientific footing."[4]

Yet there is a middle ground between a philosophy of history which accepts and one which rejects all generalizations and insists that the unique individuality of every historical constellation be understood immediately on its own terms without reference to general concepts. This middle ground is provided by the attempt to utilize explanations of limited or medium range to explain concrete historical phenomena. This approach recognizes the uniqueness of every historical situation, the factors of will, intentionality, and consciousness which color every historical context, and hence the need of the historian to "understand" every historical situation.

The *Annales* circle represents in many ways such a middle ground. It is not quite correct to subsume the tradition of the *Annales* under the label of analytic history, as has been done by some of its critics.[5] For the great historians in the *Annales* tradition — Lucien Febvre, Marc Bloch, Fernand Braudel, Robert Mandrou, Jacques Le Goff, Emmanuel Le Roy Ladurie — are thoroughgoing historicists in their insistence that every age must be understood as it was, that the historian must guard against presentism, and that every attempt to impose a theory of progress or of clearly discernible direction on history results in distorting historical reality. In this sense the great historians of the *Annales* tradition have taken much more seriously than Ranke himself Ranke's famous dictum that "every epoch is immediate unto God,"[6] which had not prevented Ranke from seeing in the history of modern Europe the more or less inevitable triumph of the Protestant ideas. In their concern for each historical setting for the "total" character, the work of the *Annales* historians differs sharply from that of the American New Economic Historians and in France from the "Histoire Quantitative" of Jean Marczewski and his group, both of which groups attempt to isolate segments like the economy, to which hypothetico-deductive models can be applied.[7] Indeed, the French *Annales* cannot be conceived without considering the heritage of the German historical school. The "great men" of the *Annales* read German, and Marc Bloch had actually studied in Germany. But more important, French historical studies themselves had been deeply influenced by German scholarship. Critical methods, to be sure, predated the German influence, but the seminar method was directly patterned on German practice. While Henri Berr and Lucien Febvre rejected a narrow, event-oriented narrative history, they affirmed the necessity of starting with the sources, of examining these critically, although they possessed a broader notion of what constituted an historical source.

The aim of historical studies remains for the *Annales* historians, as it did for the German historical school, the "understanding" of the past. Yet the concept *"comprendre"* as used by Lucien Febvre or Marc Bloch possessed from the beginning a very different connotation from the German term *"Verstehen"* as used in the hermeneutical tradition.[8] For Wilhelm Windelband or Friedrich Meinecke, understanding in the sense of *Verstehen* was sharply differentiated from causal "explanation." In contrast, Lucien Febvre emphasized that the "understanding" (*comprendre*) of social phenomena could never be reduced to immediate "knowledge" (*savoir*) but always involved an attempt to explain their relationships. Understanding of human behavior in its concrete manifestations did not exclude but rather necessitated causal explanations.

The striking similarities and profound differences between historical studies in France and Germany to an extent reflected the different systems of higher education and the institutional settings within which these studies were pursued in the two countries. On one level, that of the grandes écoles, higher education was even more elitist in its recruitment in France than in Germany. To be sure, the universities enjoyed less prestige than in Germany. There were no universities in the nineteenth century in France before 1896. The Revolution had abolished the twenty-two universities which had existed at that time. Individual faculties continued to exist in sixteen provincial cities, but

Napoleonic legislation left them without any real autonomy. They were "not really independent bodies simply devoted to higher learning"[9] but primarily, at least in the case of the Faculties of Science and Letters, service institutions for the secondary schools, which not only awarded the teaching *licence* but also conducted the examinations for the *baccalauréat*. In contrast to the German universities, research and the training of scholars remained secondary. Not only intellectual and cultural life but also scholarship took place largely elsewhere. This situation was only partially changed after the individual faculties in the provincial towns were united into provincial universities. Serious specialized higher education was concentrated in France in special schools, the prestigious grandes écoles, such as the École Polytechnique and the École Normale Supérieure established in the French Revolution. For the purposes of historical studies, the École des Chartes, founded in the 1820s to train archivists and the ultra elitist École Normale Supérieure are most important.[10] In contrast to the faculties and later the universities which had relatively liberal entrance policies, admission into the grandes écoles followed upon a vigorous competitive examination. The grandes écoles provided an elitist element and an esprit de corps unparalleled at the German universities. They were residential schools, whose students were subjected to rigid discipline. A number of residential lycées with national reputations prepared students for the grandes écoles. Although the number of scholarships at the grandes écoles rose over the years a larger proportion of the students than was the case at the German universities came from well-to-do families. Fritz Ringer concludes that "altogether higher education was probably less democratic in France than in Germany until around 1930."[11]

As in Germany, the school system closely followed class lines. If the higher primary and the normal schools fulfilled a function in some ways similar to that of the German Realschulen — from which they differed in many other respects — in perpetuating the social distinction between the middle and the lower classes, the lycées served as a training ground for a cultivated bourgeoisie. Like the German Gymnasien they sought to imbue a culture based heavily on the study of the classics and consciously removed from a practical preparation for professional life. Yet well into the twentieth century the proportion of students attending the lycées in France remained considerably below the enrollment in corresponding levels of school in Germany. The same also holds for university enrollment. The heavy stress on classical studies and the skeptical attitude toward modernity left their mark, as we shall see, even on the historians of the *Annales* orientation.

The grandes écoles were by no means intended as centers combining research and training in the way in which the German universities after the Humboldt reforms of the early nineteenth century aspired to do. They were centers intended to prepare an elite for public life. To a greater extent than in Germany, where historians, contrary to the common image, were also deeply involved in political life, in France the scholar — among historians we need mention only Guizot, Michelet, Thiers — was seen as a man of the world, involved in public and political life. The Collège de France (founded in 1530 with a chair of History and Morality established in 1769), with its distinguished faculty whose lectures were open to the public and who gave no examinations and granted no degrees, came closest to an institution devoted to research.

The movement for the reform of university education and the professionalization of research increasingly looked for its models to Germany. Significant for the transformation of historical studies was the establishment of the École Pratique des Hautes Études in 1868 and of its Fourth Section devoted to history and the philological sciences. The École Pratique des Hautes Études developed independently of the university. It held no examinations. It offered no lectures. Instruction took place in seminars patterned after the German model. With the introduction of the German seminar method there followed a rather uncritical acceptance of German hermeneutic methods. Historical scholarship in France — as was also the case in the United States at that time — identified itself closely with Rankean traditions. On the surface, Charles Langlois and Charles Seignobos' *Introduction aux études historiques* (1898),[12] the standard textbook of historical method for generations of French students, appeared narrowly inspired by German practices in its stress that there is no history without written documents and in the procedure it dictated for dealing with these. A more careful reading of it as well as of Seignobos' *La Méthode historique appliquée aux sciences sociales*[13] reveals that the authors were much more aware of the active role of the historian in formulating questions and hypotheses and more willing to recognize the role of generalizations and of social factors in historical explanation than the German school had been. Moreover, the political context in which the new critical history arose in France after the national catastrophe of 1870 was different from that in Germany. The "new history" was pursued by historians, such as Gabriel Monod, Ernest Lavisse, Charles Seignobos, and Charles Langlois, who openly recognized the political function of historical science and wished to replace the theological and dynastic bases of patriotism linked to the monarchical order with the national credo of the French Revolution.[14] Nevertheless, despite their critique of the German ideal of historical science, which they regarded as too narrowly philological in its approach and too far removed from serious attempts at historical synthesis, they provided models in their writings for an event-oriented history which, in proceeding almost exclusively from official documents, viewed the political and military history of the European states through the perspective of the governments, not unlike their German precursors.

The organization of historical studies in France encouraged scholarly conformity in ways not unsimilar to those prevailing in Germany. The highly selective recruitment of the students for the lycées and the grandes écoles favored candidates with similar social and educational backgrounds. The rigid discipline of life and study in the grandes écoles, which contrasted sharply with the "academic freedom" of the German universities, nevertheless did not appear to have prevented considerable diversity in political outlook. A republican tradition in France moreover guaranteed that a greater diversity of political opinion was represented at the university. Nor were Jews excluded from academic posts to the extent that they were in Germany. Nonetheless, the manner in which the professorate was recruited in France did not encourage methodological innovation. Young scholars remained dependent on their mentors well into middle life while they completed the ambitious theses for the Doctorate of State, generally necessary for an appointment to a professorial post. Yet in France a challenge to the historicist orientation existed by way of a positivistic tradition in sociology, with deep roots in nineteenth-century thought and a firm base in the French academic structure.[15] It was the sociologists and the philosophers who provided the first significant challenge to the historicism of the historians.

From the standpoint of this French tradition of positivism, the theory of knowledge congruent with the Rankean tradition appeared irrational and unscientific; for the positivistic conception of science presupposed that all statements were capable of inter-subjective validation. The hermeneutic tradition accepted that such validation was possible in the critical examination of sources but not in the understanding of a historical context. For Dilthey, for example, the personal experience (*Erlebnis*) was the final criterion of truth. French positivists since Auguste Comte, while recognizing that the subject matter of the natural sciences and of history was different, had maintained that the logic was the same whether the sciences dealt with men or nature. For the French analytical tradition of historical studies in the twentieth century, Émile Durkheim was perhaps the most important transmitter of the positivistic conception of social science. Durkheim's theory of knowledge[16] is of particular interest to us here because important aspects of this theory were assimilated by Marc Bloch — to a lesser extent also by Lucien Febvre — and through Bloch became a part of the intellectual heritage of the *Annales* circle. In contrast to German historicism, both Durkheim and Bloch proceeded from the assumption that the individual could only be under-

stood within the context of a society and that this society manifested itself in concrete forms which could be observed from the
outside very much like phenomena of nature.

From this position Marc Bloch, one of the founders of the
Annales, was later to ask whether it is really true, as conventional historians have maintained, that "the observation of the
past even of the most distant past is always indirect" and could
be mediated only through documents, documents which first
had to be "understood."[17] Bloch agreed with the hermeneutic
school that "it is human consciousness which in the last analysis
is the subject matter of historical studies" and that history, in
contrast to nature which knows of no intentionality, "always
has to deal with beings who are capable of pursuing conscious
goals" which the historian has to "understand."[18] But historians or social scientists were not primarily concerned with
the content of the consciousness of isolated individuals or even
the consciousness of groups of individuals but with concrete
social modes of behavior in which social norms are reflected.
The historian and the social scientist thus dealt with "social
facts" (Durkheim's term) which were often capable of direct
observation without the mediation of written documents. It was
conceivable that the individual event or the specific content of
consciousness could be understood only indirectly from written
or oral statements; but the structure of the society manifested
itself in concrete institutional and material remains. Bloch,
therefore, rejected Seignobos' assertion that no history was possible without documents.[19] The historian pursued the concrete
traces of the past. The written documents with which conventional historians had worked were for the most part only secondary sources which were insufficient for scientific or scholarly
purposes because they reflected the events only through the
subjectivity of the observer. They could be viewed as primary
sources only insofar as they themselves provided observational
material for the structure of consciousness, the mentality of a
society, or if — as in the case of laws or business papers — they
constituted a concrete constituent part of the actions of the
society. However, neither Durkheim nor Bloch believed that

this reality revealed itself simply to the passive observer. Objective reality, whether in nature or society, answered only the questions which the researcher posed. Science, therefore, could never dispense with questions, selections, analysis, or abstraction. Bloch, as had Durkheim before him, thus shifted the emphasis from the individual to the collectivity.

2

THE ACTUAL HISTORY of the *Annales* does not begin with the foundation of the journal *Annales d'histoire économique et sociale* in 1929 but in an important sense much earlier, namely, with the foundation by Henri Berr in 1900 of the *Revue de synthèse historique*. Lucien Febvre became a collaborator on the journal in 1907; Marc Bloch in 1912. The *Revue de synthèse historique* grew out of the critical attitude which found expression in the 1890s toward the conventional historical scholarship following German models. Durkheim's journal *L'Année sociologique* became one of the centers of this critique. Durkheim himself and François Simiand initiated the attack against the event-oriented historical writing centering on politics which dominated the French schools of higher learning.[20]

Henri Berr, technically a philosopher concerned with the theory of historical knowledge, considered Durkheim's sociology to be too unhistorical but agreed with Durkheim "that there is no science which does not deal with generalizations."[21] Without theory, he maintained, no science was possible, also no science of history. Berr considered one of the main purposes of the *Revue de synthèse historique* to be the discussion of the theoretical aspects of historical science, but of theory oriented toward empirical observation and sharply distinguished from speculative philosophy of history. The historians who defined the task of history as consisting of the investigation of the singular and its changes in his opinion overlooked the fact that without criteria of selections that presupposed certain regularities in history, history would be pure chaos and no science of history would be possible. History not unlike the natural sciences had to consider "similarities, recurrences, and conformities," even if these did not constitute the whole of history and even if laws were not to be understood as absolute necessities either in the natural or the historical sciences.[22] A method of understanding not subject to some rules of logic was for Berr as inadmissible in the historical sciences as in the natural sciences.[23] Both types of science worked with hypotheses. Analysis and synthesis could not be separated.[24] "A collection of facts has no more scientific value than a collection of stamps or seashells," he wrote.[25] The individual historian would be incapable of achieving historical synthesis; this would require teams of investigators.[26] History became a science to the extent that it began to explain, instead of contenting itself with description. Explanation was not possible without comparison, although the historian had to keep in mind the elements of uniqueness and individuality in historical phenomena. In conscious opposition to Nietzsche, Berr emphasized that "history has not lost its contact with life because it has been too scientific but on the contrary because it has not been scientific enough."[27]

In 1920 the important series, "Evolution and Mankind," founded by Henri Berr, began to appear. In this collection, which still continues today, a new orientation in historical writing found expression. The contrast with the eighteen-volume *Histoire de France*[28] edited by Ernest Lavisse is clear. The stress on Europe remained; but in the place of the event-oriented, chronologically organized history of politics of nation states, the attempt was made here to place social and cultural history, topically approached, into a central position.

Berr's idea received an important further theoretical development in Lucien Febvre's *La Terre et l'évolution humaine*,[29] which appeared in 1922 with a preface by Berr. In this book Febvre emphasized the close link between geography and history but at the same time emphatically rejected the geographic determinism which had been advanced by the German geographer, Friedrich Ratzel. Febvre associated himself with the conception of a "human geography" as it had been advocated by Paul Vidal de la Blache in France, a belief that the geographical environment indeed constituted an important part of the framework of human possibilities but that man himself participated in the shaping of this environment. The past decades, Febvre stressed, had seen a radical change in the basic conceptions of geography and of history. The historians and the geographers at the time of his writing he found no longer interested only in the development of "the political, legal and constitutional framework of the peoples of the past or the military and diplomatic events. They are interested in the whole life of these peoples, in their material and moral culture, the total development of their sciences, arts, beliefs, industries, trade, social divisions and grouping."[30]

In his thesis of 1912 on *Philippe II et la Franche Comté*[31] Febvre had already made a contribution to such a history. He was concerned here with a history of a region, of Franche Comté — not as purely geographical but as a historical region at a definite point in time. The purpose of the study was to investigate a crisis, which manifested itself at one and the same time in the political conflict between "provincial privileges and Catholic absolutism," in the social and economic confrontations between nobility and bourgeoisie, and in the religious struggle, between Protestants and Catholics. Febvre sought in this book to reconstruct "the inner life of a political entity, the region of Franche Comté," to write a political history which "sought out the obscure and deep seated causes of human decisions in the humble realities of provincial existence and in the changes in the social order"[32] thus far concealed from the learned historians who had devoted their efforts to diplomatic and military history and the religious conflicts. Febvre avoided the term structure and recognized the influence which great personalities had had on history; yet he was nevertheless primarily concerned with changes in political, social, and intellectual structures. He did not recognize the primacy of any single sector of social reality, of economics, religion, politics, or geography. These aspects of the total social role and the life-style of nobility and bourgeoisie could not be separated. He began to be interested in prices, income, and population growth which he used to illustrate his observations. Strikingly absent in Febvre's investigation of the "whole life" of an age and of a region were the lower classes of the population.

This primary concern with the upper classes recurs in Febvre's later works in his study of *Martin Luther un destin* (1928) and especially in his great work on *Le Problème de l'incroyance au XVI siècle: La religion de Rabelais.*[33] In the latter, Febvre is not attempting a history of ideas in the manner of Meinecke or Croce but rather an analysis of an intellectual climate, of a mentality, centered however on the educated classes who in this book, in contrast to his work on Luther, are viewed relatively isolated from social and political forces. Febvre examines the assumption underlying much of the research on Rabelais, that Rabelais was an atheist. Whether this was indeed the case cannot in Febvre's judgment be determined on the basis of the texts which have come down to us. We can however determine whether it was possible in Rabelais' day to be an atheist.[34] Febvre here proceeds from a radically historicist position which presupposes the unique character of every epoch. He regards as "unhistorical" the question whether Rabelais had been an atheist or an unbeliever. "The whole book" he stressed, "is directed against these illusions and these anachronisms."[35] In Rabelais' age, belief and unbelief, Greek philosophy and Christian religion, natural science and theology could simply not be separated from each other. Febvre tries to demonstrate this partly by conventional methods, through a hermeneutical examination of the texts, partly however by means of an "archeology of language," which examines the "mental tools" of the age on the basis of their concepts and syntax.[36]

While Febvre in his later works assigns an ever greater role to consciousness, Bloch increasingly emphasizes the material framework within which consciousness expresses itself. His first major book *Les Rois thaumaturges* (1924)[37] is concerned with a problem of collective mentality, the emergence of the belief in the practical ability of the kings through their miraculous gift of touch to cure the disease of scrofula and the assimilation of this belief into the medieval conception of kingship. Even

more from a methodological point of view, Bloch's *Les Carac-
téres originaux de l'histoire rurale*[38] (1931) constitutes an historiographical breakthrough which translates the Durkheim-
ian concept of the social fact into a tool of historical research.
Bloch's point of departure was no longer the hermeneutic interpretation of documents but the archeological analysis of the
material remains of the past. In contrast to conventional agrarian histories, Bloch proceeded not from legal and institutional
relationships but from agriculture as it had been practiced. Taking into consideration field patterns, cropping systems, and
farming techniques, Bloch attempted to reconstruct a social
history of agriculture since the Middle Ages. Such a history,
Bloch thought, required a "regressive method": information
which we possess of recent times with the help of archeological
material enables us to reach conclusions about agrarian structures of the more distant past. Also needed was a comparative
method as a means of defining more clearly the unique character of these structures. In contrast to Febvre, Bloch was not
primarily concerned with the mighty, the wealthy, or the cultured but with serfs and peasants. Also in contrast to Febvre,
Bloch was much more intensively interested in the problem of
historical change, in this case in the continuity and development of agriculture and of rural life from the Middle Ages to
the present.

In his great work of synthesis, *La Société féodale* (1939–
1940),[39] Bloch viewed feudalism from a perspective quite different from the conventional studies which conceived it from
the standpoint of military services and also from Marx's conceptions of feudalism as a social mode of production. Bloch
attempted here to reconstitute what he calls "a total social am-
biance." Feudalism was presented as an integral part of the
social climate of the times and of a mental structure in which
modes of work and thoughts and relations of domination and
dependence, of wealth and poverty were closely interwoven.
By means of a comparison of different forms of feudalism,
mainly in Europe but also elsewhere, Bloch attempted to redefine the concept of feudalism as a form of society. He pro-

ceeded topically and only in part chronologically; but in contrast to the later works of Febvre, Bloch's primary concern was the rise and decline of a social structure. He did not, however, claim to possess a model of explanation for historical change. In this respect Bloch's procedure remained descriptive rather than explanatory, even if he was concerned with the description of complex social structures and not with narrating events.

3

THE *Annales d'histoire économique et sociale* were founded in 1929 jointly by Lucien Febvre and Marc Bloch. We shall divide the history of the *Annales* into two periods, one prior to 1945, in which what Le Roy Ladurie has called a "qualitative structural history" predominated, and a second period after 1945, in which the "quantitative history of *'conjonctures'* " comes increasingly to the foreground without replacing the older direction entirely. (The term *"conjonctures"* so belabored by the *Annales* is difficult to translate. Borrowed from the economists, it combines the notions of trend and cycle.) There are also clear institutional differences between these two periods. The different organizational circumstances under which the *Annales* appeared contributed to the changes in the direction and methods of *Annales* research. Before 1945 the journal itself stands in the foreground, edited by Febvre and Bloch, who at the time — Febvre until 1936, Bloch until 1939 — were still in Strasbourg. The *Annales* should not be identified exclusively with "its great men" even in this period, as some of the historians of the journal have done. From the very beginning, the *Annales* constituted an international forum for new directions in social history. The war then became a turning point. Bloch, of Jewish descent, had to leave Paris, fought in the Resistance, and in June of 1944 was executed as a hostage by the Gestapo. Febvre continued the journal in Paris. While in hiding from the Nazis, Bloch wrote his important reflections on the nature of historical science, *Apologie pour l'histoire,*[40] which remained a fragment, and his analysis of the French debacle of 1940, *L'Étrange défaite.*[41] The causes, he believes, were to be traced in the intellectual and spiritual inflexibility and narrowness that characterized the leadership classes of France, a narrowness reflected in the mentality and practice of French historians.

War and Resistance contributed to the reorientation of French scholarship. Bloch's critical stance toward traditional French intellectual and scholarly attitudes, which he had castigated in *L'Étrange défaite,* was shared in the postwar period by a generation of younger scholars. After 1947 the development of the *Annales,* renamed in 1946 *Annales, Économies, Sociétés, Civilisations,* is closely interwoven with an institution, the Sixth Section of the École Pratique des Hautes Études, founded in 1947, under the direction of Lucien Febvre and after Febvre's death in 1956 by that of Fernand Braudel until his retirement in 1972. As we had indicated, it was at the École Pratique, founded in 1868, that historians had first been trained in seminars after the Rankean model. The new Sixth Section of the École Pratique was to serve as a center for interdisciplinary teaching and research in the social sciences. The Sixth Section, which counted among its members not only historians but also structuralist anthropologists and linguists — including Claude Lévi-Strauss, Roland Barthes, Pierre Bourdieu, and others — as well as economists, geographers, and sociologists, now became the best financed and most significant center for social science and historical studies in France. While in the period before 1945 the *Annales* had fought against the historical establishment represented by the event-oriented historiography of Seignobos, now the *Annales* themselves became the establishment. The new title of the journal expressed the belief of its editors that history and the social sciences could no longer be separated and that both had to be merged in a "science of man" which dealt with the structure as well as with the dynamics of historical existence.

The works of Febvre and Bloch belong not only in terms of time but also in terms of methodology to the first of the two periods mentioned above. The same is also true for the *Annales* of the 1930s and 1940s. Bloch and Febvre promised in the first issue that the new journal would tear down the high walls which separated historical studies from the social and economic sciences and would do this not by means of "long theoretical essays" but by "facts and examples."[42] Bloch and Febvre in fact kept that promise. As Bloch wrote in a critical obituary of the German social historian Georg von Below, the need existed to come closer to the "human realities." Von Below, who had thought so largely in legal and constitutional terms, had never succeeded in making apparent "the close relationship between political order, social structure, mentality, feelings and ideas."[43] Bloch agreed that these relationships could not be reduced to a simple formula. The *Annales* undertook many-sided investigations of agrarian structures; the interaction of technology, science, and mentalities; the changes in the structure and the function of the nobility since the Middle Ages; and the development of early capitalistic business methods.

More space was devoted than in later volumes to the economic and political problems of the nineteenth and especially the twentieth century: the world economic crisis, Fascism and Socialism, the modern megalopolis, and the developing countries. Of great interest to the *Annales* were the beginnings of quantitative economic history. There were frequent reports about yet unutilized "private" archives, which contained documents needed for a quantitative social and economic history. Throughout, the close relationship between economic and social history and the history of mentalities was stressed. The *Annales* were interested in early capitalistic business practices, not solely from an economic perspective but in connection with the history of collective consciousness. Febvre began the section "Words and Things" in which he sought to investigate the close relationship between "mental tools" and social and economic reality. In the 1930s the *Annales* began the great discussion — still continuing today — on the significance of magic in European history.

Fernand Braudel's monumental thesis *La Méditerranée et le monde méditerranée à l'époque de Philippe II*,[44] which appeared in 1949, signified in certain respects a transition from an emphasis on the history of mentalities to an "emphasis" on structures as quantities which were relatively independent of human action. Much more radically than his teacher Lucien Febvre, or than Marc Bloch, Braudel distinguishes between different historical times, an almost stationary geological time, the "long duration"[45] of social institutions, and "the short time" of events. He does indeed, especially in the second edition of 1966, emphasize that geographical and climatic factors do not determine history but that men impress their character on geographic space.[46] But at the same time he stresses how powerfully the great social structures resist human intervention and in the second edition raises the possibility that political and intellectual events — for instance, wars, the persecution of the Jews, cultural movements like the Renaissance — are dependent on long-range cyclical oscillations.[47] To a much greater extent than Bloch or Febvre, Braudel regarded political history as uninteresting and irrelevant. To be sure, a third part of his book on the Mediterranean deals exclusively with political and military conflicts of the late nineteenth century, but Braudel refuses to establish the relationship between events and structures. Politics, he argues, has its own time, the time of "short duration." Political events are like dust — irrational and ephemeral. He acknowledges in the second edition that this part of his book on the Mediterranean "frankly stands in the tradition of conventional historical writing" in the sense of Ranke.[48]

What is decisive for history in Braudel's opinion are the long-range developments. Not that Braudel would like to see these developments reduced to mathematical abstractions of the sort employed by the newer behavioral sciences. As a historian he is interested in concrete reality, in "the sources of life themselves in their most concrete, most everyday, most industrial and humanly most anonymous form."[49] In the 1960s Braudel spurred extensive investigations by the Sixth Section of the material and biological bases of the daily life of the broad masses, of nutrition, health, clothing, fashions, production, and class distinctions.[50]

The "quantitative history of economic cycles" originated outside the *Annales*. Very early however, in the 1930s, the *An-*

nales devoted considerable attention to the international research on economic cycles. In the 1950s they followed with great interest the developments in historical demography. Very quickly, quantitative economic and demographic methods were integrated into the *Annales* concept of structure. Quantification in economic or social history was not new. What however distinguished the new quantitative history from previous attempts to utilize statistics in historical writing was that the concern became not with the description of a unique historical situation but with the analysis of social or economic processes. The new quantitative history thought in causal terms. Numbers were to be used in the comparison of differing variables. In order to make this comparison possible, quantifiable factors had to be isolated and long quantitative series reconstructed from the sources. These series, involving a variable, often extended over hundreds of years and made visible long as well as short trends and oscillations, which could be compared with other parallel series in each of which a variable was similarly isolated. Quantitative history was therefore conceived of as a "problem oriented, not a descriptive history."[51] Such a history, in fact, would approach the sources at least as critically as the conventional historical science did, indeed in some ways even more critically,[52] since it regarded literary evidence with great skepticism and preferred hard empirical data from which the elements of subjective bias could be more readily excluded. But it would also recognize much more consciously the role of the historian in approaching the sources with questions and working hypotheses.

Only in the 1950s did the historians of the Sixth Section begin to work seriously with quantitative methods. But already in the 1930s the *Annales* had followed with great interest the work of Earl Hamilton, François Simiand, and Ernest Labrousse. The interesting aspect in Hamilton's contribution[53] consisted less in the resuscitation of an old thesis, already advanced by Jean Bodin in the late sixteenth century — that the price revolution of the sixteenth century was a result of the flooding of Europe with precious metals from America — than in the quantification of the thesis. Hamilton, working in the Spanish archives, had calculated exact amounts of gold and silver imports and then compared them graphically year by year with the development of prices. On the basis of a long series of prices and wages, Simiand,[54] who had been a close collaborator of Durkheim early in the century, arrived at a periodization of European economic history since the fifteenth century. The series revealed so-called A phases of long duration when prices rose and B phases of declining prices which Simiand related to social and political changes. Ernest Labrousse[55] then refined the methodology of wage and price studies even further and investigated the influence of price movements on the outbreak of the French Revolution. This work was later continued by the Sixth Section, of which Labrousse became a member. Within the framework of or inspired by the Sixth Section, ambitious team projects were undertaken which sought to reconstruct not only a quantitative history of prices and wages but also of production and trade for important towns and regions in France, Spain, and Italy during the Old Regime — as, for example, in the astonishing ten volumes of the thesis *Sevilla and the Atlantic, 1550–1650*[56] of Pierre and Huguette Chaunu. By utilizing the archives of Sevilla, they quantified the business records of the Spanish merchant fleet in the Atlantic and thus obtained a better picture of the economic cycles in Spain than did Hamilton.

In the 1950s the great publication series of the Sixth Section began to appear: *Ports, routes, traffics; Monnaie, prix, conjonctures; Affaires et gens d'affaires; Hommes et terres; Sociétés et civilisations.* Simiand's dream, of which Febvre had written in the *Annales*[57] in 1936, of a "social science laboratory in which a director supervises the research of his assistants and the material labors of his technical employees" became a reality.

One could hold against the quantitative economic history of the 1950s that, as Georges Lefebvre regretfully observed, "living, suffering man does not appear in it."[58] There is a good deal less justification when this reproach is made against the works of the 1960s, which increasingly integrated the methods

of the new historical demography into the research of economic
cycles. Historical demography was no more a creation of the
Sixth Section than the quantitative study of economic *conjonctures* had been. Serious work in historical demography began in
France in the early 1950s, in Great Britain in the early 1960s.[59]
Historical demography as developed by Louis Henry differed
from classical demography in concerning itself with the period
before demographic statistics were available, in France before
the Census of 1801, and reconstituting demographic data from
vital statistics contained in parish and tax records.[60] The Institut
National d'Études Demographiques, became the major center
for demographic studies in France, the Cambridge Group for
the History of Population and Social Structure a major center
in Great Britain. From the beginning close contacts existed
between the historians of the Sixth Section and the demogra-
phers of the Institut National d'Études Demographiques and
later those of the Cambridge Group.

The new demographic approach, in avoiding raw statistics
for concrete data on individuals and in seeking to reconstitute
families from these data, came a good deal closer to the study
of concrete human beings. The studies of the 1950s concentrated on villages. By means of sampling techniques some attempts were made relatively soon to gain a view of demographic developments on a regional or national scale. Demographic factors were introduced into the study of economic and
social history. The main concern was no longer with statistics
which served primarily to illustrate an age as in Lucien Febvre's
thesis on Franche Comté or in Braudel's first edition of his book
on the Mediterranean. Long series were constructed on the
basis of land registers, tax books, parish records, and the like.
Ernest Labrousse and in Germany Wilhelm Abel[61] had recognized already in the 1930s the influence of demographic factors
on the development of prices and wages in technologically backward countries, such as in preindustrial Europe where agricultural production remained relatively constant but where a
market economy already existed. The new demographically
oriented economic history now challenged the long held as-

sumption that the stock of precious metals and the quantity of money played a determining role in the movement of prices.

The new demographic studies not only made a direct contribution to the theory of economic development but also offered a clearer picture of the everyday life of the masses of the population. The two most important works which came out of this new orientation were Pierre Goubert's *Beauvais et le Beauvaisis de 1600 à 1730*[62] and Emmanuel Le Roy Ladurie, *Les Paysans du Languedoc*.[63] Both studies set as their aim to write a "total history"[64] of a single region during a limited period of time. Both proceeded with a Malthusian model governed by what Goubert called a demographic structure[65] in which biological factors were still determining and productive capacities remained limited but in which a market economy already existed so that the movement of prices and population increase led to pauperization and intensified class conflict. Here, perhaps for the first time, a serious attempt was made to write the kind of "history of material culture"[66] for which Braudel had called: an empirical and quantitative history which took biological, geographical, and even climatic factors into consideration — harvests, epidemics, nutrition, clothing and fashions, means of production, the distribution of commodities and wealth. The Malthusian model, however, was regarded as a working approach to the empirical data, not as a ready made theory to be imposed upon history. Again, painstaking archival work in land registers, church records, and tax books was involved.

From the long series which these sources yielded it became apparent that mental and social factors limited the determining rule of biological factors and helped shape the economic processes. Goubert's statistics showed that the fertility of women by no means followed a purely biological cycle but differed regionally in the Beauvaisis (the area north of Paris which he had analyzed) and reflected the impact of strict Catholic sexual ethics. Goubert's study made it possible for the first time to gain a clear picture of family structures, of the distribution of landed property, the exact role of the capitalistic bourgeoisie, the crisis of the rural nobility and the condition of the disinherited in one region of seventeenth-century France. But consciously missing from his "total history" was an analysis of institutions and mentalities. In Goubert's *Beauvaisis* political and religious conflicts consequently play a minimal role. Interestingly, Braudel judged Goubert's study very critically and expressed the opinion that Goubert had viewed the Beauvaisis too much in isolation from the general history of the time, that he had been too concerned with structures and too little with change, and had at times forgotten that "statistical methods are only auxiliary sciences, that the essential task consists in building the house of history itself."[67]

Le Roy Ladurie went a good step further in the direction of a study of the crises of consciousness. In *Les Paysans du Languedoc,* he studied the history of Protestantism in this region of southern France in close connection with demographic and food crises and the class conflicts which arose from these. Particularly interesting are Le Roy Ladurie's attempts to utilize concepts of depth psychology to analyze the bloody religious and class confrontation during the carnival in the southern French town of Romans in 1517 — and also the chiliastic uprisings in southern France at the end of the seventeenth and the beginning of the eighteenth centuries, with their sexual sadistic and cannibalistic symbolism — in a very concrete context of economic hardship and the suppression of Protestantism. Le Roy Ladurie succumbs even further than Goubert to the tendency to view a region in isolation from the general French and European development. Goubert had still recognized the importance of royal taxation policies on the economic life of the region. Le Roy Ladurie assumes that the role of the central government can be excluded from a discussion of the economic or the religious history of the Languedoc because in his opinion in the sixteenth and seventeenth centuries the French monarchy did not yet constitute a significant factor in this region. The investigations by Goubert, Le Roy Ladurie, René Baehrel,[68] and others, which in this form could only be conducted on a local level, nevertheless constitute important contributions to a comprehensive, comparative, demographic economic and social history of Europe. Such a history is slowly becoming possible on the basis of extensive local studies in France, Poland, England, and elsewhere. It is doubtful, however, whether the monarchy, and other national institutions were quite as insignificant for the social development of the regions as Le Roy Ladurie and Goubert have assumed and could be so totally excluded from regional history.

But Goubert and Le Roy Ladurie were fully aware that their method, with its heavy stress on demography, could not be universally used in historical studies but was applicable only to a certain type of social structure in a given period when, as in the Old Regime in France, industrialization had not yet occurred but a market economy was already well developed. Both Goubert and Le Roy Ladurie recognized that the "old demographic structure" was replaced in the eighteenth century by a new structure in which social factors began to restrict the role of biological determinism. If Le Roy Ladurie had proceeded on Malthusian assumptions, he concluded his book with an interesting chapter in which he called Malthus a "theoretician of traditional societies," a prophet of the past,[69] whose doctrines ceased to function at the very time that he formulated them in the late eighteenth century. Pierre Vilar had sought to demonstrate that even in traditional societies demographic factors were not necessarily decisive. In his quantitative analysis of eighteenth-century Catalonian economy and society[70] he showed that a rapid increase in population could be accompanied by a similarly rapid increase in productivity even under preindustrial conditions.

4

THE *Annales* approach has been subjected to considerable criticism, criticism which has come from very different political and historiographical orientations. The critics have often identified the *Annales* too narrowly with purely quantitative approaches to the study of relatively stable social structures.[71] This hardly does justice to the great diversity represented in the work of the historians associated with the *Annales* and the Sixth Section. We can easily distinguish several methodologically and conceptually different approaches, which, however, by no means exhaust the work done within the framework of the Sixth Section and the *Annales*. These approaches share certain assumptions — that the most relevant history is social history and that in social history structures and *conjonctures,* not the actions of individuals, are decisive. In the late 1950s, François Furet and Adeline Daumard had asserted categorically that "from a scientific point of view, the only social history is quantitative history,"[72] and that such a social history for the eighteenth or nineteenth century could be reconstructed from quantified or quantifiable information gathered from such archives as the Notarial Registers of Paris, which contained important clues not only to social structure and social mobility but also to family psychology and popular culture. A not entirely different approach can be seen in the attempts by Labrousse, Le Roy Ladurie, Goubert, Baehrel, and others to proceed from hard economic or biological data to a qualitative history of social and psychological structures.

It must however be kept in mind that this sort of quantitative history by no means represents the only major orientation in the *Annales* today and that an older direction of the "history of mentalities" less dominated by quantification continues to occupy an important place. This direction found expression in the late 1950s and 1960s in the investigations undertaken or directed by Jacques Le Goff on the role of the intellectuals, the bankers, the merchants, the mendicants, and the heretics in the Middle Ages; in Philippe Ariès' *Centuries of Childhood: A Social History of Family;*[73] and in Michel Foucault's *Madness and Civilization,*[74] a study of changing approaches to insanity since the Middle Ages. Here there is as yet little attempt to establish quantitative series. Robert Mandrou consciously since the late 1950s began to lay foundations for an "historical psychology" exploring changes in "collective mentalities."[75] Every collective psychology involves conduct (*comportement*) and while this can be quantified to an extent, it also involves many intangible factors. Thus, for example, not only economic *conjonctures* but concepts of status are crucial for an understanding of economic mentalities. These mentalities express themselves in human behavior. In a number of studies, Mandrou has sought to reconstruct the climate of opinion of an age (*climat mental d'une époque*) through an analysis of concrete practices, such as changing attitudes toward witchcraft reflected in the actions of the magistrates[76] or capitalist attitudes as they emerge from the account books of the Fuggers' estates.[77] Much more oriented toward measurable data in the history of ideas are the two volumes, *Livre et société*,[78] in which François Furet and a team of collaborators have undertaken a statistical analysis of book titles, reviews, the social composition of the reading public and of the provincial academies as well as the occurrence of terms and concepts in order to lay bare certain trends in the intellectual development of the eighteenth century.

If *Livre et société* represents one direction in which the history of mentalities can be explored, the attempts to utilize psychoanalytical and anthropological concepts, as in Le Roy Ladurie's *Paysans du Languedoc* or in the examination of themes from folklore and mythology,[79] represent a very different avenue of approach. Yet these *Annales* explorations into the history of mentalities differ sharply from the more strictly sociopolitical analyses of public consciousness by Marxists like Albert Soboul or George Rudé,[80] which tend to stress conscious attitudes rather than subconscious motivations, and also from recent American attempts at psychohistory.[81] For psychohistory has largely remained an analysis of the very personal childhood, adolescent, or early manhood crises of leadership figures and has done relatively little to explore the social context in which these crises took place or the motivations of the following of these leaders.

Yet neither the quantitative history of *conjonctures* nor the more subtle history of mentalities fully exhausts the rich diversity represented by the *Annales,* much less that of the Sixth Section. The *Annales* have remained a forum for international discussion on the methods of historical studies within the framework of the human sciences. If the *Annales* have been attacked by critics as methodological "dogmatists," they could with equal or greater justification be called methodological eclectics. The pages of the *Annales* have remained open to the critics of a quantitative, structural history and of a history of mentalities in the *Annales* tradition, to Marxists like Albert Soboul, and also to such defenders of a history emphasizing the role of individuals, ideas, and political figures as Raymond Aron.[82]

There are certain similarities in the criticism which has been leveled against the *Annales* by Marxists and by methodologically and politically more conventional historians. Both have pointed out that *Annales* historians have very largely ignored the role of political factors and that they have underplayed the role of conscious direction in social processes. Lucien Febvre was admittedly justified when, in the introduction to the *Journal of World History*,[83] published by UNESCO, he stressed that the new journal should consider not only the history of states but also that of peoples and civilizations. But the large-scale exclusion of political history led in the opinion of the Soviet philosopher Igor Kon "to a distorted conception of even the most purely economic processes."[84] For most *Annales* historians, political history remained surface history. In recent years, however, the *Annales* have indeed become increasingly interested in the analysis of political processes.[85] Both Marc Ferro, a director of the *Annales,* and Georges Haupt, a member of the Sixth Section, have occupied themselves with socialism, the First World War, and the Russian Revolution; François Furet and Denis Richet, with the French Revolution.[86]

Critics from very different ideological camps have questioned the adequacy of the quantitative methods employed by *Annales* historians as a tool for social and historical analysis. Roland Mousnier had sharply criticized François Furet and Adeline Daumard's earlier efforts to reconstitute social structures in the eighteenth century by a statistical analysis of economic information contained in marriage contracts in the notarial archives of Paris. The notarial archives were indeed important, Mousnier maintained, but one should put different questions to them. Furet and Daumard like Labrousse had failed to understand that "a society is not a series of cubes but an organism."[87] They had projected sociological categories of the nineteenth and twentieth centuries, when social classes corresponded closely to socio-professional groupings, the latter defined by economic criteria, into a period in which different criteria of social differentiation operated: notions of honor, dignity, birth, and social function which were less directly influenced by factors of economic wealth or function in a hierarchically ordered society. Marriage practices were indeed an important outward mark to identify a group which held common social ideas, possessed a consciousness of itself as a group, and followed a similar life-style. Hence the absolute need to use the marriage contract in the notarial records to gain insight into the social structure of the eighteenth century; but only after qualitative analysis could statistics be used meaningfully. Then, however, they became indispensable. In the Sixth Section itself, Robert Mandrou similarly stressed the role of social attitudes in an attempt to define classes and class struggles in France at the beginning of the seventeenth century. No historical explanation was possible, Mandrou argued, without taking into consideration the history of mentalities. Mandrou suggested that "French society at beginning of the 17th century did not escape a general sociological rule which I consider to be solid; a society is always defined by its dominant class."[88] The dominated classes tended to imitate the dominant class and integrate elements of its outlook. Even Furet, defending himself against the orthodox Marxist criticism of his history of the French Revolution by C. Mazauric and Albert Soboul, relied on the argument that class conflict in the Old Regime was less a problem of economic interest than of group consciousness, social status, and social domination often relatively independent of economic factors.[89]

Yet leaving aside Marc Ferro and Georges Haupt's studies on the first World War, the Socialist Movement, and the Russian Revolution, which methodologically differ markedly from the works which we have discussed in this chapter, the criticism leveled against the *Annales* historians for their failure to attempt an analysis of political behavior retains a degree of justification. Where *Annales* historians such as Braudel or Furet have dealt with political events, they have generally been unable to make a transition from structural social to political history without a radical methodological break. Braudel, as we already mentioned, could still write in 1966 that political history had not progressed since Ranke, that it remained event-oriented, "surface" history. Similarly, Furet argued in 1971 against Mazauric and Soboul that politics and ideologies functioned relatively independent of other social processes.[90] He assigned to the monarchy a central role in the dissolution and transformation of social classes in the eighteenth century and underlined the role of ideologies in the political conflicts of the French Revolution. But since politics and ideologies possess this degree of independence, Furet concluded that a scientific history of politics was impossible. The question whether a science of politics was possible had already engaged the *Annales* historians a decade earlier in a debate with Raymond Aron. Aron had been by no means as pessimistic as they regarding the possibility of such a science. But the basis of a science of politics required more than the empirical analysis of social structures. It involved the analysis of political intentions in their social context. It was the inability of the Durkheim school to overcome the abyss between events and structure which, Aron wrote, had led him to Max Weber, who had attempted to understand political history in a social framework.[91]

A further charge which has been leveled by Marxists and others against the *Annales* historians is that they have sought to turn history into a natural science in which human life would be governed by blind determinism and conscious human intervention eliminated. Such a belief in the power of anonymous, uncontrollable forces may perhaps be detected in Pierre Chaunu's recent attempt to explain in the language of demographic statistics why, unlike England, Normandy failed to achieve an industrial "take-off."[92] But the attempts which Goubert, Le Roy Ladurie, Vilar, and others have made to examine economic and demographic factors quantitatively can by no means be equated with scientific determinism. Goubert and Le Roy Ladurie are aware that their methods can not be universally applied but serve to investigate certain problems in the specifically historical setting of a preindustrial period.[93]

Indeed, the central theme of the first volume of Braudel's *Civilisation matérielle et capitalisme* (1967)[94] is an increasing liberation of men since the late Middle Ages from the necessities of nature which dominated daily life in the past, an emancipation made possible by technical, scientific, and intellectual developments that began in a specifically European historical context. Similarly Pierre Vilar in his monumental *La Catalogne dans l'Espagne moderne*[95] emphasizes that in the final analysis neither geographical, technological, nor economic factors suffice to explain the agricultural upswing of Catalonia in the eighteenth century; it can be understood only through the historical analysis of the total situation. There is a danger in regarding an isolated segment of a society, such as its economic development, as a rational whole and forgetting that the "rationality of human reality" is a totality capable of being understood only through historical analysis. This stress on the concrete historical situation led the *Annales* to take a critical attitude toward the New Economic History in the United States, which sought to explain economic growth by means of quantitative models that isolated economic variables from the broader historical context.[96]

The *Annales* circle has been reproached for its lack of interest in the history and the problems of industrial societies. Relatively few works have dealt with the nineteenth or twentieth centuries, and these — for example, Jean Bouvier's study of the *Crédit Lyonnais*[97] or Charles Morazé's *Les Bourgeois conquérants*[98]—almost entirely avoid the quantitative methods which were employed in the studies of the Old Regime. Adeline Daumard's study of the Parisian bourgeoisie constitutes somewhat of an exception.[99] Louis Chevalier's work on the *"classes dangereuses"* was written outside the circle of the *Annales*.[100] Marc Ferro is concerned with the tendency of collective psychology in interaction with economic forces in his analysis of Europe in World War I and Russia during the Revolution.[101]

The historians of the Sixth Section have expressed the opinion that the relative neglect of recent history in the *Annales* has derived in large part from the accident that almost all of the great mentors in the *Annales* tradition have been historians of early modern Europe or of the Middle Ages. But this alone probably does not explain the limited interest of the *Annales* historians in the later periods. The historical studies published under the auspices of the Sixth Section have by no means been limited to the French or even the Spanish or Italian Old Regime or to the Middle Ages. Braudel's *Civilisation matérielle et capitalisme* encompasses the whole world from the fifteenth to the eighteenth century. The interest of the older *Annales* in the history of the non-Western and underdeveloped countries continues, combined with a new anthropological concern with primitive cultures.

It is not quite correct, as one German critic maintained, that the historians of the *Annales* are concerned only with the "static structures of certain societies" and that for them the concern with historical change comes close to zero. Emmanuel Le Roy Ladurie indeed wrote recently of his interest in an "immobile history" in which demographic, technological, and social structures remain relatively stable, as he believes they did in Europe between the fifteenth and the early eighteenth century.[102] But the theme of the great *Annales* studies, including Braudel's book on the Mediterranean, which examines the relative decline of the economic and political significance of the Mediterranean area in the late sixteenth century, is change, the emergence of modern capitalism with its transformation of social relationships. However, the breakthrough from the history of early capitalist societies to the history of the industrial period never quite succeeds. This failure has been explained in part by the observation that the quantitative methods of a "serial history"[103] are suitable only for the analysis of social processes which can easily be isolated and which take place within the relatively stable structures of pre-industrial societies. But the "history of long series" has been extensively used outside the Sixth Section, particularly by theoretically oriented economic historians, to analyze growth and cyclical developments in industrial societies. In part the inability of *Annales* historians to analyze the transition from the Old Regime to the more modern period reflects the lack of a comprehensive theory of social change.

In a sense "serial history" has operated with a basis-superstructure conception: the isolation and comparison of selected variables, which it considered basic to the society, would permit the construction of a total picture of a period in a specific geographical-historical region. In the *Les Paysans du Languedoc,* Le Roy Ladurie indeed went far beyond a cumulative history of segments to a broadly conceived integrated social history, very much taking into consideration the mental climate of the age. Goubert in the *Beauvais et le Beauvaisis* proceeded from recurrent demographic and economic cycles to changes in the structure itself, for example, the growing economic power and function of the bourgeoisie. If the *Annales* historians lacked a comprehensive theory of social change, this undoubtedly was connected with their healthy skepticism of every form of "metaphysics of history" and therefore also of theories of histories which could not be formulated in the form of propositions subject to empirical verification. This skepticism is certainly justified, yet it does not remove the need for theoretical formulations which go beyond the tangible measurable series provided by demographic and economic phenomena to a consideration of some of the factors taken into account by Weberians and Marxists, such as ideologies, conflicts of power, social standards and economic interests, traditions, personalities, and others often disregarded by *Annales* historians.

These limitations on the methodological perspectives of many of the *Annales* historians can probably not be explained purely in terms of scientific considerations but must be understood in the framework of the traditions and institutional structure of the *Annales* and of the Sixth Section. The heritage of

Durkheim with its emphasis on structures and collective consciousness at the expense of the intentional actions of men still weighs heavily on the Sixth Section. The institutionalization of the *Annales* within the Sixth Section may also set limits to flexibility. The individual scholar in certain cases has been replaced by the team, his study has been transformed into a "laboratory." In France a much broader conception of what constitutes the sciences has long led to history being included among the scientific disciplines. Large sums from the National Center for Scientific Research have become available for historical research. In this National Center, the dominant outlook takes the natural sciences as the norm and encourages concrete, measurable results. To a greater extent than in other European countries historians have turned to the computer. This has led to ambitious projects like that of making available to the social historian complete, computerized military archives concerning all persons subject to military service in nineteenth-century France for selected dates of birth, approximately a generation apart.[104] The French research, moreover, has been centralized to a greater extent. This contrasts sharply with the United States where historians are scattered over hundreds of universities where, in contrast to their colleagues in the so-called behavioral sciences, they receive only small-scale support from the foundations, but where they also may enjoy a greater degree of independence in the choice of their research topics and methodological approaches. Nor do a handful of professors dominate research and control appointments to the extent to which they do in France.[105] On the other hand, the creation of the Sixth Section made possible a fusion of history and the human sciences not attained in the United States where historians have been relatively less involved in interdisciplinary research and behavioral sciences have remained more aloof from history.

It is doubtful whether the historians of the *Annales,* notwithstanding occasional statements by Bloch, Febvre, and Braudel to the contrary, viewed their function as a *science engagée* in a political sense. If there was such an engagement, it was for a secular, moderate republic. Their assumption that the historian always proceeded from the interests and perspectives of the present did not for them exclude the possibility of an honest reconstruction of the past. Their commitment to political neutrality as well as their concern with the "material history" of the broad masses made it possible for them after Stalin's death to establish, in some cases re-establish, close contacts with historians in the socialist countries of Eastern Europe. Soviet and *Annales* historians, Braudel observed, will inevitably pose different problems, but insofar as they are honest historians, they will be able to agree on the results of their research.[106] Braudel thus assumes that in its scientific procedures, historical research remains relatively independent of ideological bias.

Very different political views have been represented among the *Annales* historians, from the pronounced conservatism of the right of Pierre Chaunu to the Marxism of Pierre Vilar.[107] Yet certainly scholarship and political ideology have not been separated as clearly from each other as Furet asserted in his above mentioned controversy with Soboul.[108] The controversy between Furet and Soboul was certainly not without political overtones. In a sense, the fascination with hard data, particularly data relating to preindustrial societies, has relieved *Annales* historians of the task of critically confronting past and present. The affinity of the *Annales* historians to the structuralism of Lévi-Strauss is not surprising. The personal ties between Fernand Braudel and Lévi-Strauss go back to their days together at the University of São Paolo in Brazil in the 1930s. More important is the shift of emphasis of structuralism from dynamic growth societies to more static enduring systems in which a perennial humanity manifests itself. As event-oriented history has supposedly overlooked, "observable phenomena and available sources are not the result of a specific intention but rather the fragmentary outcrops of an underlying system."[109] Marxists, and to an extent even historians proceeding from a *Verstehen* perspective, could accept this statement in part. What distinguishes the structuralist approach is, first, the radical de-emphasis of "specific intentions" and, secondly, the de-emphasis of the unique character of modern civilization. In a sense this may reflect a fashionable value judgment in regard to Western civilization and its high regard for rationality, an attempt to question the qualitative distinction between reason and unreason (or in Foucault's case sanity and insanity), between man and nature, which has been fundamental to linear oriented historical thought from the Ancients to Marx.

The introduction to the special number of the *Annales* in the summer of 1971 on "History and Structure" warns against projecting "on all epochs, on all civilizations the value system of industrial Europe, its cult of change and innovation."[110] This orientation by no means excludes the possibility of serious studies of modern technological societies. It is rather a call for a widening of historical perspective, a turning away from a European centered concentration to a comparative approach which considers underlying structures in non-technological societies as well. Much more consciously than traditional or Marxist approaches, this orientation probes the sources of cultural and social manifestations in the collective subconscious. Nevertheless it also reflects the relative disinterest of the *Annales* historians in problems of modernization, which have been so central to the concerns not only of Marxists but also to historians in the Weberian tradition of *Verstehen*.[111]

Although the *Annales* historians have in important ways countered the imbalance which has marked the tradition of Western historiography since its beginnings in classical antiquity — with its stress on "specific intentions" of historical figures and its confusion of European with universal history — the question remains whether in their quest for a "total history" they have not again fragmented history by excluding or neglecting men as active agents. They still lack today, as they did in their debate with Raymond Aron ten years ago, a model for the understanding of politics. Yet the modern world can hardly be understood without taking into account the role of political decisions, and probably the Old Regime cannot be so understood either, as François Furet seems now ready to concede. The use of models of demographic and economic *conjonctures* have been most fruitful in dealing with the relatively stable

societies in which technical innovations and political intervention were of limited importance; but the *Annales* historians of
the Old Regime, like Braudel, Goubert, and Le Roy Ladurie,
have been intensely aware of the structural changes which occurred in the transition from the Old Regime to a modern society in which the automatism of the climatic-biological cycles
no longer functioned properly. The *Annales* historians have
rightly insisted that a descriptive approach to political decisions
remains scientifically insufficient, that "specific intentions" must
be understood within a structural framework, yet they have
often excluded these factors from their own historical analysis.
This has led them, as we have seen, to a certain methodological
irrationalism in dealing with political and intellectual history,
not entirely different from that of the conventional event-oriented historians which they have so bitterly rejected. The event,
the political decision, the idea are "dust," "ephemeral," inexpli-
cable. They have failed to solve, or, as J. H. Hexter notes in specific reference to Braudel's book on the Mediterranean, even
failed to pose the problem: "how to deal with the perennial
historiographic difficulty of linking the durable phenomena of
history with those that involve rapid change."[112] In stressing
the primacy of social structures so exclusively, they have neglected to examine to what extent men make history and have
left to the Marxists and others the task of studying under what
conditions men make their history.

On one level, the approach of the *Annales* has been remarkably free of the methodological dogmatism of which they
have been recurrently accused. The *Annales* have remained
what they have been from the beginning, a forum of international and interdisciplinary discussion. They have immeasurably
broadened the perspective of the historian, not only spatially,
by breaking through the frame of Western civilization and by
exploring non-Western as well as primitive cultures and logics,
but also topically and methodologically, by widening the scope
of the historian's interest to all phases of human social life, including the biological aspects and the realm of fantasy and myth
building, and exploring the broadest variety of non-written ex-

pressions not only for the "pre-historic" but also recent periods.[113] They have integrated historical science with the "human sciences" in the broadest sense, not only in the case of the classical social or behavioral sciences but structural anthropology, psychoanalysis, the arts, literature and linguistics in their most modern forms. They have challenged the parochialism of the classic tradition of historical writing, which since Thuycdides has centered attention so largely on the conscious actions of individuals of power and culture. Yet as we suggested, the *Annales* approaches have also led to limitations in perspective, not only in subject matter but also in methodology. The *Annales* have made little contribution to bringing greater conceptual rigor into the analysis of those elements of purposive human action which enter into specific historical change. They have in practice kept alive a concept of historical objectivity which they had questioned in theory. They at times assumed that there were objective social processes which operated independently of human will and which could be understood by strict scientific methods that transcended ideological divisions. They thus strove toward a depoliticization of history and scholarship which, Marxist critics have charged, itself involved political valuations.

The years since 1947 have seen the *Annales* movement attain further international significance. In the 1930s, Bloch and Febvre remained relatively outside the main stream of French historical studies dominated by the Sorbonne and oriented heavily toward political, diplomatic, and military history rather narrowly conceived. The establishment of the Sixth Section marked the beginning of the rapid rise of the *Annales* group to a position of dominance in French historical and social science research. In the past fifteen years the work of the *Annales* and of the Sixth Section has become widely known throughout the world. The influence of the *Annales* has known no rigid East-West frontiers. Considerable attention has been given to *Annales* methods particularly in Poland, and Polish historians have been well represented in the pages of the *Annales*. But also in Italy, Hungary, in recent years in England,

and elsewhere, the *Annales* found careful readers and students. In Great Britain, the Cambridge Group for the History of Population and Social Structures, founded in 1964, has had close contacts with the Sixth Section. In West Germany, where the *Annales* were extensively criticized but little read until recently, Braudel's *Civilisation matérielle et capitalisme* has recently been translated and a selection of *Annales* articles is in preparation.[114] In the United States, where the classic works of Marc Bloch had long been available in translation but the more recent work of the "school" had remained relatively unknown, several of the *Annales* classics as well as two collections of articles from the *Annales* have now been published in quick succession.[115] To be sure, outside of France, the *Annales* lack the institutional basis which contributes to their present position of dominance in French scholarship; nevertheless the *Annales* have become a model of scientific history to historians throughout the world today to a greater degree than any other one group of historians.[116]

III

Beyond "Historicism" — Some Developments in West German Historiography Since the Fischer Controversy

I N GERMANY the tradition of historicism which we discussed in the first chapter remained firmly established well into the twentieth century, relatively unshaken by the traumatic political upheavals of the age. Karl Lamprecht's challenge to the conventional historiography in the 1890s had done little to lead German historical studies into new paths. Rather, it resulted in an empassioned reaction against the attempts to introduce generalizations into historical writing and a conscious consolidation of the German historical profession in defense of the traditional patterns of historical study. A variety of political, social, and institutional factors contributed to preventing a serious reorientation of German historical science until very recent years. When German historical studies began to follow new directions in the 1960s and 1970s, these paralleled developments in other countries in their openness to concepts and methods of the empirical social sciences, yet at the same time, in the continued stress on the autonomy of historical phenomena, reflected a continuity with older German patterns of historical and social science thought.

In an important way, the reaction against Karl Lamprecht marked a retreat from positions already attained in German historical science in the direction of a theory-oriented history which took into account social factors. Even J. G. Droysen, Heinrich Sybel, and especially Heinrich Treitschke[1] had to a limited extent taken social and economic developments and the changing cultural scene into account in their narratives. By the turn of the century there existed a rich tradition of social and economic history — most important representative of which was Gustav Schmoller — as well as a keen interest in cultural history dating back into the early nineteenth and even the eighteenth century.[2] Karl Lamprecht's work in many ways represented a synthesis of these traditions.

German economic history as exemplified by the Historical School of National Economy shared basic assumptions of the political historians regarding the character of historical knowledge as well as the relation of the state and the economy.[3] A decade before the Lamprecht controversy, Gustav Schmoller had defended the historical perspective of the Historical School against the marginal utility theory of Carl Menger in Vienna. If Menger, in the tradition of classical political economy, had seen the possibility of formulating economic theories of general validity, Gustav Schmoller had stressed the extent to which all economic behavior took place in a concrete, historical context, reflected the values of the society, and was effected by the intervention of the state. Without denying the role of theory in economic science and the place of empirical data in the formulation of economic theory, Schmoller had nevertheless emphasized the historical character of such theory.

Yet the reaction against Lamprecht reflected a conscious attempt to minimize the role of theory and the relevance of social factors for the understanding of history. The philosophic discussion, as in the writings of Wilhelm Windelband and Heinrich Rickert, stressed the distinction between the idiographic method of the historical and cultural sciences, which sought to understand a unique course of events, and the nomothetic method of the natural sciences, which aimed at the formulation of explanatory laws. We have already seen[4] that neo-Kantian philosophers, such as Wilhelm Dilthey and Heinrich Rickert, but also Max Weber, understood this distinction differently from the historians. While the philosophers recognized that all sciences, including history, were systems of con-

cepts rather than description of reality, the historians continued to maintain the Rankean belief in the ability of the historian
to recapture the past as it really occurred.

The tenacity with which the German historical profession
clung to the traditional historical methods has to be seen within
the political context of twentieth-century Germany. An important group of historians sought consciously to go back to
Ranke's conception of the conflict of power on the international
scene as the central concern of the historian.[5] Free of value judgments, the historian was to analyze the objective power interests
of the great states. These could be understood independently of
social and economic factors. The task of history as a science
consisted in the narrative reconstruction of a course of events
as they emerged from the critical examination of documents of
state. Linked to this common concern with political history,
separated from its broader structural context, was a commitment to the defense of German national interests, narrowly
conceived, and the insistence that all aspects of domestic policy
must be subordinated to the exigencies of foreign affairs.

Lamprecht himself shared the basic commitments of the
conservative historians to the extension of German power in
the world. Yet his critics, such as Dietrich Schäfer, Georg von
Below, and others, saw in a broadly conceived social and cultural approach to history an implied ideological threat to the
established political order in which a semi-autocratic, military
monarchy, strongly tinged with an aristocratic ethos, represented the best security against the forces of social revolution.
The social stresses of Imperial Germany, intensified in the Weimar period, strengthened the hold of a historiographical tradition which had its origins in the very different historical setting
of Restoration Prussia. The institutional structure within which
historical research was carried on and history was taught contributed to the persistence of conventional patterns. The manner
of recruitment of the German historical profession — not entirely different from the one we have described in France but
operating within a different political and intellectual heritage
— contributed to ideological and scholarly conformity.

In their hostile attitude toward democratization and their fear of socialism, the German historians were by no means unique; nor were they alone in their stress on diplomatic and military history. Unusual only is the extent to which nineteenth-century historiographical notions were able at the German universities to resist change into the 1960s.[6] The organization of the university and the recruitment of its personnel made dissent more difficult than in other countries.

The aristocratic structure of the university gave extensive authority to the full professors (*Ordinarien*) over junior scholars. The *Habilitation,* by which a scholar aspiring to a professorial appointment had to write a second dissertation under the guidance of a chairholder, strengthened the control of the *Ordinarien* over the younger generation of historians. Extra-scholarly considerations regarding the candidate were an important factor in the secret vote of the faculty committee to approve the *Habilitation.* Acceptance of the *Habilitation* merely provided the successful candidate, now generally well beyond his early manhood years, with the *venia legendi,* the right to lecture as a *Privatdozent* without a tenured position or a guaranteed income. Once possessing the *venia legendi,* he awaited a "call" to a university chair. The power of the ministry of culture to select the candidates for university chairs from a list prepared by the faculty further insured stability. A remarkable similarity in social background was evident, with the history professorate — even often at Catholic universities like Munich — recruiting itself from a small, homogeneous circle of men coming from the families of medium or upper rank officials, pastors, occasionally lawyers or doctors, almost always Protestant[7] (very occasionally Jews assimilated into the Protestant milieu). These had passed through common educational experiences in the humanistic Gymnasium and in their university studies, and consciously identified themselves with the social and political aspirations of the Protestant *Bildungsbürgertum.*

After 1870 the professorate was for the most part staunchly committed to the established order, with occasional minor deviations in the direction of the greater conservatism of men like

Treitschke, the socialism of the Chair of Schmoller and others, and the liberalism of Hermann Baumgarten or Theodor Mommsen.[8] The *Lex Aron,* enacted in 1898, further limited the possibilities of ideological nonconformity by effectively barring political dissenters, for example Social Democrats, from even the lower ranks of the teaching staff at the universities. Yet more important than legal attempts to insure conformity were pressures within the universities themselves which extended beyond politics to *Weltanschauung* and methodology. Thus a man as politically orthodox as Kurt Breysig, a student of J. G. Droysen and Gustav Schmoller and a participant in the work of the *Acta Borussica,* was unable to obtain a professorship once he began to develop his interest in comparative cultural history until a Social Democratic government in Prussia in the 1920s created a new chair for him over the opposition of his colleagues. The dissenters became dissenters only after they already attained their academic chairs. The impeded careers of men like Veit Valentin, Kurt Breysig, Arthur Rosenberg, Eckart Kehr, and Gustav Mayer are only better known examples of the effectiveness of the control exerted by the profession.[9]

There did indeed develop a dissenting orientation within the profession both as to methodology and to political outlook, but it was a moderate dissent which remained well within the national tradition. It was best represented, perhaps, by Friedrich Meinecke,[10] editor of the *Historische Zeitschrift* from 1896 to 1935, who was deeply involved in his earlier years as its editor in the attacks on Lamprecht. Meinecke, like Ernst Troeltsch, Max Weber, and Hans Delbrück, was part of that loyal opposition which believed with Pastor Friedrich Naumann that an effective German *Weltpolitik* required a bridging of the gulf between the Hohenzollern monarchy and the working class. A political alternative had to be found to Social Democracy. At the same time a scholarly reply to Marxism had to be formulated. Meinecke and Weber represent diverse ends of a spectrum; both sought to escape a narrow, narrative approach to history. The contrast between Meinecke the historian and Weber the historical sociologist is, of course, striking.

Meinecke sought the "ideas" which found expressions in the great personalities who made history; Weber, while acknowledging the role of the charismatic individual, sought causal understanding of the impersonal forces operating in history. Yet these explanations were to be found in human consciousness. In the final analysis, the bureaucracy, the power state, and capitalism were all driven by an inner logic of their own to accomplish the most efficient extension of their operations, a logic which was determined by a world-outlook, an inner-worldly asceticism, and was only partly affected by conflicting social interests. Moreover, Weber remained an outsider to the historians. The moderate dissenters, including Weber, remained deeply committed to a national power state standing above social interests whose actions were determined by the exigencies of foreign policy. A sense of realism led them to oppose the maximalist war aims of the Pan Germans, as the limits of German power became evident in the course of World War I, and to support the Weimar Republic after November 1918.

The German defeat in 1918 led to a consolidation of historiographical and political conservatism at the German universities.[11] The refutation of the charges of German war guilt became a primary concern of the historical profession. The chairs of history in the Weimar period were largely held by men who had held them in the Wilhelminian period and now felt even more threatened in the Republic. Even the essentially conservative state-centered approach to social and economic history in the tradition of Schmoller or as pursued in the Weimar period by Otto Hintze was viewed with distrust. Meinecke's moderate conservatism, his allegiance to the Republic, his concern to go from a narrowly event-centered to a more broadly conceived idea-oriented political history were in the minority, even if his significance as teacher of a more critical younger generation of historians must not be underestimated.

There did indeed appear in the Weimar Republic an opposing orientation more outspokenly critical of the German political past, but this orientation remained essentially within the framework of the conventional event-and-person-centered political history. If the conservatives as well as the moderate conservatives like Friedrich Meinecke had hailed the superiority of the German political and intellectual heritage, as they interpreted it, over the more democratic and rationalistic traditions of the West, the core of liberal criticism consisted in the belief that Germany had taken a mistaken and disastrous turn in its political development by failing to follow "Western" models of parliamentarization. But for these liberal critics, for example Johannes Ziekursch,[12] and Franz Schnabel[13] and a little later Erich Eyck,[14] the tragedy of Germany's political development rested in large part in the failure of leadership, of moral and intellectual principles — hence their extensive concern with Bismarck, although from a critical perspective.

The years after 1933 did not mark a radical break in German historical studies. The half-hearted attempts of the regime to force a *Gleichschaltung*[15] of the historical profession remained largely unsuccessful; a *Gleichschaltung* was also not necessary. The older conservative generation was only seldom *völkisch* in a "National Socialist" sense of biological racism; nevertheless it affirmed the authoritarian state. Yet even historians who made no secret of their hesitations regarding Nazi domestic policies, such as Friedrich Meinecke, who was pressed into resigning his editorship of the *Historische Zeitschrift* in 1935; Herman Oncken, who was forced into retirement; or Gerhard Ritter, who temporarily was forbidden to travel abroad and later taken into custody at the time of the Anti-Hitler plot in 1944, remained firm supporters of the foreign policy of the Third Reich in which they saw a continuation of traditional national policy. The year 1933 saw the permanent loss to Germany of a more critical group of historians of democratic persuasion, none in full professorial chairs, including Gustav Meyer, Eckart Kehr, Arthur Rosenberg, Hans Rosenberg, Veit Valentin, Alfred Vagts, George W. F. Hallgarten, and Hajo Holborn.

Common to the conservative and the moderate conservative historiographic positions described above was the insistence on the fundamental difference between a German and a "Western" outlook. The liberal historians, of whom we shall speak next, shared the assumptions regarding the fundamental difference between the German and Western European historical development but reversed the value judgments. For the liberals, like Johannes Ziekursch or Erich Eyck, Bismarck thus became the key to the understanding of modern German history as he did for the conservatives. Few of the liberal critics of Bismarck held professional chairs; Ziekursch and the Catholic historian Franz Schnabel were exceptions. When they aspired to university careers, as Veit Valentin, Gustav Mayer or Eckart Kehr did, they generally found these blocked.

The question of the re-examination of German history became pressing after the Nazi seizure of power, a re-examination which was undertaken by and which dominated the study of German history in exile.[16] A large part of this literature followed relatively conventional methodological lines in its stress on men and ideas. Erich Eyck's scrutiny of the moral failures of Bismarck;[17] the extensive concern with the "intellectual roots" of Nazism, which occupied German historians abroad well into the 1960s; George Mosse's *The Crisis of German Ideology;*[18] Fritz Stern's *The Politics of Cultural Despair;*[19] the essays in the volume edited by Hans Kohn not long after the War, *German History: Some New Views;*[20] but also a work written from a Marxist perspective, Georg Lukács' *Die Zerstörung der Vernunft*[21] are important expressions of this concern. While emphasizing the role of ideas, these works nevertheless recognized a relationship between attitudes and social structure broadly defined. For liberal historians, such as Kohn, Holborn,[22] Mosse, and Stern, and Marxists, such as Alexander Abusch[23] and Georg Lukács, the failure of German liberalism was related to the failure of the bourgeoisie to gain effective political power in Germany in the nineteenth or twentieth century. The democracies of Western and Northern Europe thus remained the model for German development.

The year 1945 did not mark the radical break in historical scholarship in West Germany of which some West German historians have spoken. The personnel of the universities remained largely unchanged. None of the liberal democratic historians who had been driven out of the universities and out of Germany returned on a permanent basis. Racially persecuted historians of conservative orientation, such as Hans Herzfeld, Hans Rothfels, and Hans-Joachim Schoeps, returned to the German universities, in Herzfeld's case somewhat more open to democratic positions and methodological innovation than he had been in the Weimar period. With few exceptions, such as in the cases of the once rabidly anti-Semitic Günther Franz and Erwin Hölzle, historians who had supported the historiographic efforts of the Nazis remained at or returned to the universities. The structure of the university remained unchanged, as did the manner of recruitment. A more critical attitude toward the recent past and the attempt to apply concepts of modern social science developed more generally outside the historical seminars, in the new seminars of political science, as in the case of K. D. Bracher's analyses of the collapse of the Weimar Republic.[24] Among the historians themselves, a new generation who had entered the profession during the 1930s, like Otto Brunner and Theodor Schieder, began to recognize the limits of an event-oriented history and called for a structural approach to history (Strukturgeschichte). Yet these structures, applied by Brunner to medieval regional history,[25] concerned primarily administrative and constitutional forms and emphasized the central role of concepts (Begriffe) and of world views. Werner Conze's Working Circle for Modern Social History in Heidelberg concerned itself with the impact of industrialization on politics and society, including the working class. Legal and constitutional changes following the French Revolution appeared as primary factors for industrialization.[26] The events of the years 1933 to 1945 paled in importance when seen in the perspective of the fundamental structural changes which society had undergone in an industrial age. Industrialization continued to be studied by the Heidelberg Circle within the framework of the German states of the nineteenth century in which the leadership of statesmen, including Bismarck, and of the great personalities of the labor movement continued to be decisive forces. An important theme of the works of the Heidelberg Circle was the integration of the Social Democratic worker into the German national state. Undoubtedly, the new structural approach to history and to industrialization reflected certain concerns congenial to the political and scholarly climate of the late 1950s and the early 1960s. It permitted it to combine social history, including that of the modern industrial period, with traditional historical and scholarly concepts, to view Germany as part of a Western industrial society and yet stress the uniqueness and essential soundness of the German nation state, and finally to point at a national consensus which bridged socio-economic class conflicts.

A central issue in the re-examination of the German past after 1945 was the question of the place of the Nazi period in German history. If to liberal historians abroad, like George Mosse, the Nazi seizure of power appeared not as an "accident of history" but prepared long beforehand,[27] liberal-conservative or conservative historians within the German universities who had been forced into "inner emigration," like Friedrich Meinecke or Gerhard Ritter, or for "racial" reasons into actual emigration, like Hans Rothfels, now stressed the discontinuity which the years 1933–1945 represented in German history.[28] Nazism had its root not in the German past; its continuity was rather to be sought in a tradition of political democracy, socialism, and industrialism which went back to the French Revolution. Not the lack of democratization but the excess of it were responsible for Nazism. There was broad agreement in the rejection of the Nazis; yet there was also the attempt in much of the literature on the anti-Nazi resistance to distinguish radically between army and bureaucracy in the Nazi period on the one hand and the party on the other.[29] The Institute for Contemporary History in Munich sought to document the excesses of the Nazi period but did little to analyze the period before 1933. Only a limited revision of the traditional establishment view of modern German history appeared necessary. The soundness of Bismarck's *Reichsgründung* remained unquestioned. Gerhard Ritter now began to see in the post-Bismarck period the begin-

nings of a militaristic outlook, of which Prussia had been traditionally free, which contributed to the international tensions
preceding World War I.[30] Yet German policies, while leading
to the diplomatic isolation of Germany, could not be held directly responsible for the outbreak of World War I. The system of alliances were responsible for a war into which the
nations of Europe had involuntarily slid. While conservative
historians in the Weimar Republic had castigated Bethmann-
Hollweg's supposed moderation in war aims and admired
Ludendorff's leadership, now after World War II Bethmann-
Hollweg became the wise statesman and Ludendorff the exponent of militarism. The liberal-conservatism which in the
Weimar period had represented a maligned minority position
in the historical profession now became the established position
at West German universities.

In this atmosphere, in which West German society appeared at peace with itself, seemingly to have purged itself of
its Nazi past yet saved its past traditions, Fritz Fischer's *Griff
nach der Weltmacht* (1961)[31] appeared as an unwelcome jolt.
The now famous "Fischer Controversy" marked a turning point
in historical research in the Federal Republic. Fritz Fischer's
study which set off the controversy proceeded quite conventionally by examining the state archives and in the process taking into consideration the Memorandum of September 9, 1914,
in which Bethmann-Hollweg first formulated German war
aims, which had been conveniently overlooked previously by
conservative nationalist historians. Fischer in the two introductory chapters began to ask important questions, regarding the
interrelation of foreign and domestic policies and economic
interests, which required more complex methods of social analysis and which until then had only seldom been asked by non-
Marxist historians such as Eckart Kehr and George W. F.
Hallgarten.

For non-Germans the intense emotion which Fischer's
book generated is difficult to understand. Two assertions by
Fischer raised particular controversy: 1) that the German Imperial Government not only took the risk of world war in July

of 1914, but had actively prepared for it, a conclusion which Luigi Albertini, whose work had not been translated into German,[32] had reached long before; 2) that extensive annexationist war aims were propagated not only by Pan German extremists, like Ludendorff, but had support in a broad consensus of German public opinion which reached from the Majority Social Democrats to the Far Right. If historians had stressed the sharp dividing line between Pan-German ultras and the moderate government leaders around Bethmann-Hollweg, Fischer showed that this difference was only one in "scope and methods."[33] Perhaps even more disturbing was the suggestion that German aims to establish economic and political domination of Central Europe, the Balkans, and the Near East and to establish an overseas empire in Central Africa arose not in the course of the war but represented interests which preceded the war and which continued into the postwar period. Ludwig Dehio, while editor of the *Historische Zeitschrift* in the 1950s, had aroused considerable criticism for his attempt to trace a continuity of German policy through two world wars.[34] But while Dehio still stressed the "primacy of foreign policy" and saw Germany's expansionism as the result of her role as a "hegemoniac" power in the period after the decline of France, Fischer stressed the close interrelation of foreign policy and domestic social and economic interests. Fischer suggested that it was not Germany's exposed position as a continental major power but her social and political structure that was decisive for her tragic history in the twentieth century. The implication, not spelled out by Fischer, was clear: German policies in World War I involved continuities which still in the 1960s required a critical reassessment not only of the German past but also the German present.

Fischer's book was followed by the publication of documents by his students[35] and of further studies, such as Imanuel Geiss' book on German war aims in Poland.[36] The debate reached its high point at the German Historical Convention in West Berlin in 1964. As the discussion abated, the substance of Fischer's thesis regarding the large share of responsibility which the German government bore for the outbreak of the war and the essentially aggressive character of German war aims was accepted by an increasingly large segment of the West German scholarly community. This shift in outlook reflected to an extent a change of generations, the emergence of a younger generation with greater distance from the past, but undoubtedly also certain fundamental changes in West German society itself. Ralf Dahrendorf[37] and David Schoenbaum[38] have pointed at the beginnings of a "social revolution" toward greater "modernity" in the 1930s despite the ideological opposition of the Nazis to this process. The years after the currency reform and the initiation of the Marshall Plan saw a continuation of the process of economic modernization and a decline in the social influence of agrarian, small business, and handicraft sectors from which a good deal of the opposition to political democratization had come previously. As almost all segments of the population participated in the affluence of a consumer-oriented economy, the class tensions of the past, particularly those between working-class and the so-called "bourgeois" parties, became blurred. Many in the new generation now looked critically at the authoritarian structures and mentalities of the past. At the same time, the lessening of cold-war tensions and of the cold-war mentality permitted a more critical examination of the problems of highly industrialized societies as well as those of the Third World. The pressure of the student movement contributed to getting under way the long overdue reforms of the universities. The late 1960s and early 1970s witnessed the creation of new universities, of new chairs of history, of new positions for younger scholars, greater participation of students and junior faculty in university decisions — including appointments — and of alternatives to the *Habilitation*. These reforms have not been enacted evenly throughout West Germany and almost everywhere they have met with intense opposition from the professors (*Ordinarien*) and conservative segments of the public. Nevertheless, they have weakened the pressures for conformity which were built into the traditional structure.

The 1960s witnessed a renewed interest in the writings of social theorists of the Weimar period, including those who had been forced into exile in 1933 and had been largely ignored in the 1950s, as well as an increased interest in the social science discussion outside of Germany, particularly in the English-speaking world though relatively little as yet in developments in France. An increasing number of young historians in the 1950s and 1960s visited the United States and Great Britain for study or research. The return of émigré scholars in political science, philosophy, and sociology[39] not only reawakened an interest in intellectual currents of the Weimer period but also brought a greater acquaintance with social science theory. Historical studies in the 1960s began increasingly to adopt concepts and theories from the social sciences but very selectively and pragmatically.

Hans Rosenberg particularly during his visiting professor-ships in Germany made a younger generation of German historians aware of the utility of economic growth theory and the theory of economic cycles for the analysis of political processes. In moderation of the interest in the quantifiable behavioral sciences, the Frankfurt School of philosophers and sociologists, including Theodor Adorno and Max Horkheimer, who had returned to Frankfurt after the war,[40] and also younger men like Jürgen Habermas and Alfred Schmidt, helped reawaken an interest in Marx, although a Marx whose Hegelian side was strongly emphasized. At the same time, the Frankfurt School pointed at the limits of quantitative methods without repudiating these altogether. Rejecting the "one dimensional" concern for "facts" shared by positivists, quantitative behavioral scientists, and historicists, the Frankfurt School called for a "critical theory" which would point at the political and social irrationalities in the status quo and aim at the transformation of social relations into a community of self-determining men emancipated from irrational restraints and domination.[41] Marx's vision of unalienated man merged in the theory of the Frankfurt School with a Freudian pessimism regarding the limits of meaningful social reorganization. The Frankfurt School thus provided a welcome theory to a non-Communist moderate left, particularly congenial to German intellectuals who had been steeped in the tradition of German historicism yet rejected its political heritage. It is difficult to determine the direct influence of the Frankfurt School on the historians in the 1960s, particularly since the School offered a few examples of historical writing other than in the history of ideas and of culture. Hans-Ulrich Wehler, perhaps the most influential historian of the late 1960s and early 1970s, explicitly acknowledged his indebtedness to Max Horkheimer and a "critical theory" which "in the interest of a rationally organized future society critically examines (*'kritisch durchleuchtet'*) past and present ones."[42] More important, however, as we shall see, were certain Marxist and Weberian ideas which permitted a degree of synthesis between the stress on conceptual rigor and exact measurement of the Anglo-American social science tradition and the Frankfurt School's stress on the comprehension of social processes and the critical value-oriented assessment of these.

In the wake of the Fischer controversy, historians turned to a critical examination of the recent German past but with different emphases and methods than those which had been current in the 1950s and early 1960s. In seeking to understand the phenomenon of Nazism, a good deal more attention was now paid to the problem of continuity in German history. Historians began to look increasingly to the Wilhelminian and the Bismarckian periods for an understanding of later German developments and to approach this period somewhat less in terms of the reconstruction of the actions of specific men than through the critical examination of social structures. An important early work in this new direction was *Deutschlands Weg zur Grossmacht* (1966)[43] by Helmut Böhme, a student of Fritz Fischer. Böhme viewed the events of 1866 and 1871 less as a result of Bismarck's policy than as the result of the industrial revolution and the Prussian victory over Austria in the struggle for economic predominance in Central Europe. Trade interests replaced foreign affairs as the major determinant of policy. The basis for German unification under Prussian leadership had been laid before the battle of Königgrätz by the renewal of the *Zollverein* in 1864 closely integrated with the Prussian economy.

If the Foundation of the Reich in 1871 had taken place under the aegis of proponents of free trade policies, the economic pressures of the Great Depression of 1873 led to an ever closer alliance with the large agrarian interests in the East, the demand for protectionism, and the reorientation of the Reich under Bismarck's leadership after 1879 along politically and socially conservative lines. Thus the very process of industrialization within the framework of the German situation worked to prevent the German middle classes from gaining political control, yet drew the leadership of the great emerging economic enterprises closer to a Prussian state which remained firmly in the hands of the old privileged persons and groups.

At the center of Böhme's use of the archives had been the trade policies of the German states. Beginning in 1966 a large number of works began to appear which sought to study meticulously the role of economic pressure groups in the Wilhelminian period. Therefore in a sense the questions which Fischer had posed on the effect of economic interest groups on foreign policy were being explored in terms of the archival evidence found in the files of such organizations, business corporations, and government bureaus. The authors of these new studies for the most part had received their doctoral training only in the 1960s, some in the seminars of Fritz Fischer in Hamburg but others in those of Gerhard A. Ritter (not to be confused with Gerhard Ritter) in Berlin or Münster, or even of more conventional mentors like Theodor Schieder or Werner Conze. For the theoretical basis for their studies, they went consciously back to the work of dissenting historians of the Weimar period, such as Eckart Kehr, who died as a very young man in Washington, D.C., in 1933, and of the period of emigration, such as Hans Rosenberg, who returned briefly to Germany, to the Free University of Berlin, in 1949 and 1950 as a visiting professor. Both men had been ignored by the German historians in the 1950s. Hans Rosenberg's classical analysis of the emergence of bureaucratic absolutism in Prussia, *Bureaucracy, Aristocracy and Autocracy: The Prussian Experience, 1640–1815,*[44] has remained unpublished in German until now. By the end of the

1950s, Kehr's essays, scattered in journals of the Weimar period, as well as his dissertation, *The Building of the Battle Fleet and Party Politics, 1894–1901,*[45] were already being widely read by younger historians. Here indeed there was to be found a "critical theory" applied to history, an attempt to combine Max Weber's conceptions of the development of bureaucracy and of social status with a Marxist notion of the role of the state as an agency of class domination. The publication by Hans-Ulrich Wehler in 1965 of Eckart Kehr's most important essays[46] and the republication in 1966 of Kehr's book on the construction of the battle fleet thus came at a crucial point in the reorientation of West German historiography.

Since 1966, the new literature on political pressure groups has grown rapidly to include Hans-Jürgen Puhle's study of the *Bund der Landwirte* (The League of Farmers);[47] Hans Jaeger's[48] and Hartmut Kaelble's[49] investigation of the association of industrialists; Heinrich August Winkler's[50] analysis of pressure groups of artisans and small retail traders; Volker Berghahn's study of the function of the construction of the battle fleet for domestic politics[51] — in a sense a continuation of Kehr's analysis past 1901; Peter-Christian Witt's work[52] on the financial policies of the German Reich from 1903 to 1913; and Dirk Stegman's study[53] of the role of parties and pressure groups in the "politics of anti-Socialist coalition" (*Sammlungspolitik*) from 1897–1918.

These studies are less concerned with the direct influence of economic interests, as was George W. F. Hallgarten's study of pre-1914 imperialism,[54] than with the deeper problem of social and political domination. All the just mentioned studies — with the possible exception of Kaelble — share the basic assumption of Kehr and Rosenberg that there has been an imbalance between the economic and the socio-political modernization of Germany. According to this conception, the process of economic modernization in Germany took place under conditions which, unlike those in England, the United States, or France, made it possible for preindustrial or prebourgeois groups such as the Junkers, the bureaucracy, and the military to maintain their social and political influence in an industrial society. Industrialization proceeded successfully under the guidance of the state. This, as well as certain social and political concessions, helped to satisfy important interests of the bourgeoisie. Yet in the process of industrialization under capitalistic conditions, the existing conflicts and contradictions within the society, shaped so profoundly by bureaucratic absolutism in the period of preindustrialization or early industrialization, were accentuated. Instead of a modern industrial state, an "industrial agrarian state"[55] came into being. The economic interests of capitalist industry contributed to an expansionist foreign policy and to the building of the war fleet. The latter were possible only if a compromise were effected with the agrarian interests of the Junkers, a compromise which would maintain the political and social power of an elite which had outlived itself. Such a compromise, these historians argued, made it impossible to provide a capitalistically motivated *Weltpolitik* with the social basis which it required in the long run. The situation in world affairs required social and political democratization at home. Yet the terms under which the agrarians agreed to support increased armaments on land and on the sea ruled out such democratization. It led to the attempts at an anti-Socialist coalition (*Sammlungspolitik*) of partners, industry and agriculture, with very different interests. The *Sammlungspolitik,* these studies argue, not only contributed to the events which led to World War I and the German defeat but, according to Kehr, contributed to the intensification of the "conflict between the party interests of those who governed and the substantive interests of the nation."[56] It brought about a refeudalization of the solid bourgeoisie as well as of the lower middle classes and the artisans (Winkler), and contributed according to Hans Rosenberg and H. J. Puhle to the emergence of pre-Fascist, *völkisch,* anti-Semitic attitudes, which, according to Dirk Stegmann, found their fulfillment in the Nazi state.

Kehr's generalizations regarding the political activities of economic interest groups are doubtless overly sweeping and lack adequate empirical foundation. The studies mentioned above have begun to furnish this foundation and to create a more differentiated picture of the goals and policies of the various pressure groups.[57] Nevertheless, these works perhaps appear in some ways more interesting for the critical perspective they bring to bear on this period of German history than for methodological innovations. For the most part, as Hans-Jürgen Puhle suggested, they consciously sought to employ essentially the traditional historical method of gaining understanding through a critical examination of textual evidence, but they applied this method to new material and new questions.[58]

However, the studies we have discussed have sought to go beyond "biographical or political history to an examination of the supra-individual context, which does not always become apparent from the text."[59] Except in the case of historians who consciously utilized well-developed concepts of social structure and change, such as Rosenberg, Wehler, Kocka, and Koselleck, the role of theory in these writings should not be overstated. Much of the literature on pressure groups was written by men who consider themselves in the first place as "craftsmen." Nor do the institutional bases exist for the sort of teamwork possible within the framework of the Sixth Section of the *École Pratique* in France or the Institutes of History of the Academies of Science in the socialist countries. Research is concentrated at the universities where it continues to be carried on by individual historians. Except in a few instances, such as the Institute for Social and Economic History at Göttingen, directed by Wilhelm Abel until his retirement in 1972, there were relatively few instances of closely coordinated efforts. Even larger cooperative research projects, like those on the estates in eighteenth-century Europe, undertaken at the Max Planck Institute for History in Göttingen, on nationalism in Cologne, or on industrialization in Heidelberg, involved the division of labor among individual scholars making their particular contributions as specialists to a broader topic.

Nonetheless certain general conceptions regarding method were at least implicit in the work of the historians whom we have just discussed. Like the *Annales* historians they sought to explore the structural contexts in which events occurred; but to a much greater extent the structures which interested them were those which reflected human actions and outlooks, such as constitutional, administrative, and legal institutions, rather than the more elemental, automatic demographic and economic factors which interested the *Annales*. The structures of concern to the new critical group of German historians thus required special types of generalizations or typologies which took into account the concrete, unique elements in every historical situation.

In its methodological assumptions, the new orientation to study political history in its social context in many ways draws on examples offered by Max Weber and, to a lesser extent, Otto Hintze. As we mentioned earlier, already at the time of the Lamprecht controversy Heinrich Rickert had stressed that the historian never depicts the past as it was.[60] Reality in nature or history was a chaos of events upon which the scientist or the scholar imposed an order by means of concepts. For Rickert and Weber, Windelband's distinction between the idiographic methods of the cultural or social sciences — seeking explanation of unique events — and the nomothetic approach of the natural sciences — aiming at laws — did not hold, since the cultural sciences like the natural sciences required generalizations, even if not laws. The methodological distinctiveness of the social and cultural sciences derived from their subject matter, from the condition that "every cultural event embodies some value recognized by men, for the sake of which it was either brought about or, if it already had come about is cultivated,"[61] and from the fact that dealing with cultures the historian or cultural scientist deals with systems of values. Weber agreed with Rickert that "knowledge of cultural processes is inconceivable except on the basis of the *meaning* which the reality of life, which always takes on individualized forms, has for us in specific, individual relationships."[62]

Yet the fact that the cultural sciences dealt with values and meanings which had to be understood in their concrete historical context by no means excluded the possibility of explaining them but, indeed, made such explanations possible. Weber's basic assumption, accepted at least implicitly by the historians with whom we are dealing, was that men normally act pur- positively in pursuit of ends which in themselves in the last analy- sis did not derive from rational or empirical procedure. Yet since human behavior was value-oriented, it was possible through empirical or rational procedures to explain how men collectively act in pursuit of these values. The *"verstehende Soziologie,"* as conceived by Weber, was not a part of psychol- ogy[63] insofar as it was not concerned with the sources of human motivation but with the analysis of the behavior which men would follow in pursuing most effectively the purposes which guided their behavior. This made possible the development of models of explanation, of "ideal types," heuristic models which permitted one to grasp unique historical complexes in genetic concepts. These "ideal types" were not conceived by Weber as "hypotheses," since they did not seek to depict reality but rather provided a heuristic principle by which real historical develop- ment could be assessed.

Weber's analysis of modern Western society involved a con- ception of modernization which in a modified form recurred in much of the critical literature on Germany which we are dis- cussing. The later historical literature, with its often narrow focus on German problems in the nineteenth and twentieth centuries, to be sure lacked the universal historical perspective which marked Weber's work; for Weber the analysis of ancient Judaism, classical Greece and Rome, China and India became crucial for the understanding of the uniqueness of the rational- ization process of the West. Nor was the thesis — by which the sources of modern secular rationalism were sought in Protes- tant, this-world asceticism — considered necessary for an un- derstanding of modern capitalism, which Weber himself acknowledged no longer needed the support of religious asceti- cism. Yet the critical literature accepted Weber's assumption that strong forces were operating toward a more "rational," i.e., efficient, effective organization of collective activity as expressed in the trends toward bureaucratization, the extension of capitalism, and the scientification of intellectual life. The question could of course be asked whether bureaucratization — modelled heavily here on Prussian examples — did in fact mark as clear a movement toward rationalization in government as Weber suggested or did not involve irrational elements of resistance to change and persistence to routine. Moreover, the early bureaucratization of government on the European continent when contrasted with the much slower development in this direction in England or America may in important ways have reflected the uneven modernization of political and economic conditions.

Weber was keenly aware of the uneven modernization of Germany in contrast to the West, the persistence of an aristocratic "rural society" in Germany, supported by a mandarin class, an "aristocracy of education"[64] as a political force seriously hampering the modernization of Germany and — a matter of particular concern to Weber — weakening the role of Germany on the international scene. Similarly, Weber recognized the elements of social conflict that accompanied the release of social and political aspirations resulting from modern industrialization and the maintenance of a system of domination which sought to consolidate the existing distribution of power, status, and wealth.

Weber's influence on German historical scholarship must by no means be overstressed. Certain points of contact exist between Otto Hintze's attempts in the 1910s and 1920s to introduce developmental typological concepts and to analyze by means of a comparative approach[65] the development of such European institutions as bureaucracies, capitalism, feudalism. Hintze was much more of an epistemological realist than Weber and assumed that the generalizations and typologies with which the historian worked were not merely heuristic devices invented by the historian but represented *"anschauliche Abstraktionen"* (abstractions won by contemplating the object) derived directly from the historical subject matter. But Hintze not only remained without great influence in his immediate time on the generation of young historians in the Weimar Republic but also lacked Weber's breadth and critical political stance. He focused more narrowly and uncritically on Prussian administrative institutions as they affected the economy in the period before the French Revolution and touched only peripherally on the industrial age.

The critical orientation in German political historiography of the 1960s and 1970s — of which Eckard Kehr and Hans Rosenberg were forerunners in the Weimar period and in emigration respectively — can by no means be labeled Weberian. Like Hintze, historians in this orientation, such as Kehr, rejected the neo-Kantian notion that social science concepts do not reflect reality but serve purely to organize the chaos of events for the purpose of understanding them. Nevertheless they remained indebted to Weber's analyses of status, bureaucracy, and capitalism as these related to Weber's examination of the unique character of German modernization. Weber was politically passionately committed but insisted that the scholar in his quality of scientist rather than as politician must strive for value freedom in inquiry; by contrast, the younger group has been frankly committed to a critical examination of German social and political structure and national values. Without considering themselves Marxists, they have placed the conflict of class and economic interests much more centrally into the analysis of politics than Weber and have stressed much more sharply than he the role of capitalism in intensifying the inner tensions of German society and contributing to the tragedy of 1914 and 1933.

Eckard Kehr's and to an extent Hans Rosenberg's critical studies of Prussian and German politics in the eighteenth and nineteenth centuries thus became important models for the literature on interest groups. Much more so than Weber, Kehr and Rosenberg recognized the extent to which bureaucracy operates as a force that prevents reform in the direction of a more rational social order. Kehr like Rosenberg recognized the capitalistic character of the great aristocratic estates. The absolutistic states created the bureaucracies to break the power of the aristocrats and the estates. Military pressures intensified the process of bureaucratization and centralization in the eight-

eenth century but were accompanied by the increasing aristoc-
ratization of the bureaucracy. The establishment of a *Rechts-
staat,* a state of law, in which the bureaucracy was protected by
due process provisions against the arbitrary intervention of the
king marked for Kehr "the victory of agrarian capitalism over
the monarchy." The Stein reforms confirmed for Kehr the establishment of a "dictatorship of officialdom,"[66] for Rosenberg
that of "bureaucratic absolutism."[67] The development of an independent bureaucracy was intimately interwoven for Kehr
with the development of capitalism in Prussia. The future contradictions of society were contained in the condition that Prussian bureaucracy now satisfied the economic interests of the
"bourgeoisie" yet at the same time maintained the political role
of the capitalistic agrarian classes. The fateful political result for
Germany was the "collapse of the political activity of the bourgeoisie" which for Kehr occurred with "inner necessity"[68] from
the development of capitalism under specific Prussian-German
conditions once the bourgeoisie had obtained its political demands and allied itself with agrarian capitalism. The "irresisti-
ble development of capitalistic economy"[69] consolidated this
alliance and led to the dangerous course in German foreign policy which Kehr analyzed in his book on the construction of a
battle navy. The conventional conception of the "primacy of
foreign affairs" was reversed and foreign policy seen by Kehr
as a function of domestic interest.[70] The fleet was built less as
"an instrument for the preservation of national autonomy"
than as an "instrument of economic autonomy and the struggle
for economic expansion" and, more important, as a means for
"stabilizing anew the threatened dominance of industry and
agriculture allied against the rise of the proletariat as a political
force."[71] The basic characteristic of the German situation, which
Kehr believed Marx had not fully understood, was contained
in the "contradiction between economic and political power":
the control of German politics not by the "legitimate representatives of the industrial capitalistic economic system, the
bourgeoisie, but by the legitimate representatives of an economic system, feudalism, which has essentially been bypassed

by history."[72] The growing tensions of a capitalistic social order under these conditions led by necessity (*zwangsläufig*) to the transformation of the "national state" into a "class state, and to a policy of force in international affairs."[73]

Kehr's broad analysis of German history nevertheless raised certain methodological questions. In contrast to Weber, Kehr was dealing with what he understood as an "objective" social process which follows strict inner necessities. Theoretically it should be possible to find compelling empirical evidence for these processes, which after all occur in the real world and seem to a greater extent for Kehr than for Weber to determine political behavior and fundamental attitudes than to be determined by them. Yet the methods utilized by Kehr to analyze these developments essentially involved discussions of the political opinions of rather broadly conceived economic groupings such as "capitalism" or "agriculture" and of socio-economic groupings or "estates" (*Stände*) such as the officials, the officers, and the teachers; and of political parties. Kehr's book remains an interesting thesis. However, the basic archival work needed to establish the relation of economic interests to political action has just begun to be done. Similarly the analyses of German classes requires empirical studies which are still largely lacking. Within limits quantification becomes an important tool of social analysis. Kehr's shortcomings here are in many ways also Weber's — and to an extent Marx's. Weber viewed sociology as an "empirical" discipline. Yet his analysis of social structures and developments remained impressionistic. Empirical examples could always be marshaled in support of explanatory theories such as for Weber's thesis on the religious origins of capitalism, but no criteria existed as to how this evidence should be selected to provide a convincing case. In the last analysis neither Weber nor Kehr transcended important limits of a *Verstehen* approach. The limitations in Kehr's works also hold for a part of the literature on the role of interest groups where this literature too facilely accepts Kehr's generalizations as a framework for its research.

Both Rosenberg and Wehler went beyond Kehr in seeking

to incorporate theories of economic growth, capable of a high degree of quantification, into historical analysis. To a lesser extent so have other historians, such as Helmut Böhme, who have stressed the significance for political development of cyclical development in the economy, particularly that of the depression of 1873. The depression of 1873 received a prominent place as a causal element in many of the studies of the emergence of economic pressure groups. Rosenberg in his book on the Great Depression[74] sought to study German and Austrian history in the late nineteenth century as an example of a hypothesis that the long cycles of economic activities could provide a key not only for the empirical investigation of economic processes and growth but also for the study of non-economic phases of development and of structural connectedness and thus for an understanding of "history itself" (*"der" Geschichte*).[75] Thus Rosenberg explored the impact of the depression of 1873 on the decline of both political and economic liberalism, the emergence of anti-Semitism and what he calls "pre-Fascist" attitudes, and the consolidation of the alliance of agrarian and industrial interests already observed by Kehr. The effect of the depression, he recognizes, must be understood, however, in terms of the specific political legacy of Central Europe, not merely as a mechanical reflex to a set of economic circumstances.[76]

Wehler in his *Bismarck und der Imperialismus* (1969) sought to relate German colonial policy in the Bismarck period to a broader theory of industrialization. Even more explicitly than Rosenberg, Wehler stressed that industrialization must not be viewed as a uniform, linear process of economic growth but as growth marked by uneven oscillations and crises and by national differences. Nor was the economy as such the primary factor in historical change. "The economy, society, politics and ideas form a totality, an independent cybernetic system (*Regelsystem*)."[77] Imperialism in the Bismarck period, with which Wehler is here concerned, can thus not be understood in purely economic terms but must be viewed in the light of social, political, and ideological factors. Colonialism in the Bismarck period for Wehler becomes a function of domestic politics as the navalism of a later period had become for Kehr. Bismarck did not acquire colonies to pursue *Weltpolitik*, but world power arose from the economic expansion of a great industrial state.[78] Colonial policy took the form of a "manipulated social imperialism" to offset social conflicts accentuated in a period of economic crisis and prevented the reforms necessary in an industrial society. Yet the chapters dealing with the course of events (*Ereignisgeschichte*), which follow the theoretical section of the book, show again how difficult it is to establish the links between theoretical models of explanation and actual historical events. For Wehler's narration of Bismarck's colonial policy does not differ radically from conventional accounts. As Wehler rightly points out, it is in this period that Germany acquired a colonial empire which was expanded but little after Bismarck.[79] Yet Bismarck's policy, as described in the narrative chapters of the book, seems less affected by the cyclical behavior of the market or by industrial interests than by partly accidental factors as well as considerations of foreign policy in acquiring reluctantly an empire which was of marginal significance to the German economy. Stressing the importance of the depression on foreign policy, Rosenberg and Wehler nevertheless see its effects very differently. If for Rosenberg the depressed economic situation with its social tensions motivated Bismarck to avoid "all international adventures,"[80] Wehler sees in this period the roots of German imperialism. Basically both Wehler's and Rosenberg's books — Rosenberg's study explicitly so — are conceived as hypotheses,[81] which, while they leave questions open, have nevertheless explored the possibility of a more theory-and-problem oriented approach to history which seeks to lessen the gap between empirical method and an approach which takes into account the elements of meaning and intentionality. The differences in Wehler's and Rosenberg's conclusions on foreign policy again illustrate how difficult it is to formulate concepts and methods which lead to scholarly consensus in the interpretation of historical developments.

Both Rosenberg and Wehler have been criticized, particularly from a Marxist position, for their failure to utilize a comprehensive theory of social change.[82] Rosenberg, it has been pointed out, is not concerned with explaining why cycles occur but is content to observe that they do occur and to use them as a means of periodization. Wehler seeks to explain the occurrence of crises in terms of the growth problems of capitalism, particularly the problems of overproduction and the anarchy of the market, failing from the perspective of his Marxist critics to assign proper importance to the declining rate of profits. Wehler is further criticized for treating every economic crisis as a unique occurrence, seeking to explain each crisis in terms of isolable factors, and employing a "pluralism of theories" to explain these.[83] Wehler would hardly deny this and openly admits that "a certain theoretical eclecticism will be the rule rather than the exception" in historical explanation.[84] Such an eclecticism, of course, sets limits to scientific rigor and maintains an element of subjectivity in the choice of the theories to be applied to analyze each crisis. But one can argue that at this point of development of the social sciences, this shortcoming is unavoidable if one does not wish to venture onto the unscientific plane of speculative theories of history incapable of empirical validation. In criticism of Wehler, Rosenberg, and Wolfram Fischer, Reinhard Spree from a Marxist position complained of historians "who limit themselves to the analyses of parts or to microanalyses, who arbitrarily define segments of reality and reduce complexity through the discovery of empirical regularities by subsuming great masses of data under definite categories or 'quasi laws.' "[85] Yet Spree does not solve the problem, which we have raised earlier, of how a dialectical "conception of society as a concrete totality"[86] can lessen the elements of subjectivity and arbitrariness which he discovers in Wehler's approach.

Wehler, like the Marxists, recognizes the political role of history, which he views as a "living, political, critical science of society," that both reflects the historical character of the time and acts on it.[87] The history of the nineteenth and twentieth centuries for Wehler is inseparably bound up with that of industrialization. The task of the historian in the German situation of the present, he stresses, rests in contributing to overcoming the "lags" between the economic, social, and political development which so fatefully afflicted German history from 1871 to 1945. Weber, Wehler argues, was correct in recognizing that modern science is always "anchored in certain ultimate ideas of value" which undergo revision with changing social realities. The normative decision which Weber made in favor of an individualistic system of liberal capitalism and of certain Western cultural values, Wehler feels persuaded to make today in terms of the "distant goal of a mass-democratic social state, in which, however, the claims of society to an absolute title (*Anspruch*) over the individual are resisted and the industrial world is humanized — to an extent subjected to the controls of rational planning,"[88] essentially the goals of present-day German Social Democracy.

Hans-Ulrich Wehler and Hans Rosenberg have stood out among the historians we have just discussed in their conscious attempt to integrate social science theories into historical research and thus to increase the explanatory value of historical studies. The years since 1970 have seen a regular explosion in West Germany of writings dealing with role of theory in historical studies.[89] These have been written from very different perspectives. Yet while in the 1960s, Gerhard Ritter, as the dean of German historians, was still able in the controversy with Fritz Fischer to combine a defense of national political traditions with a reaffirmation of the historicist stress on political personalities, the new literature agreed on the inadequacy of the classical heritage of German historicism. This sense of the inadequacy of the German tradition of historical science involved not only disillusionment with the German political past but also doubt regarding the cultural value and relevance of history in a modern technological society in which many of the continuities with the past had been broken.

This skepticism regarding the utility of history expressed itself in the late 1960s and early 1970s in a steady shift of students at the universities from history to sociology and political science and the replacement of history courses in the secondary schools by courses in social studies (*Gemeinschaftskunde*).[90] Related to this more general disaffection from history was the increasing conviction among historians that historical studies as they had been pursued in Germany had only inadequately met the requirements of a scientific discipline, science here understood in the broad sense of the term *Wissenschaft.* Sharp differences were reflected in the competing conceptions of the character of such a science. These conceptions reflected the conflict between neo-positivistic, hermeneutic, and Marxist dialectical viewpoints which we described in the first chapter. While Karl-Georg Faber recognizing the role of hermeneutic methods in history nevertheless sought to stress the role of generalizations based on empirical data,[91] historians of the democratic left, such as Dieter Groh[92] and the contributors to Imanuel Geiss's volumes, *Ansichten einer zukünftigen Geschichtswissenschaft,*[93] remained critical of the attempt to introduce value-free generalizations into history. Yet a general consensus emerged among historians that history could not be separated from the social sciences — although these sciences were conceived very differently — and that the social sciences in turn could not be approached purely structurally or functionally without taking into consideration the elements of time and change. Further agreement existed that historical studies to attain scientific character required the use of explicit theories, although disagreement continued on the character of theories suitable for historical studies. The task, of course, remained that of translating the demand for theory-guided historical research into actual practice. The literature on interest groups of the late 1960s had only in a limited sense pursued questions guided by theory. Its theoretical assumptions had been largely implicit and where the attempt had been made to develop explicit theories, as in H. U. Wehler's *Bismarck und der Imperialismus* and Hans Rosenberg's *Bismarck und die grosse Depression,* the link between theoretical models and events had remained tenuous.

Yet it was not enough to apply social science theories to history; what was also needed was a solid foundation of empirical social research upon which to build such theories. It is in the areas of demographic studies, theory-oriented economic history, and quantitative methods generally that scholarship in West Germany — and incidentally also in East Germany — was lagging when compared to historical scholarship in France, England, and Poland. It has been Hans-Ulrich Wehler's great contribution as an editor to make German historians aware of the attempts outside of Germany, particularly in the English- and French-speaking countries, to apply social science theories to the analysis of historical phenomena.[93] At the same time, Wehler in a series of important essays[94] explored the limitations of these methods to historical studies. These essays represent a considerable elaboration of the theoretical position developed in *Bismarck und der Imperialismus*. Wehler calls attention to the extensive work done in the Anglo-American countries and in France in quantification in demography, economic growth, and political behavior as well as attempts to introduce anthropological and psychoanalytical concepts into history. He sees the great contribution of the cliometricians, such as the New Economic Historians, in the precise formulation of problems of investigation and the rigorous examination of explicit hypotheses and models by means of quantitative methods. Yet these methods which proceed by isolating measurable variables, Wehler warns, have their limits in the complexity of historical situations with their "unavoidable qualitative aspects."[95] The danger which Wehler sees in introducing hypothetic-deductive models, such as employed in the New Economic History, is that in abstracting economics from history, they distort both economic and historical reality. For in proceeding from a theory of economic equilibrium, characterized by perfect competition and the unobstructed operation of the laws of supply and demand, they ignore the concrete political and other factors which at any moment prevent such equilibrium.

The understanding of economic processes thus requires "historical socio-economic theories in the place of theories which claim general validity in isolated economic questions."[96] Marx and Weber for Wehler continue to offer important examples of "historical social sciences." It was one of their great contributions, as it was that of the German Historical School of Political Economy, to have repudiated an economic science resting on abstractions, separated from "real history."[97] Marx and Weber, as did Schumpeter and Gerschenkron, obviously went further than the Historical School of Political Economy in formulating theories of the economy applicable, to be certain, only within a historical context, yet capable of conceptualizing an inner logic of development. The superiority of Gerschenkron's analysis of industrialization processes over that of Walt Rostow rests exactly in Gerschenkron's introduction of specific historical factors to explain the diversities of patterns of industrialization in countries in which the breakthrough to an industrial economy took place under circumstances which, compared to the classical model of the English "take-off," reflected relative "economic backwardness."[98] No general historical theory is possible. The more general a theory, the more formal and empty it is and hence the less useful to the historian.[99] Yet the use of theories in history is possible for Wehler on two levels. A multiplicity of social theories, derived from the social sciences, can be utilized to approach any specific historical problem. But beyond this, historical theories of "middle range"[100] are possible, which he believes — like those utilized by Marx, Weber, or Gerschenkron — offer hypotheses capable of a degree of empirical confirmation. While recognizing that value concepts and intellectual interests determine the problems which historians pose, Wehler nevertheless remains confident in contrast to the Neo-Kantians that the "past possesses structures independent of the inquiring subject,"[101] structures which admittedly become apparent only amid the competing interpretations which emerge in the course of scholarship. These structures nevertheless provide an objective element for the examination of historical theories.

Yet the problem remains how "middle range" theories can be applied to historical studies. While the studies of interest groups in the late 1960s were generally "critical" in Wehler's sense, they proceeded for the most part relatively conventionally as to method, centering on the decisions taken by leading personalities in economic and political life as these revealed themselves in written documents. The past five years have seen a rapid movement beyond this stage to a more conscious attempt to utilize methods and concepts from the social sciences, particularly from the international discussion on economic growth and cycles, from Weberian sociology, and to a lesser extent from recent demographic studies. An example of the new concerns is the series "Critical Studies in Historical Science,"[102] begun in 1972, which has focused on exactly the problems which Wehler has considered of prime importance to the historian today, an analysis of political and social developments in the modern industrial world with the aid of theories and methods gathered from the contemporary social sciences but from a "critical" perspective focusing on the dysfunctions in capitalist industrial societies.

The industrialization of Germany has played an increasingly central role in German historical studies since the 1960s. But these studies have seldom done what Wehler and Rosenberg have sought to do: to apply theory to the study of the interrelation of economics, social structure, and politics and place this study on a firm empirical basis. Quantitative studies are still relatively rare in Germany. This is so despite the wealth of statistics which German officials and scholars, such as those close to the Verein für Sozialpolitik — an organization of professors and others formed in the 1870s for the scientific study of the social problems caused by industrialization — accumulated in the nineteenth century. As James Sheehan recently noted: "The student of German social and political history confronts an extraordinary abundance of quantitative data, but he finds a relative scarcity of sociological or historical penetrations of this material."[103] The Weimar period saw considerable activity on the part of sociologists such as Theodor Geiger and others to compile statistical data on German social structure and mobility, but relatively little use of this work has been made by recent German social historians. The most recent *Handbuch der deutschen Wirtschafts- und Sozialgeschichte* (Handbook of German Economic and Social History) still reflected the deep hold which historicist notions held even on economic historians. The editors, apparently oblivious of the developments in economic history outside of Germany, could thus maintain as late as 1971 that the traditional methods of historical research, as formulated by Droysen in the *Historik* a century ago with the stress on the unique, continue to be adequate for economic history. The volumes of the *Deutsche Agrargeschichte* (German Agrarian History)[104] published in the 1960s, all, with one exception — Wilhelm Abel's contribution — treated agricultural history from the perspective of constitutional, administrative, and legal history. The geographical limit of the history was that of the German "nation," or after 1871 the Reich; the periodization of economic or agricultural history, that of reigns.

Wolfram Fischer in the late 1960s called for an "empirical social science" of the past.[105] He still complained in 1967 how little the German research had learned in terms of method from either Marxist or non-Marxists in the British debate on the standard of living in the period of early industrialization.[106] And he called upon historians to link quantitative methods of economic history, estimates of Gross National Product, real income, price and loan levels with sociological analysis of class in the period of early industrialization. In his own studies he sought to test Marx's assertion that industrialization under capitalistic conditions led to a simplification of class structure and questioned this conception not only for the late but also the early industrial period. In recent years regional studies, such as Otto Büsch's work on industrialization in the Berlin-Brandenburg area,[107] have become more frequent and interest has been awakened in demography. But neither Büsch's nor Walter Köllmann's[108] studies on population are marked by the theoretical interests for which Fischer and Wehler have called. Büsch frankly affirms his disinterest in a "theoretical discussion regarding the relationship of industrialization, economic growth and social change"[109] but prefers to provide the neighboring disciplines with the empirical material needed to test their theories, hypotheses, and models.

There continues to persist a strong, even if lessening, resistance to the application of empirical social sciences to historical studies. The younger, socially and politically more critical historians have quite often accepted from their elders a good deal more than they admit of the idealistic conception of history, particularly the hostility to empirical and quantitative research. The work of the French *Annales* circle has been little understood in Germany but emphatically rejected by older conservative historians like Gerhard Ritter and younger adherents of a "critical theory" like Dieter Groh.[110] Groh's arguments parallel those of Frankfurt School philosophers, such as Adorno and Habermas in their famous controversy with the "positivists," Karl Popper and Hans Albert.[111] Groh accuses the *Annales* of objectivism and stresses that history as a "critical social science," whose aim is "emancipation," must combine analytical and empirical with "hermeneutic" *Verstehen* methods. Groh is undoubtedly right that quantitative series do not carry their own explanations with them and cannot take into account the extent to which "men make their own history." Yet Groh like Habermas has few methodological guidelines for the study of history to offer which possess greater methodological rigor than the intuitive *Verstehen* approach of the classical historians. Here again Wehler's work represents a welcome attempt to bridge the gap between explanatory social science approaches, model building, quantification, and the like as they have emerged in historical work, particularly but not exclusively in economic history, and German *Verstehen* approaches stressing the role of consciousness and human decisions.

Indeed, it is striking that in contrast to Great Britain, where Marxists such as Eric Hobsbawm have been very much involved along with non-Marxists in assembling extensive empirical and quantitative material on the condition of the working class, in West Germany this kind of research until recently has been conducted almost entirely by such historians as Wilhelm Abel and his circle, who consider themselves as scholars to be value-neutral and politically non-engaged. Wilhelm Abel's highly quantitative approach to the history of agriculture and the economy remained a rather isolated phenomenon. Entirely free from the *völkisch* romanticism which surrounded studies of the peasant in the Nazi period, Wilhelm Abel in 1935 had published a quantitative study[112] of cycles of agricultural depressions and prosperity since the late Middle Ages. On the basis of long series of data on population, wages, prices, and food consumption, he sought to investigate on a comparative European basis the interrelation of demographic and economic factors from the beginnings of a market economy to the beginnings of industrialization. Abel's work was consciously ignored in Germany, not only in the Nazi period but well into the 1960s when his investigations and methods had already attracted considerable attention in France, Great Britain, and Poland; and he himself, until the early 1960s, remained isolated in the faculty of agriculture. His Institute of Social and Economic History in Göttingen has since then unearthed an impressive amount of data for German towns. Yet while these data throw considerable light on the well-being of the common man, the extent and cycles of poverty with a particular stress on the artisans, and are therefore of great value to the sociologist as well as the economist — Abel has also made an important contribution to the controversy on the causes of pauperization in the early industrial period[113] — his studies consciously avoid political as well as sociological factors, such as questions of social status, which cannot be easily quantified.

Until recently histories of the working classes written in West Germany — or, as we shall see in the following chapter, East Germany — were primarily histories of the organized working-class movement, that is, for the pre-1918 period primarily the SPD. German scholarship until recently lacked the radical tradition which inspired the English "history from below." Recent years, however, have seen a number of studies which have dealt concretely not only with the economic conditions of the working class but also with such topics as family life and reading patterns as undertaken by Rolf Engelsing in his articles on the social history of the German middle and lower strata in the period of transition from a corporative to a modern capitalistic society in the eighteenth and nineteenth centuries.[114] Engelsing has been concerned not only with questions of the standard and cost of living but also with political consciousness, education, choice of reading matter. The methodological differences between Engelsing's attempt to study the "history of the reading public in the modern period" and the similar themes in the *Livre et société* studies which we discussed earlier are striking and interesting. Engelsing largely avoids quantification; rather, he seeks examples from a broad selection of literary sources — letters, diaries, memoirs of the famous and the unknown — which present a broadly international yet impressionistic picture of reading matter and reading habits. Similarly, his concept of class and social status avoids the criteria utilized by the French group intended to enable quantification. This attempt to reconstruct the consciousness of a broad segment of the population, generally ignored by the historians, on the basis of literary evidence recurs in a different form in the studies undertaken or directed by Walter Grab on Jacobinism and radical democratic movements in Germany in the late eighteenth and the nineteenth centuries.[115]

Important studies of the early industrial period continued to stress the methods of a *verstehende Soziologie* deeply indebted to Max Weber and to a certain extent to Karl Marx. Two studies need to be mentioned: Reinhart Koselleck's *Preussen Zwischen Reform und Revolution*[116] and Jürgen Kocka's study of the white-collar employees at Siemens from 1847 to 1914,[117] which both appeared in the series edited by Werner Conze at Heidelberg, "The Industrial World." Koselleck sees in Prussia the one state whose "growth to power coincided with its industrialization."[118] Yet the process of industrialization remains in fact very much on the periphery of Koselleck's study. The key to an understanding of the social and political consequences is to be found in an analysis of Prussian legislation and administration. Koselleck sees the roots of later social and political tension in the reform policies of the Prussian bureaucracy. These policies, on the one hand, by dismantling the old system of estates, prepared the way for a social and economic order better suited to industrialization; they, on the other hand, by thus having eliminated the protection to the poor which the guilds and corporations assumed traditionally, brought about a direct confrontation of the poor and the state in a period of increasing industrial poverty which set the stage for the revolution of 1848 and contributed to the opposition to democratization afterwards. Koselleck explicitly intends to go beyond "biographical and political history" to a social history which makes "lasting structures" visible. Yet such a structural history in the final analysis, he insists, must base itself on the interpretation of texts, on traditional "historical-philological methods,"[119] even if the latter may be supplemented, as in fact they are by Koselleck, by considerable quantitative material. In the final analysis history is the history of consciousness. For Koselleck as for Conze, a major key to the social history of an epoch, including that of the modern industrial world, is to be found in the conceptions which guided an epoch. Social history is therefore necessarily "concept history" (*Begriffsgeschichte*), to be clearly distinguished from the history of ideas (*Ideengeschichte*), which has much less to offer the historian. Conze's institute has thus been engaged in the publication of a major dictionary of "Basic Historical Concepts,"[120] the first volume of which has now appeared, as a contribution to the understanding of the industrial world through its language.

Jürgen Kocka in his analysis of the development of the relations of white-collar employees and management in the Siemens firm over three generations[121] goes a good step further to link theories of bureaucratization and social stratification with archival research. Central to Kocka, as to much of the critical literature on German history in the half century before 1914, is the problem of the industrialization of Germany under conditions in which preindustrial bureaucratic attitudes and traditions were still more pervasive than in other countries such as Great Britain or the United States. From this perspective, Kocka examines the emergence of a white-collar "middle-class" and a white-collar mentality in Germany, and in a more recent study, not yet published, the corresponding classes in the

United States. This interest in comparative history is shared today by a large number of the younger historians. While for over a century, from approximately 1848 to the 1960s, comparative historical studies were rare, at least among historians proper in contrast to historical sociologists such as Max Weber, the years since 1965 have seen a plethora of studies which seek to view German developments, the ancien regime, early industrialization, parliamentarization, organized capitalism, imperialism, fascism within a comparative international framework — to be certain, almost always with a focus on the developmental problems of modern Germany.

A remarkable change had thus occurred in the climate of German historical scholarship since the time of the Fischer controversy. This change reflected not only a reassessment of the national past but also a methodological reorientation which cannot be entirely separated from the changes in political and social outlook. Yet the historiography of the mid-1970s reflected both a convergence with tendencies in historical sciences internationally as well as the persistence of traditional German themes. The insularity which marked German historical scholarship well into the 1950s, with its almost exclusive concern with German problems and its ignorance of the methodological discussion abroad, was partly ended. Indicative of the new openness to social science research abroad was the attempt of a research team formed in 1973[122] at the Max Planck Institute for History to utilize methods developed by the *Annales* and the Cambridge Group for the History of Population and Social Structure, including those of family reconstitution neglected until now in Germany, in a projected in-depth regional study of proto-industrialization. Other studies of proto-industrialization and early industrialization, resting more exclusively on economic data and seeking to analyze the role of leading sectors of the economy in industrial "take-offs," have been undertaken by Richard Tilly and his students at Münster. The Göttingen group intends an intensive microhistorical study utilizing a variety of social data relating to population, agriculture, manufacture, political and social institutions, social and cultural norms to be quantified wherever possible "to avoid the uncertainties of the idiographic method." The attempt is to be made by means of hypotheses to establish the relation between historical theory and empirical data.

A similar openness marks the series, "Critical Contributions to Historical Science," which we mentioned above, as well as the announcement of the new journal, *Geschichte und Gesellschaft. Zeitschrift für Historische Sozialwissenschaft,* to appear in 1975, intended to serve as a forum for "social-scientific historical research" among German and non-German scholars. "History," the prospectus announces, "is to be understood as a historical social science in close relationship with neighboring social sciences, especially sociology, political science and economics." Yet much more consciously than in the case of the studies of the *Annales* circle or the Cambridge Group, the effort is to be made "not to lose sight of political perspectives." If the focus of the *Annales* studies was on social processes in preindustrial Europe, the editors of *Geschichte und Gesellschaft* and of the "Critical Studies" intend to concentrate on the period following the industrial and political revolutions of the eighteenth century. Marx and Weber continued to inform the social science conceptions of the "Critical Studies" although these studies in principle, even if markedly less so yet in practice, strongly acknowledged the need for empirical corroboration.

In this respect Jürgen Kocka's volume in the "Critical Studies," *Klassengesellschaft im Krieg, 1914–1918,*[123] is of particular interest as an attempt in the analysis of the politics of World War I to go beyond the work of Fritz Fischer and his students as well as beyond the studies of the historians dealing with economic interest groups. For both of these groups, in Kocka's view, had continued with the "aid of traditional methods of textual interpretation" to understand decisions of leading personalities in economic and political life rather than to explore the "social economic structures of change *per se.*"[124] Still, it is the political dimensions of these processes which concern Kocka in this essay. Kocka seeks to approach these by means of a model derived from Marx's theory of class, yet separated from the

broader context of Marx's philosophy of history, and supplemented admittedly somewhat eclectically by more recent theories of conflict. As utilized by Kocka, Marx's theory of class
operates on three levels — a material basis on which class membership and the opposition of classes is determined in terms of
the ownership and control of the means of production, a "subjective" level on which the objective "position of the classes"
contributes to the "subjective" awareness of their class interests,
and finally the organization of classes in terms of their interests
resulting in the concrete forms of class conflict which expresses
itself in political action.

It may be argued that the theory of class conflict taken out
of the broader context of Marx's conception of history and society loses its dialectical perspective and becomes a relatively
mechanistic explanatory scheme. Kocka would not necessarily
deny this. Yet this model, Kocka argues, is of considerable use
in understanding the growing political conflicts in Germany
during the First World War which led to the German Revolution of 1918–1919. It does not offer an objective replica of an
actual course of development in the sense in which Marx
thought such was possible but formulates an ideal type which
serves to identify and analyze "certain elements and factors of a
historical reality."[125] The model is thus a heuristic device, not
capable of verification or falsification but only of comparison
with reality. The war precipitated processes which corresponded
to the Marxist model; classes became more homogenous during the war as the real income of industrial workers and white-
collar employees declined and the privileged position of the
latter in relation to the former diminished during the war.
Large enterprises generally suffered less economically than
smaller ones. Although there was no direct relation between
the extent of economic hardship and political protest, class tension rather than the desire for peace contributed decisively to
the revolution of 1918, which Kocka sees as the "consistent outcome of German social history in the First World War."[126]

To be certain, the Marxist model has to be modified, Kocka
stresses; while the state "tendentially" was an instrument of

control by the economically dominant classes, in fact the bureaucratic state functioned to a high degree as an autonomous factor. In the face of the exigencies of war, the element of autonomy in governmental decisions became more pronounced as the state established its control over the economy and in pursuit of the interests of the war effort implemented policies which more frequently than in pre-war Germany ran counter to the desires of organized capitalism in meeting the demands of the workers. The Marxist-Leninist theory of monopoly state-capitalism in Kocka's opinion does not suffice to explain economic policies during the war. Factors not included in the Marxist model must be included to explain the failure of a revolutionary working-class movement. One of these factors lay in the process of bureaucratization of large complex organizations, such as the German labor unions and the Social Democratic Party, with the resultant alienation between the bureaucracy, pursuing its own organizational ends, and its membership, a process accelerated during the war and intensified in the division between relatively conservative Majority Social Democrats, seeking the integration of the workers into the existing social order, and a growing, radicalized working class. A host of other factors had to be identified, such as the distinction between town and country or the role of religious differences and of ethnic minority groups, in order to take into account the counter tendencies which modified the operation of the class model used here to explain political change. Yet these counter tendencies do not invalidate the model in Kocka's opinion but determine its limits and thus increase its heuristic value.

Kocka's study remains an essay, and it was conceived by him as such. Kocka's model calls for and requires empirical corroboration. This corroboration can include quantitative evidence of the kind Kocka supplies in his discussion of such "objective" factors as changes in occupational distribution, real and nominal wages, food consumption or the profitability of German corporations. Kocka recognizes that the problem of evidence becomes a good deal more complex once the transition is made to what he calls the "subjective" level of political consciousness and the translation of this consciousness into political conflict. Here the limits of quantification and the remaining needs for a *verstehende Soziologie* become acutely apparent.

The difference between the conception of a "historical social science" as held by Kocka and by the contributors to the "Critical Studies" and that contained in the *Annales* conception of history as a "human science" is clear. Despite their break with the idealistic conceptions which dominated the classical tradition of German historical scholarship, their recognition of social processes relatively autonomous of conscious human direction, and their willingness to utilize empirical and quantitative methods of the behavioral sciences, the younger German historians of the new "critical" orientation in history continue in the tradition of Marx and Weber to emphasize more emphatically than the French historians of the *Annales* circle the residual differences between natural and historical phenomena and the extent to which the latter require the "analysis of meaning" never fully reducible to quantities. In seeking a rigorous historical social science, they are willing to go considerably beyond the models offered by Marx and Weber in seeking empirical corroboration, yet like them continue to be more skeptical regarding the relevance of empirical, including quantitative, data separated from a broader historical context.

On the whole the literature dealing with the Third Reich has been conceptually more conventional than that dealing with the political and social tensions accompanying modernization in the earlier period. We have thus discussed it only marginally, although important attempts by K. D. Bracher, Hans Mommsen and others to apply political science concepts to the politics of Weimar and the Third Reich deserve attention.

IV

Marxism
and Modern Social History

A SHARP CONTRAST existed until recently in the relation of
Marxist economists and Marxist historians to their respective scholarly communities. Marx had been thoroughly steeped in classical economic theory. He sought to refute
political economy, in part, with its own methods. In turn,
Marx's economic analysis, although rejected by political economists, became part of the classical body of economic literature.
Marx, although profoundly aware of the limits of empiricism in
economic analysis, nonetheless himself sought to formulate hypothetico-deductive systems, replacing those of classical political
economists, and like the latter subject to empirical examination. To an extent Marxist economic theory underwent further
development, by Rudolf Hilferding, Rosa Luxemburg, and
others, so that a continuous tradition of Marxist economics
came into existence. In contrast, Marxian historical writings,
including those of Marx and Engels themselves, lacked the
conceptual and methodological rigor of Marxian economics.
Marx's historical writings were more directly related to the
needs of an immediate political situation and guided by general
philosophical assumptions and political values. The lack of
common methodological ground contributed to the isolation of
Marxist historiography from the main currents of scholarly
historical discussion, as did the very different institutional
framework within which each functioned. Nor did Marxists

succeed in linking their strict models of economic development with the analysis of historical events, except by means of broad generalizations incapable of empirical validation.

The last several decades have seen Marxist historians enter the community of professional scholars. The process of professionalization, which in the course of the nineteenth century transformed historical studies, in the twentieth century also affected Marxist historical writings. The great Marxist historians of an earlier time such as Karl Marx and Friedrich Engels themselves, Franz Mehring, Jean Jaurès, V. I. Lenin and Leon Trotsky had been statesmen, men of action, or (in Franz Mehring's case) publicists in leadership positions within their parties, who viewed historical writings as a strategic instrument in the class struggle. Since the 1920s and 1930s, Marxist history has been increasingly written by professional historians at universities and research institutes. The conditions under which this happened were fundamentally different in societies governed by Communist parties, such as the USSR and after 1945 the Socialist countries east of the Elbe, from countries like France or Italy where Marxist historians were part of a broader pluralistic community of scholars. Yet professionalization generally, even in countries in which it was accompanied by considerable ideological direction, brought with it an increasing awareness on the part of Marxist historians of the conventional research techniques of the historical craft; it also increased the possibilities of dialogue and led non-Marxist historians to take seriously the challenges offered by Marxists to the conventional conception of scientific history.

This essay does not intend to present a comprehensive survey of Marxist historiography today. The diversity within Marxist historical studies prevents us from defining Marxism in abstract terms. We have thus chosen a historical approach. A first section will briefly examine the historical work of Marx and Engels themselves, which proves to be much more difficult to reduce to a common formula than has generally been assumed. A second section will seek to examine several directions in recent Marxist historical scholarship. The main emphasis will be on historical studies in the West, because there the conditions have been most favorable for the dialogue with the historical orientations which we have discussed in the preceding two chapters.

I

Marx had been convinced that both economics and history had to be raised to the level of rigorous sciences, that both moreover, except for heuristic purposes, could not be separated from the broader total context in which they occurred. What Marx understood by scientific method has, however, been the object of considerable interpretation.

There are clear points of agreement between Marx's concept of science and the nomological conception of science.[1] Marx certainly in his economic writing sought to formulate "laws" of development which formed an important cornerstone of the process of history. "The ultimate aim of this work," Marx wrote about *Capital*, "is to unveil the economic law of motion of modern society."[2] The scientific formulation of laws required theory, theory which permitted a degree of quantitative formulation and was subject to empirical validation. In *Capital* Marx sought to formulate sets of laws, such as "the law of the tendency of the rate of profit to fall," which he was convinced could be expressed in formulae that historical development would prove to be correct or false to the satisfaction of economic scientists of whatever conviction.

But Marx nevertheless emphatically rejected a correspondence theory of truth and the empiricism which such a theory involved. He consistently distinguished between the essence (*Wesen*) of things and their appearance (*Erscheinungsform*), cautioning in *Capital*, that "the general and necessary tendencies of capital must be distinguished from their form of manifestation."[3] He similarly warns the historian in the *German Ideology* against taking historical evidence at its face value.[4] The critique of empiricism is perhaps most explicitly developed in the section on methodology in the "Introduction to a Critique of Political Economy," in which Marx specifically warns that if "we commence with the real and concrete aspect of conditions as they are; in the case of political economy with population" as the basis of productive activity, we arrive at empty "abstraction," at a "chaotic conception of the whole." This occurs if we deal with the concrete, for example with population, apart from class and other factors which give it content. But "the concrete is concrete," Marx observes, "because it is a combination of many objects with different destinations" and the task of science is to grasp the concrete in its relation to the whole (*Totalität*).[5]

The "concrete" as an expression of the "totality" can only be apprehended by means of theory. Yet every theory, Marx recognizes, is in fact an abstraction of essential but nevertheless partial aspects of the whole. Historical understanding is made even more complex by the fact that "human history," as "Vico says, differs from natural history in that we have made the former, but not the latter."[6] Nevertheless it is made by men under circumstances not of their own choosing, "circumstances directly found, given and transmitted from the past."[7] Man's actions create forces which at a point in historical development arrive at operating independently of the will of men and in fact control them. This makes it possible for Marx to view the "development of economic formations of society," which for him constitutes history," a "process of natural history" governed by laws.[8] These laws are, however, not laws in the sense of the natural sciences but laws of social formations at a specific point of development.[9] As such they are constructs won from reality providing explanatory theories for behavior under certain historical circumstances. But the concrete historical situation is always more complex than the theory. Thus when Marx conceptualizes general "laws" of capitalist development, such as the law of the falling rate of profit, he recognizes that there are always influences to be taken into consideration which "counteract" these laws and give the laws "merely the characteristics of a tendency."[10]

Empirical analysis thus proves insufficient for the understanding of concrete historical situations. The link between law and event is contained for Marx, as for Hegel, in the dialectic.

Marx, to be sure, wishes to free the dialectic from the idealistic "mystifications" it suffered in Hegel's hands and place it on the firm ground of the "material world."[11] The driving force of the dialectic for Marx is thus not to be found in the "process of thinking"[12] but in the contradictions created by the development of the "material productive forces" and the "property relations within which they have been at work hitherto."[13] Yet at the same time, the very concept of dialectic presupposes a process toward increasing rationality, rationality understood not only in terms of more efficient organization of material and human resources for the purposes of production but in terms of the creation of "those material conditions, which alone can form the real basis of a higher form of society in which a full and free development of every individual forms the ruling principle."[14]

Marx's approach to society, while thoroughly historicist in its stress on change, is nevertheless normative. These norms, to be sure, are not the ahistoric standards of natural law theory since man in "acting on the external world and changing it, at the same time changes his own nature."[15] All science of society for Marx is historical science, proceeding from the material basis of human existence; yet insofar as all social science examines social states not only in terms of economic but also of social dysfunctionality, it is critical and normative.

It is important to understand the normative aspect of the dialectic because the polarity between the normative and the existing order forms an essential element of Marx's method in economics as well as in history. The humanism of the Parisian manuscripts, with their conception of man as a "species-being" who "considers himself to be a universal and consequently free being" but who under conditions of private property has been "alienated" from his "human essence"[16] is well known. But a similar polarity between normative conditions in terms of human values and the substantively "irrational" circumstances of a given historical formation of society that have "no natural basis" runs through *Capital* and the *Grundrisse*. Marx's basic critique of political economy is as much philosophical as economic. Political economy, he charges, operates with a false conception of value, which measures wealth as "a property of things" rather than in terms of its "value to men."[17] "Political economy," Marx wrote, "has indeed analysed, however incompletely, value and its magnitude. . . . But it has never once asked the question why labour is represented by the value of its product and labour-time by the magnitude of that value."[18]

Capitalism, Marx argues in *Capital* as in the *Economic and Philosophic Manuscripts,* represents the extreme form of the development "in which the process of production has the mastery over man, instead of being controlled by him"[19] and social relations are reduced to "the relations between things."[20] The "simple labour process, [in which] the labourer stands in relation to the means of production, not in their quality as capital, but as the mere means and material of his own intelligent productive activity" is replaced by the capitalist labor process in which "it is no longer the labourer that employs the means of production, but the means of production that employ the labourer."[21] Capitalism is doomed ultimately not merely because it proves in the long run to be economically self-destructive but because at one and the same time it is humanly destructive. Based on the creation of "surplus value" which requires that "the value of labour must always be less than the value it produces,"[22] capitalism is caught in the contradiction that within its system "all means for the development of production transform themselves into means of domination over, and exploitation of, the producers; they mutilate the labourer into a fragment of man."[23] But the very demands of the capitalist production process "compels society to replace the detailed worker of today . . . by the fully developed individual . . . ready to face any change of production"[24] and drives the "centralization of the means of production and socialization of labour"[25] to the point where these become incompatible with the capitalist system itself. Thus for the "mature" Marx of *Capital* in 1867 as for the "young" Marx of 1844, capitalist production begets its own "negation."[26] In the last analysis, science, ethics, and the course of historical development thus coincide for Marx as they did for Hegel, even if the driving force of this process is no longer to be found in spontaneously operating thought but in the "real" life world, in the contradictions generated by material forces.[27]

The question arises how this dialectical conception can be translated into scientific historical inquiry. The writing of history, Marx noted in *German Ideology,* must proceed from the "material conditions" under which men live and "their modification in the course of history through the action of men."[28] Nevertheless it is doubtful whether Marx in his historical work succeeded in linking empirically the material conditions under which men lived with the course of historical events or of testing his historical hypotheses. Marx, despite his demand that all social phenomena must be seen in their dynamic, total context, wrote two very different kinds of history: on the one hand, economic and social history, within the framework of the first volume of *Capital,* from which a consideration of political factors was largely excluded; on the other hand, political history, such as the *Eighteenth Brumaire of Louis Bonaparte,* in which Marx assumes that all political conflicts represent class conflicts but does little to base his analysis of class on empirical inquiry.

The first volume of *Capital* is a work of economic theory as well as of economic and social history. The historical sections dealing with the development of the working day, the factory system, and wage legislation occupy a major part of the volume and do not follow as clearly from the theoretical sections as Marx had intended. In the theoretical sections Marx consciously abstracts capitalism from its concrete historical setting to work out the inner logic, the "inexorable laws"[29] governing capitalism as a system wherever it may appear in time or place. Once the process of "primitive accumulation" during which the worker was forcefully separated from the means of production has established a sufficient fund of capital, a self-generating process begins to operate in which "every accumulation becomes the means of new accumulation"[30] until the contradictions within the system lead to its destruction.

In analyzing the laws of capitalist development, Marx, as we noted, has sought to abstract these from a concrete historical setting. Yet for Marx, capitalism had emerged only in one specific historical context, that of Europe. Marx in a famous letter in 1877 emphatically rejected attempts "to metamorphose my historical sketch of the genesis of capitalism in Western Europe into a historical-philosophic theory of the general path imposed by fate upon every people whatever the historic circumstance in which it finds itself."[31] Yet were capitalism to emerge in other societies, such as Russia, it would follow a similar development.

A sharp contrast becomes apparent, however, in *Capital* between the development which capitalism in Marx's analysis would undergo were it permitted to follow its own inner logic and the actual course of the economic and social development of England as traced by Marx. The "inherent tendency of capitalist production," Marx writes, is "to appropriate all twenty-four hours of the day";[32] "the constant tendency of capital" as to wages is "to force the cost of labour back to . . . zero."[33] But the long historical sections on the working day and on the development of wages give a much more complex picture than Marx's model suggests. Marx relates how from the Black Death until the eighteenth century, under largely or partially pre-capitalist conditions, legislation tended to lengthen the working day and repress wages. The very point at which with the Reform Act of 1832 Parliament became an effective instrument for the pursuit of capitalist interests was also the point at which this trend was reversed and factory legislation limiting the length of the working day and regulating working conditions introduced. The intensification of labor made possible by mechanization and the circumvention by factory owners of the laws off-set many of these gains. It is England, however, which, as Marx freely admits, in the mid-nineteenth century led countries less advanced in capitalist development, such as France, in regulatory legislation. If the tendencies inherent in capitalism toward longer working days and lower wages were unable to assert themselves unambiguously, this occurred according to Marx because factors other than the inherent laws of capitalist production counteracted these tendencies. The contradictions of capitalism had created a modern working class, and the consciousness of this class became an important force in historical development. The length of the working day was never the result of purely economic forces, but always "the product of a protracted civil war, more or less dissembled, between the capitalist class and the working class."[34] Political history therefore became the key to the understanding of economic history, even if in turn political history could be understood only in its socio-economic context.

It is striking that Marx and Engels wrote little on the political history of England or on the economic history of France and Germany. Marx's and Engels' analyses of German and French political history proceeded with little of the careful examination of the economic development of these societies which *Capital* had provided for England. The basic thesis was, of course, that the political sphere was the scene in which conflicting class interests were fought out and that the outcome of these conflicts was in its general outline determined by the overall direction of history which in the European world led to the replacement of the "feudal" by the "bourgeois" mode of production, until the inner dynamics and contradictions of the latter led to the abolition of a class society. Yet the actual course of political history, as analyzed by Marx and Engels in their writings on nineteenth-century Germany and France and by Engels in his book on the German Peasant Wars of the sixteenth century, remained immensely more complex than the above theory of stages, outlined by Marx and Engels only in its most general form, suggested.[35] The problem which confronted Marx in the *Eighteenth Brumaire of Louis Bonaparte* and the *Class Struggles in France* and Engels in *Revolution and Counter-Revolution in Germany* but also in the *German Peasant Wars* was why the liberal-bourgeois revolution which they had predicted in the *Communist Manifesto* had not led to proletarian revolution. The answer lay in large part in the economic and political backwardness of both countries, e.g., in "the misfortune of the German bourgeoisie to have come too late."[36] But this explanation conflicted with Marx's assumption, repeated in the preface to the first edition of *Capital,* that all capitalist countries went through similar stages of development and that thus "the country [England] that is more developed industrially only shows, to the less developed, the image of its own future."[37] In both Germany and France, the bourgeoisie gripped by fear of a revolutionary proletariat and, as Marx goes to pains to demonstrate in the *Eighteenth Brumaire,* deeply divided within itself by conflicting economic interests, sought support either, as in Germany, in the pre-capitalist social and political order or, as in France, with its strong peasant base, in Bonapartism. Although Marx stresses the rootedness of political parties in property relations,[38] he recognizes that the victory of Bonaparte in France cannot be fully explained in terms of class interests but requires an understanding of the weight of political traditions and memories and is influenced by the cunning of individuals, such as Louis Bonaparte and the members of the Society of December 10, a group with no well-defined social base, scheming for political power.[39] Once firmly in power, the Bonapartist state manages to function to an extent independently of the direct pressure of economic interest groups or classes. More moralistic than Marx, Engels sees the failure of the German revolution of 1848 as a result of the "cowardice" of the bourgeoisie unwilling to assume its objective historical role, thus making "forever impossible in Germany" the establishment of "political liberalism, the rule of the bourgeoisie, be it under monarchical or republican form of government."[40]

The *Eighteenth Brumaire* came closest to a careful effort, free of Engels' moralism, to attempt an economic interpretation of history. Yet Marx did not lay claim to "discovering" the class struggle — this "bourgeois historians had described long before me," he wrote — but to "proving" the historical direction which this struggle would take.[41] The *Eighteenth Brumaire* is *histoire engagée,* surpassing in the acuity of its interpretation and the brilliance of its style earlier attempts by A. Thierry, François Guizot, Louis Blanc, and Lorenz von Stein to analyze French politics in terms of class conflict. Yet although Marx and Engels assumed a relationship between economic crisis and political unrest, there is little attempt to study the events of 1848 to 1851 in their relationship to cyclical economic movements of the period. Analysis of the classes remains impressionistic, devoid of empirical investigation — which a Marxist conception of science, despite its recognition of the limits of empiricism, theoretically demanded. The task to write critical political and social history from a Marxist perspective in closer relation to economic theory and empirical evidence remained for later historians.

2

As WE have indicated, Marxist historiography in the past several decades has participated in the general process of professionalization. In the USSR and later in other countries east of the Elbe, this occurred with the reorganization of the scholarly profession after the accession to power of a government dominated by the Communist party. In western countries and Japan, historians of Marxist orientation trained in conventional methods began to appear within the universities and to work within historical professions that reflected diverse ideological and methodological positions. They were thus almost from the beginning forced into dialogue with non-Marxists, utilizing methods which were common to both. In the socialist countries these conditions did not exist in this form. An important role in the coordination of research was often assigned to the academies of science with general guidelines for historical interpretation frequently offered by the parties which also maintained separate research institutions of their own. One should be careful, however, not to reduce scholarship in the socialist countries of eastern Europe to a common denominator. Profound differences existed from country to country, reflecting the differences in scholarly traditions as well as in political conditions. While in the USSR and the German Democratic Republic,[42] the topics of research, methodological approaches, and interpretation were subject to a high degree of party and state direction, this was generally less the case in Yugoslavia, in Poland and Hungary after 1956, and in Czechoslovakia in the 1960s. In East Germany where the historical profession had been most seriously compromised politically and intellectually by Nazism, the years after 1945 led to an almost complete change in the personnel of the historical profession and the accession to professorial chairs and key positions in the institutes by persons who had spent many years in the active struggle against Nazism. In other countries, such as Poland,[43] where a rich tradition of social history existed before the war, non-Marxist historians such as Jan Rutkowski and Henryk Łowmiański could return to the universities and participate significantly in the rigorous training of a young generation of Marxist historians. In France historical scholarship emerged without a radical break within the framework of the established universities and their conventions of historical scholarship.

The professionalization of Marxist historical scholarship opened the possibilities of scholarly dialogues with non-Marxists, although the ideological and political direction of scholarship in certain socialist countries contributed to preventing or delaying such discussion. Within the Western countries this dialogue was, of course, facilitated by membership in a common scholarly community with a shared historiographical heritage. But even in countries in which historical studies remained closely guided by party and state, as in the USSR and the German Democratic Republic, professionalization led to an awareness of standards for the critical examination of evidence. Nancy Heer in a recent study has illustrated with the aid of statistics the increasing shift from party-trained to university-trained historians in the USSR and suggested the extent to which since 1956, notwithstanding the absence of significant institutional changes of a liberalizing nature, "the process of historical writing and rewriting in the USSR has become less of a reflex action and more of a dialogue between historians and politicians."[44]

Already in the 1950s a serious debate could take place between Roland Mousnier in France and the Soviet historian Boris Porshnev, using complementary bodies of documents, on the character of the peasant uprisings in the seventeenth century, a debate which although leading to little agreement in interpretation raised important conceptual and methodological questions.[45] The community of language maintained despite ideological divergence between Porshnev and Mousnier was even greater a decade later between French historians of the *Annales* and Polish and Hungarian economic and social historians seeking to construct structural models of social and economic development. The increasing insistence of Marxist historians on scholarly rigor and their openness to social science concepts made possible the meeting and partial merger of Marxist and non-Marxist orientations of labor history, such as in Great Britain. A dialogue with Marxism became possible at the point at which the left tradition of working-class history, which in Great Britain had developed relatively independently of Marxist inspirations, became intensely aware of the conceptual limitations of its essentially narrative, chronological approach; and a new generation of Marxist historians, critical but free of dogmatism and possessing sufficient methodological sophistication and acquaintance with modern social science, was able to offer reasonable hypotheses for the analysis of the changing role of the working class under conditions of industrialization.

Despite the increasing professional independence of historians in the socialist countries, a discernible line of distinction still exists even today between historical studies in states such as the USSR and the German Democratic Republic in which scholarship, although by no means monolithically controlled, nevertheless remains subject to considerable ideological direction, and others such as Poland, Hungary, or those of the West, in which the autonomy of scholarship is relatively well established. Two different conceptions of objectivity tend to dominate. Almost all Marxists would agree with the East German *Einführung in das Studium der Geschichte* (1966) that "a science of history free of all presuppositions is impossible," and that the "study and teaching of history is conditioned and fulfils certain social purposes."[46] Yet the more open Marxists would question a conception of partisanship (*Parteilichkeit, partijnost*) which reduces historical science to "a chief ideological weapon"[47] in the service of the party, viewed as the repositor of objective consciousness.

This latter stance, which has dominated Soviet and East

German official historiographical theory until now (although not always historical writing) and which denies the separation of ideology and science, has made it difficult to link historical interpretation and detailed evidence in a manner convincing to scholars who do not proceed from the momentary guidelines of the party. Thus Peter Bollhagen in the *Einführung in das Studium der Geschichte* posits as an essential assumption of Marxist historiography that "logic" and "history" are one,[48] that "history takes place as a unitary, dialectical process of natural history in a lawful context,"[49] and that this lawful process permits of the "periodization"[50] of history according to the stages of development outlined by Marx and Engels. But while Eric Hobsbawm in Great Britain has argued that "there is nothing in Marx's theory of stages to authorize us to look for a general law of development,"[51] East German historians argue that the task of the Marxist historian is to demonstrate the lawfulness of "historical development as progress from a lower to a higher state."[52]

Marxism has thus been viewed less as a method than as a philosophic system. The stress on the ideological and political function of historical science has provided an approach to political history, which despite its materialist presuppositions, seems remarkably conventional in its concentration on men and ideas. This is very noticeable both in the twelve-volume textbook *Lehrbuch der deutschen Geschichte. Beiträge,*[53] the first attempt at a comprehensive synthesis of German history from a Marxist point of view, and in the eight-volume history of the German labor movement. The latter, as the introduction explains,[54] bases itself heavily on the works of Marx, Engels, and Lenin, the "resolutions of the party of the working class and the speeches and essays of the leading functionaries of the German worker's movement."[55] Despite occasional accounts of strikes, references to working conditions, what is presented is not a "history from below," such as Jürgen Kuczynski had undertaken in his multi-volume history of the conditions of the workers under capitalism,[56] but the history of the institutionalized party dominated by its great men and by the confrontation of ideologies.

At the same time, the "materialist conception of history," as understood by official Marxist historians, has led to impressive accumulations of historical information on such topics as the economic and social conditions of peasants and artisans during the preindustrial period, of working-class conditions and workingmen's associations in the period of industrialization, of strikes and social protest movements, and of the role of economic interests in the shaping of foreign and domestic policy in the "age of imperialism." The recent volume on historical research in the German Democratic Republic, from 1960 to 1970[57] illustrates the impressive accumulation of information in these areas. Research in the German Democratic Republic provided important bases for a social history of German politics. Under Jürgen Kuczynski's guidance an impressive collection of data on the living conditions of workers since the late eighteenth century has been worked out. Hans Mottek's studies of early industrialization[58] provided not only important factual information, but by pointing at investments in such areas as the railroads offered a correction of the overly simplified English model previously applied by Marxists and non-Marxists to German early industrialization according to which the industrial revolution began with the use of machines in light industry.

The *Jahrbuch für Wirtschaftsgeschichte* founded in 1960 by Jürgen Kuczynski served as a forum for the critical, international discussion of recent work in economic history. In its pages there also appeared Karl Obermann's essays on the role of demographic factors in the revolutionary movement of the 1840s.[59] Obermann's contribution lay in part in placing the study of revolutionary consciousness in a concrete social context, which lent itself, to a degree, to the application of quantitative methods. The incipient demographic researches in the German Democratic Republic have, however, been a subject of controversy.[60] Very valuable have been the extensive studies in the G.D.R. not only of Communist but also of liberal and democratic movements and individuals in Germany who had been studiedly neglected by conventional German historians since the mid-nineteenth century.[61] As in the Federal Republic, a great deal of interest has been devoted in recent years to the study of the interrelation of economic interests and foreign policy before and during World War I and the domestic politics of that war.[62] Despite the different doctrinal presuppositions from which this research has proceeded, it has been remarkably similar in its reliance on textual evidence from firms, parties, and governmental agencies to the West German literature we have discussed in a previous chapter. While the archival work has been solid, many of the studies discussed above have tended to utilize overly schematic explanatory models or, dispensing with these, have proceeded essentially empirically. What has been lacking has been the serious attempt, which has been undertaken by Polish Marxists, to formulate Marxist theories in a form in which they are capable to a greater extent of empirical controls.

3

A MUCH MORE conscious attempt to overcome the gap between theory and empirical observation was undertaken by a group of Polish economic and social historians, of whom we shall here single out Witold Kula, Jerzy Topolski, and Andrzej Wyczański. Marxists, they nevertheless in many ways carried further a tradition of social and economic history which before the war was represented by Jan Rutkowski and Franciszek Bujak. Close contacts had existed in the inter-war period between Rutkowski and Bujak and Bloch and Febvre. The journal *Rocznike Dziejow Spolecznych i Gospodarczych* (Annals of Economic and Social History), founded in 1926, reflected many concerns similar to those of the *Annales d'histoire économique et sociale*. Like Bloch and Febvre, Rutkowski and Bujak sought to move from an event-oriented to a structural economic and social history. Their postwar disciples remained very fully aware of the international discussion in all the social sciences, particularly in economics. After 1956 close scholarly contacts were resumed between the Poles and the French historians. The *Annales* became a frequent forum for the presentation of their findings in French. Like the historians of the *Annales,* Kula, Topolski, and Wyczański were structurists but from the perspective of historical materialism more centrally concerned than their

French colleagues with the processes of production and "appropriation of economic surplus."[63] They regretted, as Kula suggested, that "Marxist science," while in its programs opposed to any "idiographic" history, in practice often unfortunately approached such an attitude.[64] Yet in contrast to East German pronouncements, they stressed the primacy of "methods" over "laws" in Marxist historical inquiry.[65]

Marx, Kula and Topolski agreed, sought to construct explanatory "models" won from the analysis of "real" economic and social processes. The model method, Kula and Topolski acknowledged, was by no means unique to Marx but was shared by a large segment of modern economic theory. Topolski accepted Braudel's definition of models as "simplified schemes," "hypotheses or explanation systems solidly linked by equations or functions; this is equal to that or determines that."[66] A great deal of modern economic theory and quantitative method — e.g., the definition of secular and short-term trends, of cycles and growth — was of use to Marxist history, and broad points of agreement existed between Marxist and non-Marxist history. Marxist economic history must however be aware, both Topolski and Kula stressed, as traditional political economy has not always been, that "the economic historian must constantly bear in mind that he is interested above all in dynamic processes" and is thus not concerned with "time in general (the latter is used in pure economic models and models used in the natural sciences), but with so-called dated time, that is located at a definite place in the flow of time."[67] He must thus avoid the two extremes of "ahistorical abstraction" and "atheoretical historicism," Kula warned.[68] A similar note was recently voiced in Pierre Vilar's attempt to establish points of community between the history of the *Annales* and Marxism.[69] The Marxist method of seeking to work out "real models" which take into account an abstract logic of development, as well as the concrete historical factors within which this development takes place, Topolski argues, differs sharply from the abstract instrumentalist models used by quantitative economic historians such as Marczewski or Fogel.[70]

The Polish historians thus work with a concept of law

quite different from that of official East German and Soviet historical studies. They are unwilling to raise the "law of stages" to a world historical principle. "Let us not worry whether the world evolution of culture has moved in one or several directions," Kula comments. "Let us take as departure the astonishing fact that the world today has taken as its model the type of industrial civilization to which all the societies of the planet aspire."[71] Marx's economic history, he insists, knows no laws applicable to every society. Rather, it seeks to construct the laws governing economies in a specific, spatial-temporal setting. It does this by means of models which seek to isolate the essential elements of both stability and change in social structures. These models are first formulated in qualitative terms, which can then be partially "concretized" with quantitative information.

The prime concern of the Polish school has been the analysis of "feudal," defined as pre-capitalist, predominantly agricultural, economies in which the fundamental unit of production is great landed property.[72] The classical work on the economy of feudalism thus conceived has been Kula's attempt to construct a theory for the Polish economy from the sixteenth to the eighteenth century.[73] This model uses certain theoretical statements applicable to the functioning of all economic systems, then tries to consider certain specific characteristics of the Polish economy in this period. Such characteristics, among others, include the predominance of agriculture, the existence of peasant and gentry farms, the place of serfdom and the corvée in the agrarian economy, the unique role of handicraft within the framework of land ownership, and the guilds. The study then tries to construct a model which makes it possible to calculate the profitability of agrarian enterprises in an economy in which the marketplace plays a limited role and unpaid labor has to be taken into account. Jerzy Topolski has sought to "concretize" the model even further by modifying it to fit the conditions operating in western Poland in this period.[74] At the same time in his book on the genesis of European capitalism,[75] he has sought again by means of "concretized" models of economic development to lay the basis for a comparative study of capitalist accumulation in zones of "dynamic growth" (England), "moderate growth" (France), and "stagnation" (Poland). A. Wyczański, utilizing various quantified data, including foreign trade information, has sought to compute gross production figures for Poland, to compare these with other European areas, and in a study of the sixteenth-century gentry farms has sought to construct a quantitative model for such a farm taking into account such factors as size, labor performed, and volume of production. Wyczański has sought to probe into aspects which Braudel characterized as "material history" as a basis for a "history from below," such as food consumption figures, but also literacy, centered on Poland but viewed in a comparative European context.[76] Going beyond economic structures to a study of mentalities, Kula has sought by means of a historical analysis of changing weights and measures since primitive times to find a key to the study of changing as well as persisting outlooks in the course of world civilization.[77]

Certain of the criticisms which have been leveled against the *Annales* can also easily be raised in regard to these Polish studies. The history of structures is relatively isolated from that of events, particularly political events. In fact, however, the relation of economic developments and political structures plays a more important role in the work of Topolski than of Kula, and both Topolski and Kula have laid increasing stress on the role of subjective factors of social consciousness in historical change. Nor do these economic historians divorce structural aspects of history as freely from movement in time as *Annales* historians frequently have done. The stress on Polish economic history in the preceding pages should not give an overly narrow picture of Polish Marxist historiography. We have selected the above historians because they have gone considerably further than other Polish Marxist historians in seeking to combine empirical research and theory. As in the German Democratic Republic, a Marxist perspective contributed to a broadening of the questions asked by historians, an increasing concern with the material foundations of culture — which in 1951 led to the foundation of the Institute for the Study of Material Culture

— of social and economic conditions and of class conflict. These concerns were all reflected in Henryk Łowmianski's monumental study of the origins of the Polish state[78] as well as in the multi-volume history of Poland prepared by the Historical Institute of the Polish Academy of Sciences beginning in the 1950s.[79] Yet 1956 in many ways marked a reorientation in Polish Marxist historiography. If on the one hand it led to attempts to free historical writing altogether from explicit Marxist assumptions and marked a return to conventional monographic studies or to the use of econometric or demographic methods, often similar to those of the *Annales,* relatively isolated from clearly articulated theoretical contexts, on the other hand it was also marked by a reinterpretation of Marx by the philosophers — e.g., by Adam Schaff, Leszek Kołakowski, and more recently Leszek Nowak — which left its impact on Marxist historiography. As long as Marxist social and economic history had uncritically accepted an overly simplified scheme of historical development ascribed to Marx, it had tended rather positivistically to accumulate data on the basis of archival research. Theory and empirical research had existed side by side with little attempt to integrate the two. The emancipation from a narrowly deterministic interpretation of Marx's conception of history now left the way open to a historiography which became increasingly aware both of the role of theory in history and the need of formulating theories of limited or medium range capable of being confronted with empirical evidence. Polish historiography after 1956 thus became increasingly receptive to methodological discussions in philosophy and in the social sciences within and outside of Poland.

4

A RELATIVELY wide, complete gap existed in France until 1945 between ideologists and publicists within the Communist Party — or other political groupings on the Left — and professional historians. Professionally trained historians within the French Communist Party, such as Jean Bruhat, one of the party's most important — and doctrinaire — theoreticians of history as well as interpreter of the French revolutionary past in the Stalin period, were few. After 1945 a number of younger historians joined the party. Yet the continued dogmatism of the party, its relative lack of interest in historical research, its reinterpretations of the crucial revolutionary moments in French history since the French Revolution in accordance with the gyrations of the party line and the momentary tactical demands of the political situation prevented a meaningful symbiosis of party activism and intellectual work. As David Caute observed, "active in Party work as these historians might be, in their professional capacity they too often resembled their non-Marxist colleagues."[80]

This gulf was narrowed in the 1950s. As in other countries, the dogmatism of the party gave way to a greater openness in questions of historical method and interpretation. The party's intellectual journal *La Pensée* organized a series of colloquia on the application of Marxist principles to history. In 1953 Pierre Vilar, at a colloquium on "Marxism and History" sponsored by *La Pensée,* could complain about the lack of original research done by Marxists and the failure of Marxist historians to use statistical techniques.[81] Under the direction of Roger Garaudy, the Centre d'Études et des Recherches Marxistes organized by the party, in a continuing series of topical *cahiers* endeavored from a Marxist perspective seriously to take into account developments in the modern social sciences dealing with questions of historical development as well as problems of contemporary Western and non-Western societies. Yet for the purpose of this essay with its focus on the Marxist contribution to the development of a modern historical social science, the internal discussions within the party, as they occurred in these colloquia and publications,[82] still often remain too rigidly wedded to a Marxist theory of stages and to Marxist terminology to make possible a fruitful methodological dialogue between Marxists and non-Marxists.

We have therefore chosen to concentrate on the discussion outside the party, in the academic world. This admittedly creates much more serious problems in determining what belongs

in an examination of Marxist historiography than we encoun-
tered in the previous sections of the chapter on historical studies
in the socialist countries of Eastern Europe, where a well-defined
Marxist academic establishment existed. A certain diffuse Marxism, stressing the economic determination of politics and the
role of class conflicts, had characterized a great deal of French
historical writing, particularly that dealing with the French
Revolution and the revolutionary uprisings of the nineteenth
century. The history of the French Revolution in twentieth-
century studies had undergone a marked transformation from
the essentially political interpretations by republican and anti-
republican historians of the early twentieth century such as
Alphonse Aulard and Louis Madelin to the increasing emphasis on economic and class factors by Albert Mathiez and Georges
Lefebvre. Yet what made this new approach significant was
less the introduction of a Left political point of view than the
attempt to see political events within their structural context.
This led Pierre Vilar, who has sought to establish the compati-
bility of *Annales* notions and methods of inquiry with Marxism, to comment in 1971 that "when we look about us today
we find that the history historians write is more like history
according to Marx (or according to Ibn Khaldun) than it is
history according to Raymond Aron (i.e., history in the manner of Thucydides)." Vilar considered central to the modern
approach to history "one basic hypothesis: that the subject matter of history is structured and accessible to thought, is scientifically penetrable like any other sort of reality."[83] But this does
not really distinguish Marxist historical science from the historical science of the *Annales* or the German social historians
of politics whom we have discussed. For Marxists, as Vilar is
the first to recognize, proceed with a distinctive conception of
the structure of historical reality, which views the mode of production as the core of the social structure marked by the "economic principle of social contradiction which bears within it
the necessity of its destruction as a structure."[84] Marxism thus
involves the application of a theoretical framework for understanding dialectically the "mechanisms of human societies" but

simultaneously a practical political commitment to the transformation of these societies arising from insight into the objective exigencies of the historical situation.

But Marxism does not view itself primarily as praxis but as praxis informed by scientific theory. Vilar is right in pointing at the Marxist concern that history is capable of scientific analysis, a concern which the Marxists share with other social science oriented historians. The basis for a dialogue between Marxist and non-Marxist historians is thus given, although clear differences remain on basic questions regarding the limits of empiricism, the role of values in historical inquiry, the political relevance and function of social scientific study, and others. Nevertheless, a Marxist interpretation of any set of historical events to satisfy its own demands for adequate explanation requires that the relationship it assumes between structures and events exists not only in theory but is reflected in empirical evidence.

We have concentrated in the following pages on the literature on the French Revolution because this literature reflects a continued discussion in which Marxist and non-Marxist historians have participated in the attempt to establish such a relationship between social and economic structures and political events. In this connection Ernest Labrousse's work in the 1930s and 1940s must be mentioned again. His work, although Marxist neither in its intent nor in the extent of its empiricism, was crucial for the Marxist analysis of the French Revolution which was to follow. Labrousse in his *Esquisse du mouvement des prix et des revenus en France au XVIIIe siècle* (1933) had documented the upward movement of all prices from 1730 to 1817 and the relatively slower growth of wages. More important for our concern was his attempt in a second work, *La Crise de l'économie française à la fin de l'Ancien Régime et au début de la Revolution* (1944),[85] to relate the cyclical development of prices and wages to political events. Labrousse sought to demonstrate that the outbreak of the French Revolution had to be seen in the framework of the recession which from 1778 to 1787 had interrupted the rise of prices and wages, the bad harvests of

1787 and 1788, and the large-scale unemployment in manufacturing, especially textiles, in 1789. The "economic conjuncture" thus contributed to the "revolutionary conjuncture." To be sure, as Labrousse stressed in a comparative discussion of the revolutions of 1789, 1830, and 1848,[86] economic crises led to a revolutionary situation only if, as in these years, they coincided with a political crisis growing out of social conflict and structural contradictions and were precipitated by "provocative acts of imprudence by the government."

Labrousse's analysis of price movements laid an important foundation for later Marxist and non-Marxist studies of the Old Regime and the French Revolution. Nevertheless, Labrousse's explanation of political behavior has been criticized as overly mechanistic with some justification from very different perspectives — for example, by Roland Mousnier and the Soviet philosopher Igor Kon.[87] A more important pattern for a political history of the French Revolution in its economic and social setting was provided by Georges Lefebvre, who went considerably further than Labrousse in the analysis of socio-economic class structure and in taking into consideration factors of consciousness in their social setting.

Lefebvre had received a great deal of his inspiration from Jean Jaurès. Jaurès in the introduction to his *Histoire socialiste de la revolution française* (1904),[88] itself an attempt at an economic and social history of the Revolution, had complained that the history of the Revolution had until that date rested primarily on the analysis of documents of a political nature, such as the proceedings of the national legislative bodies, the Parisian Commune, or the meetings of the Jacobin clubs. Yet since Marx it had become clear that economic and political history were inseparable. The need now was to utilize and publish documents which threw light on the economic and social side of the French Revolution such as rural as well as urban *cahiers,* documents relating to the sale of national land, and local information on subsistence and wages. To this purpose, Jaurès as a deputy in 1903 obtained the establishment of the "Commission for the Study and Publication of Documents Relating to the Economic Life of the Revolution."

Never a member of the French Communist Party, although often sympathetic to it, Lefebvre[89] acknowledged his debt to Marx much more clearly than did Labrousse. In fact, Lefebvre's work is unthinkable without the Marxist conception of class conflict and its role in politics. Yet at the same time Lefebvre warned against "interpreting the economic interpretation of history too narrowly" and explaining the French Revolution "solely in terms of the growth of the bourgeoisie." Marx, he noted, had never used the term "historical materialism."[90] In insisting that it "is not enough for the historian to describe, he must count,"[91] Lefebvre went beyond traditional Marxist attempts intuitively or impressionistically to discover class relationships and in his thesis *Les Paysans du Nord pendant la Revolution française*[92] placed the study of class structure in the revolutionary period on a scholarly and empirical basis. Utilizing the surviving papers of about two hundred rural municipalities, notarial records, tax assessments, manorial registers, and such for the years immediately preceding and following 1789, and using wealth and income as criteria for the division of classes, Lefebvre discerned a more complex picture of conflicting interest groups than that denoted by the conventional Marxist categorization of classes. The solidarity of the peasantry against the nobility in 1789 hid the sharp differences in political interests between a landholding "rural bourgeoisie" of peasants, interested in the removal of traditional limitations of property rights, and a landless or almost landless peasantry seeking to maintain traditional village controls and collective rights, differences which were intensified by the course of the Revolution. Lefebvre revised the traditional Marxist class analysis of the Revolution. In his subsequent works of synthesis,[93] Lefebvre developed further his thesis of an autonomous peasant revolution in 1789 distinct from the revolution in the cities. The Revolution had at no point been simply a "bourgeois revolution." "Feudal" or seignorial rights and capitalism were by no means as irreconcilable as Marxists had traditionally assumed. The second half of the eighteenth century had seen the reassertion of aristocratic rights as well as the intrusion of capitalistic practices into the countryside, which threatened collective rights.

This very process had strengthened the economic worth of seignorial rights, given impetus to the reassertion by the aristocracy of these rights, and increased peasant resentment. The financial crisis, the unemployment, the bad harvests which preceded 1789 set the stage for the outbreak; the aristocratic opposition to the reforms of privilege triggered the Revolution. Yet from the beginning, the aims of the bourgeois classes, committed to a free market economy, differed from those of the poor in countryside and town seeking to preserve collective rights and the regulation of subsistence prices.

But revolutions could not be fully understood in terms of the "external aspects of antagonistic classes";[94] they proceeded by means of the consciousness of the participants in a revolutionary situation. Lefebvre read extensively in the literature on the social psychology of the crowds, in Gustave Le Bon, Émile Durkheim, and Maurice Halbwachs. In the essay on "Revolutionary Crowds" and in his book *La Grande Peur de 1789*,[95] both published in 1932, Lefebvre helped lay the foundations for the subsequent studies of the "collective revolutionary mentality." In *La Grande Peur de 1789*, Lefebvre studied the phenomenon of a reaction of mass hysteria in the countryside against an imaginary aristocratic conspiracy, a hysteria which took place in the setting of poor harvests and unemployment, rising mendicancy and brigandage but which also had deep roots in age-old class antagonisms and which directly contributed to consolidating the peasant attack against the seigneurial regime.

Lefebvre thus, although never accepting a Marxist "system," nevertheless made two significant contributions to Marxist historical science in France. Without sacrificing narrative, he placed the analysis of class conflict on a firm archival basis which had been lacking in Marx's own class analysis and that of most orthodox Marxist historians. In conventional Marxist historiography, the link between social structure and political events had never been satisfactorily established; and the latter, even in Marx's own writings, continued to center around politicians and ideologies. Through his conception of the "revolutionary collective mentality," Lefebvre pointed a way to a history based on class analysis in which broad segments of the population, no longer conceived as an abstract mass or class, but differentiated, appeared as active agents of historical change. Albert Soboul in his study of the Parisian Sans-Culottes in the Year II[96] carried further Georges Lefebvre's studies of the political behavior of the urban populace. Soboul in a sense assumed Lefebvre's succession. A student of Lefebvre, Soboul in 1959 published the first easily accessible edition of *Les Paysans du Nord,* succeeded Lefebvre as editor of the *Annales historiques de la Revolution française,* and was appointed to the chair of the History of the French Revolution at the Sorbonne once held by Lefebvre. Unlike Lefebvre, Soboul identified himself with a Marxist perspective and was an active member of the French Communist Party. Soboul's broader interpretations of the class character of the Old Regime and the French Revolution, strongly influenced by the Marxist conception of the economic formations of society, led to intense controversy, as to an extent had Lefebvre's own more guarded analyses of the class character of the French Revolution.[97] Yet the study of the Sans-Culottes was for the most part remarkably free from sweeping generalizations regarding the general course of history. Soboul warned against the old Marxist "oversimplification," of which he believed even Jaurès had been guilty in his *Histoire socialiste,* which described the Revolution as the "result of the economic and intellectual power of the bourgeoisie which had reached maturity" and now sought to "legitimate this power into law."[98]

Soboul based his study of the Sans-Culottes on the papers remaining from the forty-eight "sections" set up by the municipal government of Paris during the Revolution. The Revolution in Paris emerged in Soboul's analysis, as did the Revolution in the countryside of Lefebvre's Departement du Nord, not simply as a revolution of the bourgeoisie but of a complex, temporary alliance of groups with different interests and aspirations. Soboul, like Labrousse, recognized the effect of bread-and-butter factors, such as the fluctuations of the price of foodstuffs, on the political activity of urban population. But he emphasized that the Sans-Culottes were not a class as such, "nor was the Sans-Culotte movement a class party." They "came from all levels of society and therefore had no class consciousness." What tied them together in Soboul's view was a common ideology and life style, a hatred of the aristocracy, a demand for equal social and political rights, and for direct political democracy. Nor did the Jacobins represent a class. Indeed, Soboul concludes, "the whole regime of the year II rested on an idealist conception of democratic policy, hence its weakness." Nevertheless, the idea of the Revolution became comprehensible for him as for Lefebvre only within the broader framework of economic development: the steady advance of capitalistic economic practices in the eighteenth century accompanied by the breakdown of social regulations of the economy. Like Lefebvre, Soboul sought to work out the "inner contradictions" which led to the "decline of the popular movement implicit in the dialectic movement of history."[99] Without the alliance between popular masses and the bourgeois classes, the bourgeois revolution would not have triumphed.[100] Yet the aims of the leadership, even in the Jacobin phase, were different from those of the urban classes. The Terror accelerated the destruction of the old society and thus, despite temporary wartime measures, the removal of social constraints on property which justice and morality demanded from the preindustrial perspective of artisans and small shopkeepers. The basis of the contradiction of a new society emerged in which industrial capital was to dominate.

Soboul's work represents an explicitly Marxist position, at times in its attempt to link the Revolution to the "dialectic movement of history"[101] not free of dogmatic notes. Yet Soboul's historicism, his attempt to reconstruct the revolutionary situation, free from schematism, as it becomes visible from the archives, contrasts sharply with certain other Marxist interpretations, such as Daniel Guérin's attempt in *La Lutte des classes sous la Première Republique, 1793–1797,* written from an avowedly Trotskyite theory of "permanent revolution," which consciously seeks to project the concerns of the present into the past and discover in the conflicts of the period an "embryonic proletariat" foreshadowing modern class struggles.[102] Despite its radical ideological stance, Guérin's work in many ways appears conventional and idealistic in much the way as certain Soviet and East German studies we have described, not only in its failure to consider economic data and social structure but in its stress on leading personalities and the clash of ideas. Like Lefebvre, Soboul conceived history on the broad basis of an analysis of collective mentality. But the need to analyze this mentality in its concrete "material" setting led Lefebvre and Soboul to adopt methods of social analysis which were not exclusively Marxist. A broad meeting point exists between Marxist historiography, as conceived by Soboul, and empirical historical sociology. All political history, Soboul stresses, is social history and in the last analysis social history, he agrees with Furet and Daumard, is quantitative history. But, Soboul adds, the data which social history utilizes must not be "disembodied and desocialized" but must suppose a "precise knowledge of structures" and of the "mechanisms" of social change, of social and economic *"conjonctures."* Marxist historiography is not in conflict with a quantitative history of social structures but rather sees in it an indispensable tool for a more precise understanding of the dynamism which moves the antagonism of social classes.[103]

In the past fifteen years, the study of the political behavior of masses in a revolutionary situation has proceeded considerably further and has engaged an increasing number of historians outside of France, particularly in the English-speaking world. Further important contributions to the social analysis of political behavior in the French Revolution have been made by Richard Cobb[104] and George Rudé. Rudé, in *The Crowd in the French Revolution* (1959),[105] dedicated to Georges Lefebvre, analyzes the composition and behavior of crowds during the various major riots and manifestations between 1789 and 1795. Arguing that the identity, interests, and aspirations of the politically active elements among the broad population "can no longer be treated as mere echoes or reflections of the ideas, speeches, and decrees of the journalists, lawyers, orators, and politicians established in the capital,"[106] Rudé uses extensively the police archives of Paris and like Lefebvre and Soboul seeks to relate, at times perhaps too mechanically, political behavior to fluctuations in food prices. Nevertheless, like Lefebvre and Soboul, he seeks through the use of archival material to restore individuality and a sense of political purpose to the popular masses lacking in the older images of a faceless crowd as portrayed heroically in Michelet's "People" or demonized in Taine's "Rabble." A very different structural, quantitative approach, void of almost all narrative, marks Charles Tilly's attempt to explain sectional differences in attitudes toward the Revolution and Counter-Revolution in the Vendée in terms of indicators of economic and social modernization.[107] The scope of inquiry has been extended in recent years from the French Revolution to the revolutionary outbreaks of the nineteenth century and backwards to the food riots of the eighteenth century. Parallel studies of unrests in preindustrial and early-industrial Great Britain have appeared.[108] Not all of these studies, e.g., those of Cobb and Tilly, have been Marxist in orientation. A lively debate has ensued between Marxists and non-Marxists on the role of economic class in the political struggles of the Old Regime and the French Revolution.[109] As Marxist historians increasingly turned to social archives and began to utilize quantitative methods and non-Marxist historians took into consideration the conflicting interests of groups in their social setting, a degree of methodological consensus emerged on what constituted social history. Yet what continues to distinguish much of Marxist historiography and social science, despite the concern for theory and generalizations which it shares with the social sciences generally, is a particular awareness of the concrete historical situation and an appreciation of the role of consciousness as an active factor in social change. It is the latter which is absent in Charles Tilly's *Vendée* with its stress on measurable, anonymous factors of modernization.

5

by NORMAN BAKER

THE HISTORICAL discussion of industrialization in Britain suggests itself as a further illustration of the convergence of Marxist and modern social history not entirely dissimilar to that which we observed in France. Before developing further this illustrative theme, it is necessary to touch on certain features which have to be taken into account in an examination of British historiography. The first such feature is the late development of an academic historical profession or, stated conversely and probably more accurately, the lengthy survival of the amateur, or non-specialist, in a position of prominence. Many of the nineteenth-century writers of British History were not professional academics. If one takes the establishment of the *English Historical Review* in 1886 as symptomatic of developing professional collectivism, the gradualism of this process is similarly illustrated by the interval of thirty-five years that elapsed before the foundation of the Institute of Historical Research. Not until well into the twentieth century had full-time professional academics established a near monopoly over serious historical writing in Britain. Many reasons could be suggested in explanation of the slow pace of professionalization, including the tradition of individualism, the oft-noted British penchant for amateurism,[110] the emphasis on literary quality in historical writing, the long dominance of a few universities, specifically Oxford, Cambridge, and London, and the generally slow acceptance of the social sciences.

The British contemporary of Rankean hermeneutical historicism, within terms of which the majority of both amateurs and professionals wrote, was the Whig School. It was based on "factual," narrative history with a political and constitutional emphasis, and members of this orthodoxy chastised positivists such as Buckle with a Rankean fervor. Yet more overtly than hermeneutical historicism in Germany with its underlying nationalistic and elitist presumptions, the Whig School rested upon a belief in the rational progression of history toward capitalistic, liberal, and parliamentary values and institutions. Spared the trauma of threats to this belief from right or left, the bulk of British historical writing continued in the same tradition until World War I. Events from 1914 onwards disturbed the liberal faith but did not have the catalytic impact experienced in intellectual circles elsewhere in Europe from the late nineteenth century. The sweeping confidence previously displayed by the Whig School evaporated, many of the more extravagant generalizations were criticized and abandoned, but the individualistic liberal values and the essentially Rankean methodology were retained and provided the basis of the emerging professional code. Professionalization precipitated specialization, in terms of subject matter, and a "scientific" thrust by way of more rigorous textual criticism and a stricter evidential methodology. However, it also involved a continuing, if not increasing,[111] insistence on the individuality of historical phenomena, and the terms of the professional code also precluded conceptual innovation, particularly such as involved social science theory.

Two somewhat related influences upon the British historical profession emerging from the inter-war years served to moderate the strictures which the accompanying code might have otherwise more permanently and forcibly imposed upon British historiography. Both the pragmatic element in British intellectualism and the claims, warranted or not, of the historical profession to an apolitical stance have served to give an ideologically latitudinarian impulse to the professional code. Thus British historiography has encompassed a range of ideologies within a generally accepted evidential code. This includes the tolerance of ideologies counter to that prevailing among the profession; and meaningful debate, and at times fruitful interaction, have been possible; differences of opinion have not always been confined to the recital of polemics.

The maintenance of a forum for debate within the otherwise restricting terms of the professional code is one of the factors contributing to a significant, though by no means total, shift in that code since the mid-1950s. Closely related in this process of change have been an increasingly sophisticated use of social science concepts, a substantial Marxist influence, and a stronger emphasis upon a new and broadening notion of social history.[112] The remainder of this chapter will be concerned principally with discussion of these elements of change in the context of historical debate on industrialization in Britain.

In broad terms there were carried into the mid-twentieth century two distinguishable, though not always totally distinct, traditions of explanation for and response toward industrialization. Both traditions developed from the first half of the nineteenth century; each has been effected over time by a series of contemporaneous concerns or preoccupations, by the more rigorous standards of professional scholarship, and by closer contact with the social sciences, but the fundamentals of each tradition have remained intact. One tradition has involved an essentially favorable valuation of the effects of industrialization, based upon primarily materialistic criteria. Within this tradition any acknowledgement of the distress arising from the process has been accompanied by an assertion of the overriding significance of the material gains achieved. The contrary tradition, developed mainly but not exclusively by socialists, has involved judgment from a more humanistic perspective, insisting that material gain, if any, was more than outweighed by the price paid in terms of human misery and hardship. Within both traditions there have been inconsistencies between modes of evaluation and explanation. With few exceptions,[113] it has only been since World War II that historians in either tradition have developed the conceptual apparatus which has enabled them to approach both causes and impact of industrialization with a continuity of perspective.

By the 1830s the first of these traditions was well developed. It rested on acceptance, implicit or explicit, of the material advance represented by industrialization and of the mechanistic theories of social and economic organization and operation represented by Smith, Malthus, and Ricardo. Even when the concerns of such writers[114] involved emphasis on the social problems raised by industrialization, and thus often acquired a humanitarian thrust, such concerns did not involve a fundamental critique or rejection of industrialization and the accompanying capitalist values. Rather, they pointed to a basic acceptance and a desire to remove perceived "problems" or obstructions to the full beneficial operation of the prevailing socio-economic system. This category of response might be characterized as materialistic in its assumptions and particularistic, albeit sometimes humanitarian, in its concerns.

The materialistic tradition with its belief in the self-evident virtue of the prevailing social, economic, and political system was carried into the second half of the nineteenth century under the aegis of the Whig School. Industrialization was seen as the consummation of individualism and the virtues of the political and constitutional system which was believed to have nurtured that quality. The political, institutional, and constitutional pre-occupations of the Whig School resulted in a concentration upon the seventeenth-century political revolutions. The approach was essentially that of narrative description resting on increasing use of documentary evidence. The sense of historicism was present but frequently lapsed in consideration of subsequent British history which was seen as a steady and inevitable progression from 1688 to the parliamentary liberalism of the late nineteenth century. Industrialization was seen as a natural and reinforcing part of the process but was rarely treated as a separate phenomenon or studied in terms of its socio-economic causation or impact. Some major figures, such as Lecky, did on occasions depart from this political preoccupation, but, as in the extensive treatment of Methodism in his *History of England in the Eighteenth Century,* such digressions rarely touched on the fundamentals of the process of industrialization.[115] While their preoccupations were more particularly political, writers of the Whig School stood in a clear line of philosophical descent from those writers who earlier in the century had accepted industrialization and its preponderant material benefits. The Whig School accepted the same tenets of classical political economy and the values inherent therein. These historians were not writing the history of industrialization but history *for* the prevailing liberal/capitalist orthodoxy of the nineteenth century.

From the experience and observation of industrialization there also developed the beginnings of a contradictory tradition. Writers in this tradition, while by no means ignoring particular and direct questions, challenged the basic assumptions of the emerging capitalist orthodoxy. As facets of this orthodoxy began to take on the aura of given "natural" laws, so its critics were driven into a search for alternative socio-economic and political theory.[116] Furthermore, because it was arraigned against the fundamentally materialistic orthodoxy, the criticism took on a distinctly more humanistic impulse. The early English critics of industrialization saw both causation and impact of the process in terms of loss, deprivation, or seizure which might include, but went beyond, the purely economic. Critical evaluation of industrialization within this more humanistic tradition continued into the second half of the nineteenth century. It encompassed William Morris, the Fabian Movement, and Arnold Toynbee, whose assertion in 1882 that "the effects of the Industrial Revolution prove that free competition may produce wealth without producing well-being,"[117] conveys a central insistence of the tradition. Although, in terms of British historiography, their influence was not to be felt fully until well into the twentieth century, Marx and Engels clearly belong within this tradition. While Marx and Engels saw industrialization as both the product and the cause of fundamental change in the economic organization of society, their analysis of its implications was founded upon the human response that change provoked, expressed particularly in terms of "consciousness." Marx and Engels also provided that which both traditions for long lacked: a method of analysis which could be applied to both explanation and evaluation of industrialization.

During the first half of the twentieth century, the evolution of both traditions was influenced by a range of contemporary events. The rising political power of both Trade Unionism and the Labour Party resulted in a concentration upon the evolution of these movements among historians of the anti-capitalist tradition. Such concentration led to a generally institutional focus in the works of the Hammonds, the Webbs, and G. D. H. Cole.[118] All viewed industrialization as a cataclysmic experience, shattering connection with the past, and they shared a strong sympathy for those who had undergone this process. There was, however, something of a mechanistic element in their view of class consciousness as the "product" of industrialization, a product whose development they traced in mainly institutional terms. Their accounts of industrialization were immensely detailed, but explanation for the process itself was generally unsystematic and tended to rest on the earlier *sense,* rather than any well elaborated *theory* of loss. Their methodology remained close to that of the Whigs, in that they were providing a narrative, a success story, even though it was for working-class organization not middle-class Victorian liberals.

The absorbtion of economic theory into historical study, the evolution of economic history and its integration with the more generalized historical discipline, all proceeded slowly in Britain.[119] Nevertheless, by the inter-war period economic theory and an economic history evolving therefrom were beginning to influence both traditions and within each were giving rise to more systematic analysis of industrialization.[120] Within the capitalistic tradition these trends are most obviously represented by the work of John Clapham and, somewhat later, of T. S. Ashton. On the basis of predominantly economic criteria, it was Clapham's judgment that industrialization had a fundamentally beneficial effect on the lives of the majority of Englishmen in the nineteenth century. A particular feature of Clapham's argument was his emphasis that judgments of conditions in the nineteenth century had to be based upon more thorough and accurate appreciation of conditions in the immediately preceding period. He argued that the golden age of the eighteenth century existed only in mythology, not fact, and that those writers who perpetuated the myth were thereby creating a false impression of the nineteenth-century decline, deprivation, or loss. It was not only in pursuit of this line of argument that Clapham paid close attention to the eighteenth century. He also sought economic explanation for industrialization in terms of commercial, institutional, and technical development contributing to the process.[121] This aspect of Clap-

ham's work was carried on by Ashton,[122] who sought to isolate
and evaluate a range of economic factors contributing to industrialization, ultimately focusing on financial factors and prevailing rates of interest as of central importance. Beyond his
own writings, Ashton played an important role in encourag-
ing a proliferation of studies of industrialization in particular
regions and industries. Such studies have produced a vast range
of detailed information on the operation of industrialization
but have made relatively little contribution to overall synthesis
of causation.[123] It is the question of how, rather than why, industrialization took place that has been answered by this body
of work. While a limited conceptual framework has been utilized, much of this work in economic history has remained
fundamentally within the terms of conventional historicism.
While making strong claims to a value-free objectivity, there is
in the work of Ashton and others the same materialistic assumptions ever-present within the capitalistic tradition. The
principle addition to that tradition as a result of an economic
focus has been mechanistic and schematic, and this has tended
to re-inforce rather than undermine its fundamentally materialistic values.

While the social science influence upon the capitalistic tradition in the post-World-War-I phase came primarily from economics, in the case of its counterpart a similar influence was
admixed with a sociological approach. Most of R. H. Tawney's historical writing dealt with the sixteenth and seventeenth
centuries, but it is relevant to the present discussion because of
its place in long-term explanation for the emergence, and in
Britain ascendancy, of industrial capitalism. Tawney gave
more systematic form to the sense of loss through industrialization which had previously marked the anti-capitalistic tradition
within British historiography.[124] Tawney saw the roots of economic change leading to industrialization as going back at
least as far as the enclosure movement and substantial shifts in
ownership of land in the sixteenth century. For Tawney, it
was not only a process whereby economic organization took
on more distinctly capitalistic forms, but one in which social

values were changing; the Acquisitive Society was developing. Although he did not rigidly follow Weber, Tawney generally believed there to be a close relationship between the ascendant social values and the general tenets of Puritanism. Political conflict leading to Civil War in the seventeenth century was seen by Tawney as a conflict of interests and beliefs, not exclusively religious, between latent capitalism emanating from the changes of the sixteenth century and the quasi-feudalism of aristocracy and monarchy; an analysis close to Marx's own. Though not necessarily through deliberate intent, Tawney's work acts as a counterbalance to the trend, displayed by contemporaneous economic historians of the opposing tradition, to explain the development of capitalism in terms of economic factors and institutions.[125]

This form of response, with a stress on economic forces balanced by an emphasis on broader social factors and humanistic considerations, was continued by Christopher Hill. Furthermore, Hill carried this forward in time, making a closer chronological connection with the actual period of industrialization.[126] Although also fundamentally an economic historian, Hill paid closer attention to the actual process of political conflict than did Tawney, and particularly to the institutional aspects of that conflict. This attention was based on an appreciation of the significance of institutions, Church, Parliament, Courts, as vital channels in the conflict of values and interests which was present in mid-seventeenth-century England.[127] Over a period of time, Hill's work has reflected the trends discussed later in this chapter as major features of historiographical development since World War II. Beginning from an economic and constitutional emphasis, Hill has gradually turned his attention to ideology, both collective and individual,[128] to attitudes and beliefs as an important element in understanding the process of change from one socio-economic system to another, from feudalism to capitalism. In doing this he has helped to break down some of the shibboleths of a caricatured Marxism frequently turned against Marxists. Hill has written primarily of an age when social, economic, and political ideas were often expressed in religious terms. He does not dismiss this as irrelevance, nor treat it as merely inconsequential in explanation of the seventeenth century. Hill recognizes and deals with religion as a real force not only for its institutional importance but also for its central role in shaping the development of ideas and attitudes. He also regards other expressions of traditional vaues as an integral part of the process of change, not as a dead weight upon that process.[129]

Professionalization brought an increasing demand for "scientific" rigor in historical scholarship and proliferation of such scholarship. These in turn imposed a complexity upon history which served to breakdown some traditional generalizations and at the same time strengthened the view of the individuality of events in the past; the capacity for broad, systematic explanation appeared circumscribed. This development challenged both simplistic forms of Marxist historical analysis and the humanistic tradition of explanation for and response to industrialization. The balance in Hill's work between an appreciation of the complexity of historical change and the belief that this can be comprehended within an essentially Marxist scheme of explanation presents a substantial response to that challenge.

A similar process of challenge and response has been going on in the work of historians dealing with industrialization in a chronologically more direct sense. During the last twenty years, while traditional approaches have by no means been abandoned, there has been brought to the study of industrialization, from within both traditions, an increasing element of innovation in both technique and conceptualization. Much of this innovation has been related to a greater sense of proximity to other social sciences. There are several reasons why this process, began before World War II, should have accelerated since the mid-1950s. The attainment of academic stature by the newer social sciences, the wider general interest in their theories, and the increasing accessibility of these through the academic forum have been of importance. Improved statistical methods, and particularly the use of the computer, have encouraged innovation by making practicable certain types of study previously so time-consuming as to be prohibitive. The rapid growth of the British universities from the mid-1950s also served to create more opportunity for new ideas to be generated. Political factors have also had a bearing upon the change. The thawing of the Cold War and the dissociation from the Communist Party of many British academics from 1956 served to remove some of the psychological and attitudinal restraints that may previously have affected debate. The search for, and movement into, less ideologically rigid positions was a process conducive to the adoption of different conceptional approaches and technical methods.

Within the capitalistic tradition the main innovations within the last twenty years have been a trend toward economic model building and a rapidly accelerating use of more sophisticated statistical techniques. The development of economic models in the process of historical explanation stemmed in part from the influence of Keynesian economic theory and also from a desire to seek out guidelines for industrialization within a capitalist context in the hope that these would be applicable to contemporary developing economies. The most ambitious example of this orientation came from the American Walt Rostow in his *Stages of Economic Growth; a Non-Communist Manifesto.*[130] The title itself explicitly set the work apart from customary claims of British historians to political objectivity and fundamentally capitalistic assumptions, such as the desirability of a "freely functioning" economy, run throughout. Rostow's work had a considerable influence, although it proceeded as much from reaction as emulation. His creation of a general model from the particular course of industrialization in certain countries, notably Britain, ran counter to the institutional and micro-economic trend within British economic history. From another perspective, Rostow was vulnerable to attack for his attempt to provide a fundamentally economic model to explain a process which was also of a social and political nature, both in its initiation and its impact.[131]

R. M. Hartwell provides an example of response to Rostow from among British economic historians of the capitalist tradition. He agrees with Gerschenkron in rejecting the idea of "uniform prerequisites of industrial development," and argues: "disguised sectoral interpretation of the industrial revolution, in the form of a stages theory, does little more than suggest some important variables of growth, and give some idea of the chronology of growth; it does not explain growth." Hartwell does, however, recognize Rostow's claims "to be the most influential of modern economic historians," and believes that "a statistically verifiable model of eighteenth-century growth can be formulated," given the compilation of evidence to permit statement of relationships between factors in "quantitative-functional," rather than currently prevailing "qualitative" terms.[132] The same emphasis on the central importance of quantitative evidence in explanation or evaluation is present in Hartwell's work on the results of industrialization. He is the most prominent contemporary optimist insisting on the fundamentally beneficial aspects of industrialization, and doing so principally in economic terms.[133] Although asserting that industrialization produced social benefits in such forms as greater literacy and a less violent pattern of social behavior, extending even to forms of social protest by the 1840s, the bulk of Hartwell's argumentation rests upon demonstration, heavily statistical, that in the first half of the nineteenth century the material conditions, in terms of diet, clothing, health, and housing, experienced by the majority of English people, were improving.

Although first applied to any extent in the context of economic history, an increasing use of statistics, of more sophisticated statistical techniques and the computer, has been, since the early 1960s, most closely associated with the development of the fields of demography and the history of social structure. Superficially the two appear closely related to each other and in some respects this is true, there is, however, a tendency for the former to be more dynamic in its concerns, focusing on change over time, while the latter has a more static emphasis seeking to "hold" a particular society still in order to subject it to analysis. Initially it would appear that both fields of study would invite the involvement of scholars from within the humanistic tradition and that they would contribute most to the development from that perspective. Such an impression could arise from the persistent desire within that tradition to penetrate in comprehension of the past to the lower levels on the social scale. Generally the development of demography and the history of social structure has not achieved this end. Rather, they have added to the knowledge of what happened to the mass of people and the physical circumstances within which they lived, but they have remained without comprehension and without agency.[134] This is very specifically asserted by Peter Laslett in his justification for reference to preindustrial society in England as a one-class society.[135] In England during the last fifteen years, the history of social structure has developed mainly under the aegis of the Cambridge Group for the History of Population and Social Structure, and the main generalized statements of its direction and findings have been made by Laslett, who has tended to be excessively assertive in his claims for the unique nature of this specialization's contribution and, at times, for its independence from the events of political history.[136] Criticism of Laslett by historians from within the humanistic tradition has been strong but selective. In countering his charge that historians had previously ignored a sociological approach to their subject, Christopher Hill cites a long list of those whose work demonstrates the falsity of Laslett's assertions and includes many "with whom I disagree on many points of interpretation but whose solid scholarship compels respect."[137] Both Hill and Edward Thompson criticize the failure to relate study of social structure to more general explanations of the past, either on static or dynamic terms. They do, however, distinguish between Laslett's culpability in this respect and the more detailed studies produced by others associated with the Cambridge Group.[138] Rather than conveying a sense of committed hostility to the history of social structure, their criticism appears to reflect a recognition of its potential contribution and disappointment that this has not yet been fulfilled. The failure of the history of social structure to provide a new dawn for historians within the humanistic tradition may not however be solely the product of particular direction within the Cambridge Group. As statistical analysis becomes more sophisticated and the use of the computer grows, so the availability of sources — of sufficient numbers and with sufficient consistency over time to make the adoption of these techniques viable — becomes a powerful force in shaping the analysis of social structure. The result is an increasing emphasis in both observation and explanation of the past upon material conditions even when broadly behavioral phenomena such as propensity to procreation are considered.[139] It is fear that such emphasis may lead to disregard for non-material forces in shaping experience on the past that probably lies behind criticism of some aspects of the work of the Cambridge Group, particularly that offered by Thompson.

Trends of the last fifteen to twenty years in economic and social structural history within the materialistic tradition have drawn response similar to that of Christopher Hill, discussed above. Consideration of such response in a particularly Marxist context will be developed further by focusing on the work of two historians, Thompson and Eric Hobsbawm. The response they are chosen to represent reflects both the contribution of, and a strong element of conceptual and methodological quandary for, Marxist historians. Both clearly believe that Marx provided the most effective conceptual tools for the broad comprehension and explanation of society and social change in the past.[140] They share an awareness that some earlier Marxist historians developed a dogmatic, mechanistic, and narrowly materialistic interpretation of Marx's own view of the past. Hobsbawm and Thompson are both involved, as is Hill, in the attempt to "rescue" Marx from "vulgar-Marxist historians" and, at the same time, to resist an alternatively narrowing materialistic emphasis among capitalist economic historians which claims precision through the adoption of economic theory and increasingly quantitative techniques. In this duality of purpose they seek some aid from other social sciences, not in the imposition of their "laws" of social behavior founded in twentieth-century experience, but through the use of general concepts to formulate questions about and seek explanation of areas of past experience, some of which had previously been neglected by historians. The attempt to see, describe, and explain the past in a more total sense than is possible within any one of the conventional specializations is nevertheless pursued within the code of evidential verification which is the basis of the profession of modern historical scholarship.

Although they share this element of purpose, the respective works of Thompson and Hobsbawm reflect some variation of emphasis in pursuit of their common goal. Both historians write in that tradition which is critical of industrial capitalism and particularly of the impact of industrialization upon nineteenth-century Britain. It was Hobsbawm who engaged R. M. Hartwell in the 1963 *Economic History Review* debate which remains the most succinct general statement of pessimist and optimist opinion over the standard of living in early nineteenth-century England. Hobsbawm, basically an economic historian, was prepared to engage Hartwell on economic grounds; to dispute the latter's statistically dominated argument for recognizing an improvement in the material standard of living. Yet his strongest insistence was upon the social costs of industrialization expressed in terms of emotional and psychological upheaval and distress.[141] Thompson is prepared to take an even stronger stand for the preponderance of humanistic values in any judgment of the impact of industrialization; he appears willing even to concede to the "optimist" claims of improvement in material conditions but argues further that this does not have sufficient weight to carry an overall judgment in favor of industrialization as a beneficial force upon the lives of the majority of English people in the first half of the nineteenth century.

> . . . it is perfectly possible to maintain two propositions which, on casual view, appear to be contradictory. Over the period 1790–1848 there was a slight improvement in average material standards. Over the same period there was intensified exploitation, greater insecurity, and increasing

human misery. By 1840 most people were 'better off' than their fore-runners had been fifty years before, but they had suffered and continued to suffer this slight improvement as a catastrophic experience.[142]

Hobsbawm and Thompson view capitalism as both an economic and value, or attitudinal, system, each part dependent upon the other and both operating through a wide range of political and social institutions. While they see such system in operation in a historical context and as a dominant theme of the history of the last 450 or more years, they do not view such operation as purely mechanistic but as a force whose progress and impact has been subject to variation and the intrusion of human agency. Yet within these broad terms there are differences of emphasis between the two historians, in part at least leading to and resulting from differences of concern or preoccupation. Economic factors and forces are given a more central role by Hobsbawm than by Thompson, and they are more insistently present in his explanation of historical change. In Thompson's work, although such forces are acknowledged as of fundamental importance, they do not provide the focus for his attention, and they intrude less into his mode of explanation. Such differences as well as their similar intents are evident in both historians' explanation of industrialization and consideration of its impact.

From the mid-1950s, Hobsbawm played a prominent part in the historical debate on the seventeenth-century crisis in Europe.[143] His view was that the crisis was essentially economic, "the last phase of the general transition from a feudal to a capitalist economy," and that it led to, "as fundamental a solution of the difficulties which had previously stood in the way of the triumph of capitalism as that system will permit."[144] Yet the product of the crisis was not uniform, and Hobsbawm recognized the importance of political institutions and dominant individuals in shaping such variety. For Hobsbawm the rise of capitalism as value system to influence, direct or indirect, over powerful institutions, particularly but not exclusively that of government, was a vital factor in the growth of industrial capitalism. In *Industry and Empire,* a general study of British economic history since 1750, he laid substantial emphasis, as had Marx,[145] on the importance of expanding overseas trade in precipitating industrialization in Britain, and he also stressed the important role of government in this process, in part at least through its policy of "systematic aggressiveness."[146] The government's role in the stimulation of industrialization was not, however, confined to the pursuit of an aggressive and commercially oriented foreign and colonial policy; Hobsbawm also emphasized the more general provision of "systematic support for merchant and manufacturer, and some by no means negligible incentives for technical innovation and the development of capital goods industries."[147] Thompson has also described the increasing commitment of both national and local authorities in eighteenth-century Britain to the social and economic values of capitalism and the steady abandonment of legislative provisions based on an older value system.[148] Such trends were carried through into the period of industrialization, and Thompson insists that the distress experienced by English working people in that period was not the result of the mechanistic operation of the "natural" laws of classical economies nor the "accident" of war but of the distribution of economic and political power and of choices made about the use of that power.[149] Hobsbawm and Thompson regard the development of both organization and values as essential to the growth of capitalism and its evolution into industrial society, but Hobsbawm's explanation involves an institutional and legislative perspective while Thompson places greater emphasis on the marketplace and draws attention to the need to qualify assumptions regarding the general acceptance of apparently ascendant values.

Thompson sees the growth of industrial capitalism against a background of competing values and the perspective remains the same in his consideration of the impact of industrialization. In the preface to his main work, *The Making of the English Working Class,* Thompson describes his conception of class and class consciousness. Class is not a static phenomenon capable of categorization or isolation as part of a social structure. Class is not a "thing," and Thompson makes it clear that he does not attribute such a misconception to Marx. Class is a relationship evolving over a period of time from a shared experience which "is largely determined by the productive relations into which men are born . . . or enter involuntarily." Class consciousness is likewise a historical development; it is the way in which these experiences are handled in cultural terms."[150] For Thompson, such consciousness is the product of particular experience and a response shaped, in part at least, by particular "traditions, value systems, ideas and institutional forms."[151] Human agency — whether working through or outside of institutional forms, whether in a specifically political, or more generally cultural, context — plays an important part in shaping the conditions experienced and the response to that experience.

Developing, first, a description of the political, religious, and social traditions inherited by the English working class and, then, extensive discussion of their experiences in the early nineteenth century, distinguished by the reality and perception of exploitation, Thompson describes in detail the range of responses and their assimilation into a working-class consciousness which, in his estimation, brought English society to the verge of revolution by 1830. He does not see this consciousness as a mechanistic creation of industrialization but a formulation of the working class itself. Thompson stresses the importance in this process of the role of traditional modes of thought, not as predeterminants but as ingredients. He warns against "underestimation of the continuity of political and cultural traditions."[152] Thompson's analysis is essentially a sophisticated expression of the dialectic. The conditions experienced by English working people during industrialization stood in contradiction to a range of long-held assumptions, part real, part abstract, as to how society ought to function. From experience and realization of this contradiction emerged a working-class consciousness which attacked both the material conditions and philosophical presumptions of industrial capitalism.

Since the publication of the *Making of the English Work-*

ing Class in 1963, Thompson has paid particular attention to the traditional attitudes and values of what are normally termed the "lower orders" of eighteenth-century English society. In "The Moral Economy of the English Crowd in the Eighteenth Century," Thompson presents an interpretation that moves away from assumptions of the innate irrationality of the preindustrial mob and of its significance solely as a tool of politicians and agitators. He also seeks to move beyond a purely mechanistic analysis of the relationship of hunger and high food prices to crowd action. Such action is given a more meaningful quality by Thompson's development of the crowd's belief in the moral necessity of the economic system to operate to general advantage. He describes the hostility of the crowd not only toward middle men seen to be negating that necessity in pursuit of individual profit but also toward authorities who were failing to use the powers they possessed to enforce the moral economy. In "Time, Work Discipline and Industrial Capitalism,"[153] Thompson discusses the preindustrial concept of time in terms of hours of the day and seasons of the year with particular attention to notions about its use and thereby emphasizes a particular and important aspect of the trauma of transition to the environment of the factory. In some of his work Hobsbawm has remained closer than Thompson to the institutionally formed perspective on class prominent in the work of the Fabian historians of labor and the often overlapping view of class as particularly the product of economic conditions. However, particularly in *Primitive Rebels*,[154] his approach is similar to Thompson's. In a series of essays for which he specifically disclaims full comprehension of the subject matter, Hobsbawm outlines the historical development, in a variety of Western European contexts, of the tradition of what he terms social banditry. This involves a discussion of the responses of certain social groups to a sense of alienation from their political, social, or economic situation. The groups are selected to illustrate "the adaption of popular agitations to a modern capitalist society,"[155] and they represent an interim stage of development prior to the emergence of a broad working-class consciousness. While the strongly comparative element in Hobsbawm's *Primitive Rebels* is distinct from Thompson's concentration upon English experience, they are both seeking to rescue certain social groups and movements from the obscurity to which they have been consigned by what Thompson terms "the enormous condescension of posterity."[156] Obscurity came about from the failure of such groups in their own time and also from their apparent irrationality in terms of — or irrelevance to — subsequent preoccupations. Whether it is the Sicilian or Catalonian bandits or "the poor stockinger, the Luddite cropper . . . and even the deluded follower of Joanna Southcott,"[157] what is involved is the attempt to give some meaningful account of the actions and ideas of people who have traditionally been dismissed as absurd or irrational. Such "rescue operations" have formed a significant part of what has been termed "the new social history." The process of establishing a place for such history within the professional code, of gaining recognition for both its evidential validity and its potential contribution to the study of history in general, is marked by obstacles. From a nomological viewpoint such studies are suspect partly because the people on whom they frequently concentrate seem to defy historical trends and partly because the nature of such defiance, the motivations for it, cannot be reduced solely to materialistic terms on which the nomological viewpoint itself rests. Despite the very strong sense of historicism displayed in such studies as those of Thompson and Hobsbawm, from the perspective of the hermeneutic tradition, criticism can be raised on the grounds that there is not the evidence available from which to construct the kind of explanations attempted within the ambit of the new social history. In part, this criticism also extends to the conceptualization which is necessary to give credence to sources used and relate them to explanations offered; the process is sometimes regarded as unhistorical or unscientific; in the most critical terms it is considered to be fundamentally mere conjecture.[158]

In contending with such obstacles to some level of acceptance within, or influence upon, the professional code, social historians, including Marxists, have developed a relationship to other social sciences different from but in some ways parallel to that between economic historians and theoretical economics. This relationship has been particularly evident with sociology, social anthropology, and some aspects of mass psychology. The nature of such relationship is sometimes elusive. It certainly does not involve the direct application of social science theory or models to historical situations. Thompson in *The Making of the English Working Class* rejects such procedure and specifically attacks certain sociologist's conception of class and the process of social change in the Industrial Revolution.[159] He disclaims the ability to "predicate any *law*," but he does argue the possibility of "a logical pattern of responses to similar situations."[160] Such logic of response may not apply consistently in a historical context, such application may ebb and flow, but the logic itself is ever present.[161] George Rudé[162] in *The Crowd in History* discusses the relationship between the social historian and other social scientists. He welcomes the tendency for sociologists to avoid treatment of the crowd as a merely generalized abstraction and their prospensity to "break it down and classify it according to goals, behavior, or underlying beliefs."[163] Nevertheless, he warns against the sociologists' creation of their own stereotypes to replace those of historians and their continuing preoccupation with the "mob" notion of the crowd, carried over from Burke and Taine and evidenced in analysis of crowd behavior preoccupied with abnormalities or irrationalities.[164] Rudé's own work, which seeks to rescue the crowd from mindless anonymity, relates closely to Thompson's, although the latter places the aspirations and attitudes of the crowd in a more central position within a pattern of evolving industrial capitalism and the reactions it provoked. Despite Rudé's qualifications, the socio-psychological influence is clear when he discusses the main constructs of his own study and formulates the questions he is seeking to answer.

The emergence of a new social history, the product of many influences, including a distinct contribution from the merging of Marxism and social science, has been the most significant historiographical development in Britain and elsewhere in the last fifteen to twenty years. However, it is not a development which has passed without criticism, and its extent, permanence, and value have all been questioned. Is it merely a passing "fashion" in historical writing? Is it peculiarly the product and "possession" of left-wing ideology? Does it threaten the establishment of its own restrictive orthodoxy, through adoption of its methodology and distillation of its conceptual innovation?[165] Answers to these questions clearly affect evaluation of its importance in the development of a new general code, or "paradigm," conceptual and methodological. Absolute determination on these points is only capable of future judgment, but at this stage it is possible to suggest evidence which points to a negative answer to each of the questions raised and an affirmative judgment in respect to its potential role in the shaping of a future professional code. The volume of writing already produced in many topical fields within the terms of the "new social history," the range of questions raised, and the impact of new approaches on many long-standing historical debates suggest that it is no passing vogue and that it cannot be disregarded in the future. The development of interchange, in concept and methodology, that is already well established appears to deny the exclusiveness of the new social history to the ideological left or its potentiality as a new and restrictive orthodoxy. Variety within the terms of the development is, hopefully, apparent from the above discussion of the work of Hobsbawm and Thompson. The journal *Past and Present* has, in Britain, a close association with the emergence of new approaches to social history. Its activity as a forum for the debate of differing interpretations, both through its selection of articles and its organization of conferences, does not fit an image of ideological exclusiveness nor the establishment of a narrow orthodoxy. While Marxist historians have played a prominent role, these developments have not been the monopoly of any one ideology. Thus historians such as Lawrence Stone, Asa Briggs, and Harold Perkin have all made a contribution: Stone in terms of a more imaginative use of structural analysis in relation to change than offered by the Cambridge

Group; Briggs primarily, though by no means exclusively, in the area of urban history; and Perkin in providing a general study of British history in the period of industrialization that has as its central theme social rather than political evolution.[166]

Social history as it has developed during the last twenty years has the potential to contribute to a broadening of the professional code and an expanding professional capacity to comprehend the past. Hobsbawm himself has argued that neither the interrelationship of history and the social sciences, nor the progression toward a broader comprehension for history, the movement that he terms "from Social History to the History of Society," has yet progressed even a fraction of the way toward fulfillment.[167] This process has, however, begun, and the continuing existence of historical controversy or even its expansion do not negate the suggestion that historians are gradually adopting a more scientific approach to the study and explanation of the past. In fact, much of the scientific impulse of the last twenty years has derived from the efforts of contending groups of historians, among whom Marxists have been prominent, to advance, in initiation or response, their particular viewpoints. It is very unlikely, and for that matter undesirable, that the development of an historical science will produce one, agreed history. What it is beginning to do is to ask a broader range of questions in seeking description and explanation of the past and to develop a correspondingly wider range of concepts as aids in providing answers.

Conclusion

THE PRECEDING essays have pointed both at deep differences in perspective as well as to a degree of convergence in modern historical studies. They have in a sense given support to Hayden White's assertion that there "appear(s) to be an irreducible ideological component in every historical account of reality" which excludes the extent of agreement in historical studies which marks the exact sciences. For historians "disagree not only over the laws of social causation that they might invoke to explain a sequence of events, but also over the question of the form that a 'scientific' explanation ought to take."[1] Yet in our opinion, it does not necessarily follow from this lack of agreement that history is in no sense a science, as Hayden White and certain of the French structuralists have maintained, and that its generalizations are products of a historical or poetical imagination in no way capable of being "refuted" or "disconfirmed" by evidence.[2] Rather, we have viewed history as a reality-oriented study into human affairs which may permit a variety of scientific strategies.

These chapters have illustrated how deep are the divisions in perspective which "predetermine" the presentation of the past by historians. The very conceptions of time presupposed by the historians under scrutiny differ fundamentally. Thus while *Annales* historians have challenged the conception of a linear time which guarantees continuity of development and have asserted instead the multiplicity of historical "times," each finite, differently structured, proceeding at different velocities, and marked by ruptures, the German social historians of politics whom we have discussed as well as the Marxists have continued to assume the fundamental continuity and unity of history. The result of these contrasting senses of time has been very different histories. The attention of the German historians and the Marxists we have examined has been focused on the technological society of the West, which, for better or for worse, remains for them the central phenomenon of the modern world, of relevance not only for the understanding of the technological West but also of the preindustrial and non-Western societies in process of transformation. The *Annales* historians have questioned whether the "history of the world can be measured from the one particular experience" of the industrial revolution and raised the possibility of a history in which the concentration of change would be suspended in a study of the "immobile" elements of a society in a given epoch.[3]

These different conceptions of time entail contrasting views of the political function of history. *Annales* historians from Lucien Febvre to Fernand Braudel, Pierre Goubert and Emmanuel Le Roy Ladurie have been much more consistently historicists than Wehler or the Marxists in insisting that each epoch be seen not as part of a chain of development but as a structure to be studied in its own terms. Hence *Annales* historians have been much more adamant about value neutrality in historical inquiry, have refused to depict the history of the modern West as the culmination of world history, and have stressed the multiplicity of history. In contrast, Wehler and the Marxists have ascribed to historical science itself a critical role as an agent of change. This emphasis on the activist side of history carried with it an intensive interest in the sources of conflict within social structures and in the role of political consciousness and action which contrasted with the preference of the *Annales* for the analysis of anonymous factors involved in the functioning and transformation of social structures.

Yet in spite of these fundamental differences in outlook,

which have been reflected in divergent methodological approaches, broad areas of agreement have emerged among practicing historians in the past several decades, agreements which transcend ideological lines. *Annales* historians, Marxists, and German social historians of politics alike have sought to reestablish the link between events and structures for which the Enlightenment historians had groped unsuccessfully and for which the scientific historians of the nineteenth century ceased to search. However diverse the available approaches to this complex relationship, historians proceeding from very different perspectives have ended up employing similar methods and concepts when struggling with the event-structure problem. Thus the *Annales* historians through the extensive empirical studies of the material basis and the mental climate in which the life of broad segments of the population took place created an important model for the later critical social histories attempted by Marxists and others. In practice the nomological, hermeneutic, and dialectical approaches to history which we examined in the introductory chapter have by no means been mutually exclusive. The historical traditions we analyzed in the preceding three chapters have all integrated nomological and hermeneutical approaches in differing ways. While there is little common ground between the strictly nomological history of the New Economic Historians and the individualizing, hermeneutic methods of the conventional event-and-idea-centered political and intellectual historians — who have now become rare — the historians we have examined from Lucien Febvre and Emmanuel Le Roy Ladurie to Hans-Ulrich Wehler, Eric Hobsbawm, and E. P. Thompson occupy a middle ground in which the analysis of meaning and purposeful action is integrated with an attempt to understand these in a structural, historical context which requires the utilization of the concepts of the generalizing social sciences. Historians of different orientations have thus drawn from a common fund of modern social science concepts, theories, and methods. A broad area of communication has thus become possible between Marxists and Annalists and more recently the German social historians of politics whom we have discussed. It is to be expected that this area of understanding will widen as historians of various orientations will increase their attempts to integrate into their studies quantitative methods and concepts taken from the systematic social sciences.

Obviously there are limits to possible convergence within the present framework of these traditions. The ideal of a social history as a purely quantitative history expressed by certain *Annales* historians — although not pursued to its logical consequence in the great *Annales* studies — conflicts with the conviction of critical social historians that in the final analysis all isolable variables must be seen in a historical context in which a residue of uniqueness of meaning and purposeful action defies the transition which *Annales* historians have sought from the hard data to the structural contexts. Yet, as we saw, both intellectual and political history have moved from the older hermeneutics, which sought to proceed almost exclusively from the critical interpretation of textual evidence, to one which takes into consideration the structural — social and even biological — context within which these purposeful actions occur and which, to be understood, require the utilization of the generalizing sciences of man.

These essays have suggested that, within modest limits, historical studies since the eighteenth century have been characterized by increasing methodological rigor and widening of conceptual scope. The community of historians, in its commitment to verisimilitude and understanding, is admittedly much more loosely constituted than other scholarly or scientific communities, subdivided within itself, yet, as we saw, not without certain shared assumptions about what constitutes rational discussion. The conceptual schemes with which historians approach past reality indeed reflect the divisions and interests of the social, political, and intellectual contexts within which historical studies are pursued to perhaps an even greater extent than that of other scholarly or scientific communities. It is unlikely, therefore, that the ideological component will be eliminated from historical scholarship. Yet the very fact that historical studies themselves are so deeply rooted in the historical context within which they are undertaken may be conducive to an enriched understanding of history. Thus the social and cultural concomitants of a technological society under conditions of modern capitalism, the widening of the cultural perspective from Europe to a world scale, the end of European preeminence, the decline of old elites, the awakening to political and cultural consciousness of previously submerged classes and peoples, the manifestations of conflict which accompanied these transformations have all provided a real basis for the reorientation of historical studies. The result has in many ways been an enlargement of our picture of the past, a new interest in aspects of life, social classes, and cultures which had been neglected by the conventional historiography, a deeper probing into the psychological and anthropological bases of historical behavior, and, in a limited but not negligible way, an expansion of the conceptual range of history and a more critical attitude within the profession regarding the methodological procedures of the historian. This extension in perspective cannot be understood alone in terms of the internal development of historical science but reflects the impact of the collective experience of the twentieth century on its historical perspective. In this sense history cannot be separated from its basis in the social and intellectual realities and conflicts of its time, and historical science itself must be viewed critically within the broader context of the history of the modern world.

The term "critical" has been chosen consciously here. Any attempt to judge the past in terms of the moral or political norms of the present obviously violates the sense of historical reality; so does any attempt to interpret the past within the framework of a preconceived scheme of historical development. Nevertheless a historical approach to the past, at least to the modern but I believe also the pre-modern past, cannot escape considering the elements of conflict and of change and the role which men, individually and collectively, play in this setting. In this sense not only a history which faithfully recounts events abstracted from their structural context, as the conventional historiography tended to do, but also one which concentrates on the "immobility" of structures apart from the concrete actions and aspirations of men is seriously limited in its ability to understand processes of historical change. For societies hardly ever appear as well integrated, self-regulating systems but as entities or complexes marked by structural incongruencies and dysfunctions, by patterns of exploitation, suffering and conflict which contribute to change, as becomes dramatically apparent even in the attempts by Le Roy Ladurie and Pierre Goubert to portray relatively stable structures in early modern Languedoc and Beauvaisis. These elements of conflict and change set limits to the explanatory function of a value-neutral history seeking to grasp the "immobile," repetitive aspects of a social structure abstracted from the political and intellectual context in which it functions. They justify the questions asked by Marxists and certain of the social historians of politics whom we have discussed in their attempts to penetrate behind the empirical data to the critical analysis of the dynamics of social, political, and civilizational change. At the same time they call for the methodological circumspection which the *Annales* have practiced.

Notes

CHAPTER I

1 See in particular, Michel Foucault, *Les Mots et les choses* (Paris, 1966).

2 Hayden White, *Metahistory. The Historical Imagination in Nineteenth-Century Europe* (Baltimore, 1973), 427 and xii.

3 White, *Metahistory*, 37.

4 J. B. Bury, "The Science of History," Bury's Inaugural Lecture as Regius Professor of Modern History at Cambridge in 1902, reprinted in *The Varieties of History*, ed. Fritz Stern (Cleveland, 1956), 210.

5 J. H. Hexter, "The Rhetoric of History," *History and Theory* 6 (1967), 3–13; here quoted from abstract, 11 (1972), 121.

6 Leopold von Ranke, "On the Character of Historical Science" in *The Theory and Practice of History*, ed. Georg G. Iggers and Konrad von Moltke (Indianapolis, 1973), 33. This essay is the fragment published by Eberhard Kessel as "Idee der Universalhistorie" in *Historische Zeitschrift* 178 (1954), 290–309.

7 *Poetics*, ch. 9.

8 Cf. Eduard Fueter, *Geschichte der neueren Historiographie*, 3rd ed. (Munich, 1936); G. P. Gooch, *History and Historians in the Nineteenth Century* (London, 1913); Herbert Butterfield, *Man on His Past. The Study of the History of Historical Scholarship* (Cambridge, 1955); I. S. Kon, *Geschichtsphilosophie des 20. Jahrhunderts*, translated from the Russian by W. Hoepp, 2 vols. (Berlin, G.D.R., 1964).

9 Carl Hempel, *Philosophy of the Natural Sciences* (Englewood Cliffs, N.J., 1966), 15.

10 Cf. Oswald Spengler, *The Decline of the West,* see particularly ch. II, *"The Meaning of Numbers."*

11 Cf. Gaston Bachelard, *La Formation de l'esprit scientifique* (Paris, 1938); *Le Nouvel esprit scientifique* (Paris, 1949); *La Philosophie du non. Essai d'une philosophie du nouvel esprit scientifique* (Paris, 1949).

12 *Geschichte als Sinngebung des Sinnlosen* (Munich, 1921).

13 *The Open Society and Its Enemies* (Princeton, 1950), 452.

14 *The Savage Mind,* 262, 257; but cf. his essay "Histoire et ethnologie" in *Anthropologie structurelle* (Paris, 1958).

15 T. S. Kuhn, *The Structure of Scientific Revolutions,* 2nd. enlarged edition (Chicago, 1970), 7, 85, 111–135, 167.

16 Cf. David Hollinger, "T. S. Kuhn's Theory of Science and Its Implications for History," *American Historical Review* 78 (1973), 381.

17 *Ibid.,* 392.

18 Kuhn, *Structure of Scientific Revolutions,* 170.

19 Hollinger, "T. S. Kuhn's Theory," 378.

20 Cf. J. H. Hexter, "The Rhetoric of History," *History and Theory* 6 (1967), 3–13.

21 Cf. Donald R. Kelley, *Foundations of Modern Historical Scholarship*; George Huppert, "The Renaissance Background to Historicism," *History and Theory* 5 (1966), 48–60. See also J. G. A. Pocock, "The Origins of the Study of the Past: A Comparative Approach," *Comparative Studies in Society and History* 4 (1961–62), 209–246.

22 Kelley, *Foundations,* 307.

23 Cf. Andreas Kraus, *Vernunft und Geschichte. Die Bedeutung der deutschen Akademien für die Entwicklung der Geschichtswissenschaft im späten 18. Jahrhundert* (Freiburg i. B., 1963).

24 Cf. On the eighteenth-century German historians, particularly the Göttingen group, see Herbert Butterfield, *Man on His Past*; Peter Reill, "History and Hermeneutics in the *Aufklärung*: The Thought of Johann Christoph Gatterer" in *Journal of Modern History* 45 (1973), 24–51 and his forthcoming book on the German Enlightenment historians and the brief discussion in *Aus der Aufklärung in die permanente Restauration. Geschichtswissenschaft in Deutschland,* ed. Manfred Asendorf (Hamburg, 1974) also Manfred Asendorf, "Deutsche Fachhistorie und Sozialgeschichte" in *Ansichten einer künftigen Geschichtswissenschaft,* ed. Imanuel Geiss and Rainer Tamchina (Munich, 1974), I, 31–32.

25 Cf. Johann Christoph Gatterer, *Einleitung in die synchronistische Universalgeschichte* (Göttingen, 1771), 1.

26 Gatterer, "Vom historischen Plan und der darauf sich gründenden Zusammenfügung der Erzählung" in *Allgemeine historische Bibliothek* 1 (1767), 22.

27 *Ibid.*, 24–25; August Ludwig von Schlözer, *Theorie der Statistik*, 1. Heft (Göttingen, 1804), 92.

28 Gatterer, "Abhandlung vom Standort und Gesichtspunkt des Geschichtschreibers" in *Allgemeine historische Bibliothek* 5 (1768), 3–29.

29 Here quoted from Karl Marx, *Capital*, I (New York, 1967), 372.

30 Schlözer, *Vorstellung seiner Universalhistorie* (Göttingen, 1772), I, 26.

31 Gatterer, *Einleitung in die synchronistische Universalgeschichte*, 4.

32 Cf. Reill, "History and Hermeneutics," 42.

33 Gatterer, *Abriss der Universalhistorie* (Göttingen, 1765); cf. Schlözer, *Theorie der Statistik*.

34 Cf. Asendorf, *Aus der Aufklärung*.

35 Cf. his *Versuch einer historischen Entwicklung der Entstehung und des Wachsthums der Brittischen Continental-Interessen* and his *Ideen über die Politik, den Verkehr und den Handel der vornehmsten Völker der alten Welt*.

36 Gatterer on sources, see *Abriss der Universalhistorie*, 20ff; *Einleitung in die synchronistische Universalgeschichte*, 1–4; yet Gatterer, in contrast to Ranke, is willing to accept historical accounts based on historians who used primary sources; Schlözer seems even less critical, appears ready to accept published official records, rejects other sources, including manuscripts in introductory section to *Neu verändertes Russland oder Leben Catharinae der Zweyten Kayserin von Russland aus authentischen Nachrichten beschrieben* (Riga, 1767).

37 Leopold von Ranke, "Preface to the First Edition of *Histories* of the Latin and Germanic Nations" in *Theory and Practice of History*, 137.

38 Wilhelm von Humboldt, "On the Historian's Task" in *Theory and Practice of History*, 21.

39 *Ibid.*, 5.

40 Ranke, "On the Character of Historical Science," *ibid.*, 39.

41 Ranke, "The Role of the Particular and the General in the Study of History," *ibid.*, 57.

42 Ranke, "The Great Powers," *ibid.*, 100.

43 J. G. Droysen, *Historik, Vorlesungen über Enzyklopädie und Methodologie der Geschichte*, ed. Rudolf Hübner (Munich, 1937), 24.

44 Ranke, "A Dialogue on Politics," *Theory and Practice of History*, 119, cf. 129.

45 *Ibid.*, 118.

46 "On the Relation of History and Philosophy," *ibid.*, 31–32.

47 "A Dialogue on Politics," *ibid.*, 117.

48 "On the Character of Historical Science," *ibid.*, 41.

49 "On Progress in History," *ibid.*, 53.

50 "On the Character of Historical Studies," *ibid.*, 46.

51 Cf. Charles E. McClelland, *The German Historians and England. A Study in Nineteenth-Century Views* (Cambridge, 1971).

52 "On the Character of Historical Science," *Theory and Practice of History*, 43; cf. "On Progress in History," *ibid.*, 56.

53 Cf. Georg G. Iggers, *The German Conception of History* (Middletown, Conn., 1968), ch. V on the "Prussian School."

54 *Historik, Vorlesungen über Enzyklopädie und Methodologie der Geschichte*, ed. Rudolf Hübner (Munich, 1937); cf. *Outlines of the Principles of History* (Boston, 1893). On Droysen's concept of historical knowledge, see also J. Rüsen, *Begriffene Geschichte, Genesis und Begründung der Geschichtstheorie J. G. Droysens* (Paderborn, 1969) and J. G. Droysen, *Texte zur Geschichtstheorie*, ed. G. Birtsch and J. Rüsen (Göttingen, 1972).

55 Cf. Jurgen Herbst, *The German Historical School in American Scholarship*, (Ithaca, N.Y., 1965), on the U.S.; on France, see Martin Siegel, "Science and the Historical Imagination: Patterns in French Historiographical Thought, 1866–1914," Ph.D. dissertation, Columbia University, 1965; also Allan Mitchell, "German History in France after 1870," *Journal of Contemporary History*, vol. 2, no. 3 (1967), 81–100, and William Keylor, *Academy and Community: The Foundation of the French Historical Profession* (Cambridge, Mass., 1975).

56 (Leipzig, 1889).

57 (Paris, 1898).

58 Cf. The statement by Prof. Ephraim Emerton of Harvard, who had called Ranke the founder of the "doctrine of the true Historical

method": "If one must choose between a school of history whose main characteristic is spirit, and one which rests upon the greatest attainable number of facts, we cannot long hesitate . . . Training has taken the place of brilliancy and the whole world is today reaping the benefit." ("The Practice Method in Higher Historical Instruction" in *Methods of Teaching History* [Boston, 1883], 42.) For similar statements by H. B. Adams and George Adams, see Georg G. Iggers, "The Image of Ranke in American and German Historical Thought," *History and Theory* 2 (1962), 17–40.

59 See William Keylor, *Academy and Community*.

60 Cf. Henri Berr and Lucien Febvre, "History" in *Encyclopedia of the Social Sciences*, VII (New York, 1932), 357–368.

61 For an examination of this discussion, see Iggers, *German Conception of History*, chs. VI and VII.

62 Cf. Otto Hintze, "Über individualistische und kollektivistische Geschichtsauffassung," *Historische Zeitschrift* 78 (1897), 60–67.

63 Cf. *Historische und Politische Aufsätze* (Leipzig, 1886), III, 71.

64 Cf. Iggers, *German Conception of History*, chs. IV and VII.

65 Cf. Ernst Troeltsch, "Über die Masstäbe zur Beurteilung historischer Dinge" in *Historische Zeitschrift* 116 (1916), 1–47.

66 Cf. Reill, "History and Hermeneutics," 26.

67 Carl Hempel, "Function of General Laws in History," *Journal of Philosophy* 39 (1942), 45: see also Maurice Mandelbaum, "Historical Explanation: The Problem of 'Covering Laws'," *History and Theory* 1 (1960), 229–242; and Alan Donagan, "Historical Explanation: The Popper-Hempel Theory Reconsidered," *ibid.* 4 (1964), 3–26.

68 Cf. Joseph Paul Lacombe, *De l'Histoire considérée comme science* (Paris, 1894).

69 Cf. Karl Lamprecht, *Alte und neue Richtungen in der Geschichtswissenschaft* (Berlin, 1896), 71.

70 Karl Popper, *The Open and the Closed Society*, 453.

71 Adeline Daumard and François Furet, "Méthodes de l'histoire sociale. Les Archives Notariales et la mécanographie," *Annales* 14e année (1959), 676.

72 Mannheim, *Ideology and Utopia*, 24.

73 Cf. *Economic Backwardness in Historical Perspective* (Cambridge, Mass., 1962).

74 (Baltimore, 1964).

75 As important models for this historiography, see Erik Eriksen's *Young Man Luther; a Study in Psychoanalysis and History* (New

York, 1962) and *Gandhi's Truth; on the Origins of Militant Non-Violence* (New York, 1969); cf. R. G. L. Waite, "Adolf Hitler's Guilt Feelings: A Problem in History and Psychology," *Journal of Interdisciplinary History* I (1971), 229–250; Rudolf Binion, "Hitler's Concept of *Lebensraum*," *History of Childhood Quarterly* I (1973), 187–215; for an attempt at a socially based psychoanalytical interpretation of the popularity of Nazism, see Peter Loewenberg, "The Psychohistorical Origins of the Nazi Youth Cohort," *American Historical Review* 76 (1971), 1457–1502.

76 See e.g., *Studien über Autorität und Familie* (Paris, 1936) published by the Institut für Sozialforschung under the direction of Max Horkheimer.

77 Cf. Dieter Groh, *Geschichtswissenschaft in emanzipatorischer Absicht* (Stuttgart, 1973); Alfred Schmidt, *Geschichte und Struktur, Fragen einer marxistischen Historik* (Munich, 1971).

78 Cf. Isaiah Berlin, "History and Theory: The Concept of Scientific History," *History and Theory* I (1960), 1–31.

79 Mannheim, *Ideology and Utopia*, 45, 50–51.

80 Cf. Paul Veyne, "L'Histoire conceptualisante" in *Faire l'histoire*, ed. Jacques Le Goff et Pierre Nova (Paris, 1974), I, 62–84.

81 "Preface to the First German Edition," *Capital*, ed. Friedrich Engels, vol. I (New York: International Publishers, 1967), 8, cf. "Notwendigkeit eines Naturprozesses," *Das Kapital* (Berlin: Ullstein, 1969), 705; the English translation speaks of "the inexorability of a law of nature," *Capital*, I, 763.

82 *Philosophisches Wörterbuch*, ed. Georg Klaus and Manfred Buhr (Leipzig, 1965), 219, 221–222.

83 *Capital*, I, 177.

84 In *Writings of the Young Marx on Philosophy and Society*, ed. Loyd D. Easton and Kurt H. Guddat (Garden City, N.Y., 1967), 402.

85 For a critique of a historicist interpretation of Marxism from a Marxist perspective, see Louis Althusser and Étienne Balibar, *Lire le Capital*, 2 vols. (Paris, 1970) and the critique of Althusser's "structuralism" by Marxists of different orientation including "Pierre Vilar, histoire en construction," *Annales* 28e année (1973), 165–198; English as "Marxist History, a History in the Making: Towards a Dialogue with Althusser," *New Left Review* 77 (1973), 64–106; as well as the works by Groh and Schmidt cited above.

86 E. J. Hobsbawm, "Karl Marx's Contribution to Historiography"

in *Ideology in Social Science,* ed. Robin Blackburn (New York, 1973), 274.

CHAPTER II

1 Carl Hempel, "Function of General Laws in History," 45.
2 Henry Thomas Buckle, "General Introduction" to the *History of Civilization in England,* quoted from Fritz Stern, *The Varieties of History* (Cleveland, 1956), 124.
3 Ranke, "On the Character of Historical Science," 38.
4 *Ibid.,* 36.
5 Cf. Dieter Groh, "Strukturgeschichte als 'totale' Geschichte," *Vierteljahrschrift für Sozial- und Wirtschaftsgeschichte* 58 (1971), 289–322.
6 "On Progress in History," 53.
7 Cf. R. W. Fogel, *Railroads and American Economic Growth,* 246; Jean Marczewski, *Introduction à l'histoire quantitative* (Geneva, 1965).
8 Marc Bloch, *Apologie pour l'histoire ou métier d'historien,* Cahiers des Annales, 3, 6th ed. (Paris, 1967), xii [English translation: *The Historian's Craft* (New York, 1953), 10]. Hans-Dieter Mann, *Lucien Febvre. La Pensée vivante d'un historien,* Cahier des Annales, 31 (Paris, 1971).
9 Theodore Zeldin, "Higher Education in France, 1848–1940," *Journal of Contemporary History,* vol. 2, no. 3 (1967), 60.
10 On the French universities with references to the literature, see Zeldin's article, *ibid.,* 53–80 and particularly Terry Nichols Clark, *Prophets and Patrons, The French Universities and the Emergence of the Social Sciences* (Cambridge, Mass., 1973); Paul Gerbod, *La Condition universitaire en France au 19e siècle* (Paris, 1965) deals primarily with the socio-professional position of secondary teachers.
11 Unpublished manuscript.
12 (Paris, 1898).
13 (Paris, 1901).
14 William Keylor, *Academy and Community: The Foundation of the French Historical Profession* (Cambridge, Mass., 1975).
15 See T. N. Clark's discussion of academic recruitment in French universities cited fn. 10. Clark stresses that individual members were less important in determining academic appointments than certain small informal "clusters" of professors of similar orientation and interests.

16 Cf. Émile Durkheim, *Les Règles de la méthode sociologique* (Paris, 1895) [English translation: *The Rules of Sociological Method* (New York, 1938)].

17 *Historian's Craft*, 50–55.

18 *Ibid.*, 147.

19 Cf. *Ibid.*, 89, also 55.

20 Cf. François Simiand, "Méthode historique et science sociale, étude critique à propos des ouvrages récents de M. Lacombe et de M. Seignobos," *Revue de synthèse historique* 6 (1903), 1–22, 129–157.

21 Introduction to *Revue de synthèse historique* (1900); see also *La Synthèse en histoire*, nouvelle édition (Paris, 1953), 29. On Berr see also Martin Siegel, "Henri Berr's *Revue de Synthèse Historique*," *History and Theory* 9 (1970), 322–334. See also Martin Siegel, "Science and the Historical Imagination in French Historiographical Thought, 1866–1914," an unfortunately still unpublished Ph.D. dissertation (Columbia University, 1965), the best existing study of the crisis of "scientific" history in France.

22 *Ibid.*, 29.

23 *Ibid.*, 227.

24 *Revue de synthèse historique* 1 (1900).

25 *La Synthèse*, 19.

26 *Ibid.*, 253.

27 *Ibid.*, xii.

28 *Histoire de France depuis les origines jusqu'à la Revolution* (Paris, 1900–1911), 9 vols.; *Historie générale du 4e siècle à nos jours*, ed. Ernest Lavisse and Alfred Rambaud (Paris, 1893–1901), 12 vols.; *Histoire de France contemporaine de la Revolution jusqu'à la paix de 1919*, ed. Ernest Lavisse (Paris, 1920–22), 10 vols.

29 *La Terre et l'évolution humaine, introduction géographique à l'histoire* (Paris, 1922) [English translation: *A Geographical Introduction to History* (New York, 1950)].

30 *Geographical Introduction*, 57.

31 *Philippe II et la Franche Comté* (Paris, 1912); Paris, 1970 edition cited here.

32 *Ibid.*, 7–11.

33 *Un Destin, Martin Luther* (Paris, 1928) [English translation: *Martin Luther. A Destiny* (New York, 1929)]. *Le Probleme de l'incroyance au XVIe siècle, la religion de Rabelais*, here cited: Paris, 1968 edition.

34 *Le Problème de l'incroyance*, 29.

35 *Ibid.*, 419.

36 *Ibid.*, 328ff.

37 *Les Rois thaumaturges. Étude sur le caractère surnaturel attribué à la puissance royale particulièrement en France et en Angleterre* (Paris, 1924) [English translation: *The Royal Touch: Sacred Monarchy and Faith Healing* (Montreal, 1972)].

38 *Les Caractères originaux de l'histoire rurale français* (Oslo, 1931) [English translation: *French Rural History* (Berkeley, 1966)].

39 *La Société féodale* (Paris, 1939–1940) [English translation: *Feudal Society* (Chicago, 1964), 2 vols.].

40 See fn. 8 above.

41 *L'Étrange Défaite* (Paris, 1957) [English translation: *The Strange Defeat* (New York, 1957)].

42 "A nos Lecteurs," *Annales d'histoire économique et sociale* 1 (1929), 1–2.

43 *Ibid.* 3 (1931), 556.

44 *La Méditerranée et le monde méditerranéen à l'époque de Philippe II* (Paris, 1949); 2nd rev. ed. (Paris, 1966) [English translation: *The Mediterranean and the Mediterranean World in the Age of Philip II*, 2 vols. (New York, 1972–1974)].

45 See also Braudel's essay, "Histoire et sciences sociales. La Longue durée," *Annales* 13e année (1958), 725–753, also in Braudel, *Écrits sur l'histoire* (Paris, 1969), 41–83.

46 Cf. *La Méditerranée*, 1st ed., 303; 2nd ed., I, 206.

47 *Ibid.*, 2nd ed., II, 218.

48 *Ibid.*, 2nd. ed. II, 223.

49 *Ibid.*, 2nd ed., II, 520.

50 See e.g., the series "Vie matérielle et comportements biologiques" begun in the *Annales* in 1961.

51 Cf. François Furet, "Quantitative History," *Daedalus*, vol. 100, no. 1 (Winter, 1971), 151–167. Also "Histoire quantitative et fait historique" *Annales* 26e année (1971), 63–75; Pierre Vilar, "Pour une meilleure compréhension entre économistes et historiens: Histoire quantitative et économetrie retrospective," *Revue historique* 233 (1965), S. 293–342; also Pierre Chaunu, "L'histoire sérielle. Bilan et perspectives," *Revue historique* 243 (1970), 297–320.

52 The role of non-written sources is discussed by Emmanuel Le Roy Ladurie in his essay on the methodology of climatic history, "Histoire et climat," *Annales* 14e année (1959), 3–34; see also his *Histoire du climate depuis l'an mil* (Paris, 1967) or the English translation

entitled *Times of Feast, Times of Famine* (Garden City, 1971); see the extensive section devoted to "histoire non écrite" in *Annales* 28e année (1973), 3–164.

53 Earl Hamilton. *American Treasure and the Price Revolution in Spain, 1501–1650* (Cambridge, Mass. 1934).

54 François Simiand, *Le Salaire, l'évolution sociale et la monnaie* (Paris, 1932).

55 *Esquisse des mouvement des prix et des revenus en France du XVIIIe siècle, Paris 1933; La crise de l'économie française à la fin de l'Ancien Régime et au début de la Revolution,* Tome I (Paris, 1944).

56 *Séville et l'Atlantique (1550–1650)* (Paris, 1959).

57 "François Simiand — ou: Des conditions faites à la recherche en 1936," *Annales* 8e année (1936), 42.

58 "Le Mouvement, des prix et les origines de la Revolution française," *Études sur la Revolution française,* 2nd ed., (Paris 1963), 216 [English translation: "The Movement of Prices and the Origins of the French Revolution" in *New Perspectives on the French Revolution,* ed. Jeffrey Kaplow (New York, 1965), 103–135].

59 See the special issue, "Historical Population Studies," *Daedalus,* vol. 97, no. 2 (Spring 1968); see also Richard T. Vann, "Historical Demography," *History and Theory, Beiheft* 9 (1969), 64–78.

60 Cf. Louis Henry, "Historical Demography," *Daedalus,* vol. 97, no. 2 (Spring 1968), 385–396.

61 *Agrarkrisen und Agrarkonjunkturen in Mitteleuropa vom 13. bis zum 19. Jahrhundert* (Berlin, 1935), 2nd rev. ed. (Hamburg, 1966).

62 *Beauvais et le Beauvaisis de 1600 à 1730, contribution à l'histoire sociale de la France du XVIIe siècle* (Paris, 1960).

63 *Les Paysans du Languedoc,* 2 vols. (Paris, 1966) [English translation: *The Peasants of Languedoc* (Urbana, Ill., 1974)].

64 Cf. Goubert, *Beauvais et le Beauvaisis,* 15; Le Roy Ladurie, *Les Paysans du Languedoc,* I, 11.

65 Cf. Goubert, *Beauvais et le Beauvaisis,* 25ff.

66 Cf. Braudel, *Civilisation matérielle et capitalisme. XVe–XVIIIe siècle,* Tome I (Paris, 1967) or the English translation entitled *Capitalism and Material Life, 1400–1800* (New York, 1973).

67 *Annales* 18e année (1963), 767–778.

68 René Baehrel, *Une Croissance: La Basse-Provence rurale (fin XVIe siècle–1789)* (Paris, 1961).

69 Cf. Goubert, *Beauvais et le Beauvaisis,* 59–67; Le Roy Ladurie,

"Malthus viendra trop tard," *Les Paysans du Languedoc*, I, 652ff.

70 *La Catalogne dans l'Espagne moderne. Recherches sur les fondements économiques des structures nationales*, 3 vols. (Paris, 1962).

71 Cf. Dieter Groh, "Strukturgeschichte als totale Geschichte," *Vierteljahrschrift für Sozial- und Wirtschaftsgeschichte* 58 (1971), 289–322.

72 "Méthode de l'histoire sociale. Les Archives notariales et la mécanographie," *Annales* 14e année (1959), 676.

73 Ariès, *L'Enfant et la vie familiale sous l'Ancien Régime* (Paris, 1960) [English translation: *Centuries of Childhood: A Social History of Family Life* (New York, 1962)].

74 *Folie et déraison, histoire de la folie à l'âge classique* (Paris, 1961) [English translation: *Madness and Civilization; A History of Insanity in the Age of Reason* (New York, 1965)].

75 *Introduction à la France moderne (1500–1640). Essai de psychologie historique* (Paris, 1961).

76 *Magistrats et sorciers en France du XVIIe siècle* (Paris, 1968).

77 *Les Fuggers, propriétaires fonciers en Souabes, 1500–1618. Étude de comportements socio-économiques à la fin du XVIe siècle* (Paris, 1969).

78 G. Bollème, H. Ehrard, F. Furet, *et al., Livre et société dans la France du 18e siècle*, 2 vols. (Paris and The Hague, 1965–1970).

79 Cf. the section, "Mythes" in the special number, "Histoire et structure," *Annales* 26e année (1971), 533–622, including Jacques Le Goff and Emmanuel Le Roy Ladurie, "Mélusine maternelle et défricheuse," *ibid.*, 587–622.

80 E.g. Albert Soboul, *Les Sans-culottes* (Paris, 1958); George Rudé, *The Crowd in History, 1730–1848* (New York, 1968); E. P. Thompson, *The Making of the English Working Class* (New York, 1963).

81 Cf. Robert Coles, "Shrinking History," *New York Review of Books*, February 22 and March 8, 1973.

82 Interesting is Raymond Aron's very critical review in the *Annales* 26e année (1971), 1319–54, of Paul Veyne's attempt in his book, *Comment on écrit l'histoire* (Paris, 1971) to break with his *Annales* mentors and return to a radically individualizing, narrative *Verstehen* approach.

83 "Avant Propos" in *Journal of World History* 1 (1962), 6–9.

84 I. S. Kon, *Die Geschichtsphilosophie des 20. Jahrhunderts* (Berlin, G.D.R., 1964), II, 223.

85 See Jacques Le Goff, "Is Politics Still the Backbone of History?,"

Daedalus, vol. 100, no. 1 (Winter, 1971), 1–19. See the critical examination of classical *Annales* approaches to political events and the attempt to find an alternative in B. Barret-Kriegel, "Histoire et politique ou l'histoire, science des effets," *Annales* 28e année (1973), 1437–62.

86 Cf. Marc Ferro, *La Grande Guerre 1914–1918* (Paris, 1969) and *The Russian Revolution of February 1917* (Englewood Cliffs, N.J., 1972); Georges Haupt, *Socialism and the Great War. The Collapse of the Second International* (Oxford, 1972); F. Furet and D. Richet, *La Revolution française*, 2 vols. (Paris, 1965–66).

87 Roland Mousnier, "Problèmes de méthode dans l'étude des structures sociales des 16e, 17e et 18e siècles" in *Spiegel der Geschichte, Festgabe für Max Braubach*, ed. Konrad Repgen and Stephan Skalweit (Münster, 1964), 550–564.

88 *Classes et luttes de classes en France au début du XVIIe siècle* (Messina, 1965).

89 "Le Catéchisme de la Revolution française," *Annales* 26e année (1971), 255–289.

90 Cf. *ibid.*, 286.

91 "Pour ou contre une politologie scientifique," *Annales* 18e année (1963), 119–132, 475–499.

92 "Malthusianisme démographiques et malthusianisme économique," *Annales* 27e année (1972), 1–19.

93 Cf. Le Roy Ladurie, *Les Paysans du Languedoc*, I, 11.

94 Tome I (Paris, 1967).

95 I, 14.

96 Cf. Maurice Lévy-Leboyer, "La 'New Economic History'," *Annales* 24e année (1969), 1035–69.

97 Jean Bouvier, *Le Credit Lyonnais de 1863 à 1882* (Paris, 1961).

98 *Les Bourgeois conquérants* (Paris, 1957) [English translation: *The Triumph of the Middle Classes* (Garden City, N.Y., 1968)].

99 *La Bourgeoisie parisienne de 1815 à 1848* (Paris, 1963).

100 *Classes laboureuses et classes dangéreuses à Paris pendant le première moitié du XIXe siècle* (Paris, 1958).

101 *La Grande Guerre 1914–1918.*

102 Groh, "Strukturgeschichte," 318; cf. Emmanuel Le Roy Ladurie, "L'Histoire immobile," *Annales* 29e année (1974), 673–692.

103 Cf. Pierre Chaunu, "L'Histoire sérielle."

104 Cf. Emmanuel Le Roy Ladurie and Paul Dumont, "Quantitative and Cartographical Exploration of French Military Archives, 1819–1826," *Daedalus*, vol. 100, no. 2 (Spring, 1971), 397–441.

105 Cf. Clark, *Prophets and Patrons*, ch. II.

106 "Les Annales vues de Moscou," *Annales* 18e année (1963), 103.

107 Cf. Pierre Vilar, "Marxisme et histoire dans le developpement des sciences humaines. Pour un débat méthodologique," *Studi storici* 1 (1960), 1008–48 and "Histoire marxiste, histoire en construction. Essai de dialogue avec Althusser," *Annales* 28e année (1973), 165–198, or the English translation in *New Left Review* (July-August, 1973), 64–106.

108 Furet, "Le Catéchisme de la Revolution française," 279.

109 Cf. Maurice Aymard, "The *Annales* and French Historiography (1929–1971)," *Journal of European Economic History* 1 (1972), 508.

110 Andre Burguière, "Présentation," iv.

111 Cf. Burguière's warning: "Peut-on mesurer l'histoire du monde à l'aune d'une experience particulière, de cet emballement accidentel ou du moins récent que represente la revolution industrielle?" (*ibid.*) with Wehler's disinterest, at least in regard to economic history, with the period "between the neolithic age and the Industrial Revolution," see *Geschichte als historische Sozialwissenschaft* (Frankfurt, 1973), 46.

112 J. H. Hexter, "Fernand Braudel and the *Monde Braudellien*," *Journal of Modern History* 44 (1972), 553.

113 See the section "Histoire non écrite," *Annales* 28e année (1973), 3–164.

114 Gerhard Ritter repeatedly took issue with the *Annales*; see his report at the International Historical Congress in Rome, "Leistungen, Probleme und Aufgaben der internationalen Geschichtsschreibung zur neueren Geschichte (16., 17. und 18. Jahrhundert)," *Relazioni del X. Congresso Internazionale degli Scienze Storiche* (Florence, 1955), VI, 169–330; more recent discussions: Karl Erich Born, "Neue Wege der Wirtschafts — und Sozialgeschichte in Frankreich: Die Historikergruppe der Annales," *Saeculum* 15 (1964), 298–307; Manfred Wüstemeyer, "Die 'Annales' Grundsätze und Methoden ihrer 'neuen Geschichtswissenschaft'," *Vierteljahrschrift für Sozial- und Wirtschaftsgeschichte* 54 (1967), 1–45 and the above cited article by Dieter Groh, "Strukturgeschichte als 'totale' Geschichte." A selection of essays from the *Annales* is being prepared by K. F. Werner. See also Volker Rittner, "Ein Versuch systematischer Aneignung von Geschichte, die 'Schule der Annales'" in *Ansichten einer zukünftigen Geschichte*, ed. I. Geiss and R. Tamchina (Munich, 1974), I, 153–172.

115 E.g., Fernand Braudel, *The Mediterranean and the Mediterra-*

nean World (cited n. 44) and *Capitalism and Material Life* (New York, 1974); Emmanuel Le Roy Ladurie, *The Peasants of Languedoc* (cited n. 63); Lucien Febvre, *A New Kind of History*, ed. Peter Burke (New York, 1973); *Economy and Society in Early Modern Europe, Essays from "Annales,"* ed. Peter Burke (New York, 1972); *Social Historians in Contemporary France: Essays from Annales*, ed. Marc Ferro (New York, 1972); see also the issue of *The Journal of Modern History*, vol. 44, no. 4 (December, 1972), dedicated in part to Braudel.

116 A significant collection of articles containing important restatements of *Annales* positions is contained in the three-volume *Faire l'histoire*, ed. Jacques Le Goff and Pierre Nora (Paris, 1974), which appeared as this volume was ready to go to press. Emmanuel Le Roy Ladurie, *Le Territoire de l'histoire* (Paris, 1973) came to my attention too late.

CHAPTER III

1 Jörn Rüsen, "Johann Gustav Droysen" in *Deutsche Historiker*, ed. H.-U. Wehler, 5 vols. (Göttingen, 1971–72), II, 7–23; Helmut Seier, "Heinrich von Sybel," *ibid.*, II, 24–38; Georg G. Iggers, "Heinrich von Treitschke," *ibid.*, II, 66–80; also Andreas Dorpalen, *Heinrich von Treitschke* (New Haven, 1957); Hans Schleier, *Sybel und Treitschke* (Berlin, G.D.R., 1956).

2 On Gothein and the tradition of Kulturgeschichte, see Gerhard Oestreich, "Die Fachhistorie und die Anfänge der sozialgeschichtlichen Forschung in Deutschland," *Historische Zeitschrift* 208 (1969), 320–363; see also the journal *Zeitschrift für Kulturgeschichte* going back into the 1850s. In general a sharp distinction was maintained between political and cultural history.

3 On Schmoller, see Pauline R. Anderson, "Gustav von Schmoller," *Deutsche Historiker*, II, 39–65.

4 See above, pp. 28–29.

5 On the Neo-Rankeans, see Ludwig Dehio, "Ranke and German Imperialism" in his *Germany and World Politics in the Twentieth Century* (New York, 1967), 38–71; also Hans-Heinz Krill, *Die Rankerennaissance* (Berlin, 1962).

6 For a discussion of the institutional and social framework of German scholarship, see Fritz Ringer, *The Decline of the German Mandarins: The German Academic Community 1890–1933* (Cambridge, Mass., 1969).

7 Cf. the "Biographical Appendix" in Charles E. McClelland, *The German Historians and England. A Study in Nineteenth-Century Views* (Cambridge, 1971), 239–256.

8 See the articles on Treitschke by Georg G. Iggers, on Schmoller by Pauline Anderson, and on Theodor Mommsen by Albert Wucher in *Deutsche Historiker*; also Andreas Dorpalen, *Heinrich von Treitschke*; Alfred Heuss, *Theodor Mommsen und das 19. Jahrhundert* (Kiel, 1956); H. Schachenmayer, *Arthur Rosenberg als Vertreter des Historischen Materialismus* (Wiesbaden, 1964). On the situation in the universities, including the *Lex Aron*, see Ringer, *Decline of the German Mandarins*.

9 On Valentin, Breysig, Rosenberg, Kehr, and Mayer, see again *Deutsche Historiker*.

10 On Meinecke's politics, see Robert A. Pois, *Friedrich Meinecke and German Politics in the 20th Century* (Berkeley, 1972) and Imanuel Geiss, "Kritischer Rückblick auf Friedrich Meinecke" in his *Studien über Geschichte und Geschichstwissenschaft* (Frankfurt, 1972), 89–107.

11 On the politics of the historians in the Weimar Republic, see the forthcoming extensive study by Hans Schleier.

12 See Hans Schleier, "Johannes Ziekursch," *Jahrbuch für Geschichte* 3 (1969), 137–196; also Karl-Georg Faber on Ziekursch in *Deutsche Historiker*, III, 109–123.

13 See F. H. Schulert, "Franz Schnabel und die Geschichtswissenschaft des 20. Jahrhunderts," *Historische Zeitschrift* 205 (1967), 323–357.

14 See William H. Maehl, "Erich Eyck, 1878–1952" in *Some 20th Century Historians*, ed. S. William Halperin (Chicago, 1961), 227–253; Erich Eyck, *Bismarck: Leben und Werk*, 3 vols. (Zurich, 1941–44) [abridged English edition: *Bismarck and the German Empire* (London, 1950)].

15 Cf. Helmut Heiber, *Walter Frank und sein Reichsinstitut für Geschichte des Neuen Deutschland* (Stuttgart, 1966) and Karl Ferdinand Werner, *Das NS-Geschichtsbild und die deutsche Geschichtswissenschaft* (Stuttgart, 1967); also Werner "Die deutsche Historiographie unter Hitler" in *Geschichtswissenschaft in Deutschland*, ed. Bernd Faulenbach (Munich, 1974).

16 See Iggers, "Die deutschen Historiker in der Emigration" in *Geschichtswissenschaft in Deutschland*, 97–111.

17 See above, n. 14.

18 (New York, 1964).

19 (Berkeley, 1963).

20 (Cambridge, Mass., 1954).

21 (Berlin, G.D.R., 1954).

22 *A History of Modern Germany*, 3 vols. (New York, 1959–1969).

23 *Der Irrweg einer Nation* (Berlin, 1946).

24 *Die Auflösung der Weimarer Republik* (Villingen, 1955); also *Die deutsche Diktatur* (Cologne, 1969) [English translation: *The German Dictatorship* (New York, 1971)].

25 Cf. Otto Brunner, *Land und Herrschaft* (Brno, 1939).

26 See the volumes in the series *Industrielle Welt* published by the "Arbeitskreis für moderne Sozialgeschichte."

27 *The Crisis of German Ideology*, 8.

28 Cf. Meinecke, *Die deutsche Katastrophe* (Wiesbaden, 1946); G. Ritter, *Carl Goerdeler und die deutsche Widerstandsbewegung* (Stuttgart, 1955), 92; H. Rothfels, *Die deutsche Opposition gegen Hitler* (Frankfurt, 1960).

29 Cf. Ritter, *Carl Goerdeler* and H. Rothfels, *Die deutsche Opposition* (above, n. 18).

30 Cf. "Das Problem des Militarismus in Deutschland" in *Historische Zeitschrift* 177 (1954), 21–48; see also *Staatskunst und Kriegshandwerk*, I (Munich, 1954).

31 (Düsseldorf, 1961) [shortened English version: *German War Aims in the First World War* (New York, 1967)].

32 Luigi Albertini, *Le Origini della guerra della 1914*, 3 vols. (Milan, 1942).

33 Imanuel Geiss, *Studien über Geschichte und Geschichtswissenschaft* (Frankfurt, 1972), 127; see also John A. Moses, "The War Aims of Imperial Germany: Professor Fritz Fischer and His Critics," *University of Queensland Papers, Departments of Government and History*, vol. 1, no. 4 (1968), 213–260; Konrad H. Jarausch, "World Power or Tragic Fate," *Central European History* 5 (1972), 72–92.

34 Cf. Dehio, *Gleichgewicht oder Hegemonie* (Krefeld, 1948) [English translation: *The Precarious Balance. Four Centuries of European Power Struggle* (New York, 1962)]; also *Deutschland und die Weltpolitik im 20. Jahrhundert* (Munich, 1955) [English translation: *Germany and World Politics in the 20th Century* (New York, 1960)].

35 E.g., *Julikrise und Kriegsausbruch 1914*, ed. Imanuel Geiss (Hanover, 1963–64.

36 Imanuel Geiss, *Der polnische Grenzstreifen 1914–1918, Ein Beitrag zur deutschen Kriegszielpolitik im Ersten Weltkrieg* (Hamburg, 1960).

37 *Gesellschaft und Demokratie in Deutschland* (Munich, 1965) [English translation: *Society and Democracy in Germany* (New York, 1967)].

38 *Hitler's Social Revolution* (Garden City, N.Y., 1966).

39 E.g., Max Horkheimer, Theodor Adorno, Ossip Flechtheim, Ernst Fränkel, Helmuth Plessner, *et al.*

40 On the Frankfurt School, see Martin Jay, *The Dialectical Imagination. A History of the Frankfurt School and the Institute of Social Research, 1923–1950* (Boston, 1973).

41 Cf. Max Horkheimer, "Traditionelle und kritische Theorie" in *Zeitschrift für Sozialforschung* 3 (1934) [English translation in *Critical Theory* (New York, 1972)].

42 *Bismarck und der Imperialismus* (Cologne, 1969), 14.

43 (Cologne, 1966).

44 (Cambridge, Mass. 1958).

45 *Schlachtflottenbau und Parteipolitik 1894–1901. Versuch eines Querschnitts durch die innenpolitischen, sozialen und ideologischen Voraussetzungen des deutschen Imperialismus* (Berlin, 1930).

46 Eckart Kehr, *Der Primat der Innenpolitik*, ed. H.-U. Wehler (Berlin, 1965).

47 H.-J. Puhle, *Agrarische Interessenpolitik und preussischer Konservatismus im Wilhelminischen Reich 1893–1916* (Hanover, 1966); also "Von der Agrarkrise zum Präfaschismus," Institut für europäische Geschichte Mainz. *Vorträge.* Nr. 54 (Wiesbaden, 1972).

48 Hans Jaeger, *Unternehmer in der deutschen Politik 1890–1918* (Bonn, 1967).

49 Hartmut Kaelble, *Industrielle Interessenpolitik in der Wilhelminischen Gesellschaft, Der Centralverband Deutscher Industrieller 1895–1914* (Berlin, 1967).

50 Heinrich-August Winkler, *Der rückversicherte Mittelstand, Die Interessenverbände von Handwerk und Kleinhandel im deutschen Kaiserreich* in *Zur sozialen Theorie und Analyse des 19: Jahrhunderts*, ed. Walter Ruegg and Otto Neuloh (Göttingen, 1971).

51 Volker Berghahn, *Der Tirpitz-Plan* (Düsseldorf, 1971). See also his *Germany and the Approach of War in 1914* (New York, 1973).

52 Peter Christian Witt, *Die Finanzpolitik des Deutschen Reiches von 1903 bis 1913: Eine Studie zur Innenpolitik des Wilhelminischen Deutschlands* (Lübeck, 1970).

53 Dirk Stegmann, *Die Erben Bismarcks: Parteien und Verbände in der Spätphase des Wilhelminischen Deutschlands: Sammlungspolitik 1897–1918* (Cologne, 1970). Also important: the collection of essays edited by Michael Stürmer, *Das kaiserliche Deutschland, Politik und Gesellschaft 1870–1918* (Düsseldorf, 1970); Fritz Fischer, *Krieg der Illusionen. Die Deutsche Politik von 1911 bis 1914* (Düsseldorf, 1969); Hans-Ulrich Wehler, *Krisenherde des Kaiserreichs 1871–1918* (Göttingen, 1970); Dieter Groh, *Negative Integration und revolutionärer Attentismus. Die deutsche Sozialdemokratie am Vorabend des Ersten Weltkrieges (1909–1914)* (Berlin, 1972). *Deutschland in der Weltpolitik des 19. und 20. Jahrhunderts. Festschrift für Fritz Fischer*, ed. Imanuel Geiss and Bernd Jürgen Wendt (Düsseldorf, 1973) appeared too late to be considered.

54 *Vorkriegs-Imperialismus: Die soziologischen Grundlagen der Aussenpolitik der europäischen Grossmächte vor dem ersten Weltkrieg*, 2 vols. (Munich, 1951); a first version had been published in Paris in 1935.

55 Cf. Helmut Böhme, *Prolegomena zu einer Sozial- und Wirtschaftsgeschichte Deutschlands im 19. und 20. Jahrhundert* (Frankfurt, 1968), 82ff.

56 Kehr, *Schlachtflottenbau*, 7. For critical examinations of the adequacy of the concept "Sammlungspolitik," see Puhle, "Von der Agrarkrise zum Präfaschismus" and Wolfgang J. Mommsen, "Domestic Factors in German Foreign Policy before 1914," *Central European History* 6 (1973), 3–43.

57 E.g., E. Böhm, *Überseehandel und Flottenbau, Hanseatische Kaufmannschaft und deutsche Seerüstung von 1879–1902* (Düsseldorf, 1972); see also the study by a historian in the G.D.R., Helga Nussbaum, *Unternehmer gegen Monopole* (Berlin, G.D.R., 1967).

58 Cf. H.-J. Puhle, *Agrarische Interessenpolitik*, 11.

59 Cf. Reinhart Koselleck, *Preussen zwischen Reform und Revolution*, 17.

60 Cf. Otto Hintze, "Wesen und Wandlung des modernen Staates" in Preussische Akademie der Wissenschaften, Philosophisch- Historische Klasse, *Sitzungsberichte*, 1931, 790. On Hintze see J. Kocka in *Deutsche Historiker*; Dietrich Gerhard, "Otto Hintze: His Work and His Significance in Historiography," *Central European History* 3 (1970), 17–48; Walter Simon, "Power and Responsibility: Otto Hintze's Place in German Historiography" in *The Responsibility of Power*, ed. Leonard Krieger and Fritz Stern (New York, 1968),

199–219. In the process of publication, Oxford University Press, *The Historical Essays of Otto Hintze*, ed. and with an Introduction by Felix Gilbert.

61 Cf. Rickert, *Kulturwissenschaft und Naturwissenschaft*, 4th and 5th ed. (Tübingen, 1921), 33–36, 21–23.

62 Max Weber, "Die 'Objektivität' sozialwissenschaftlicher und sozialpolitischer Erkenntnis" in *Gesammelte Aufsätze zur Wissenschaftslehre*, 2nd ed. (Tübingen, 1951), 180; cf. *Max Weber on the Methodology of the Social Sciences* (Glencoe, Ill., 1949), 80.

63 "Der Sinn der 'Wertfreiheit' der soziologischen und ökonomischen Wissenschaften," *Gesammelte Aufsätze zur Wissenschaftslehre*, 3rd ed., 489–540 [English translation: "The Meaning of 'Ethical Neutrality' in Sociology and Economics" in *Max Weber on the Methodology*, 1–47]. "Über einige Kategorien der verstehenden Soziologie, *ibid.*, 432.

64 "Capitalism and Rural Society in Germany" in *From Max Weber, Essays in Sociology*, ed. Hans Gerth and C. Wright Mills (New York, 1946), 371.

65 See *Historical Essays*, above, n. 60.

66 "Zur Genesis der preussischen Bürokratie und des Rechtsstaats. Ein Beitrag zum Diktaturproblem" in *Der Primat der Innenpolitik*, 31–52.

67 *Bureaucracy, Aristocracy and Autocracy.*

68 "mit innerster Notwendigkeit": "Zur Genesis," 43.

69 "der ökonomisch unaufhaltsamen Entwicklung der kapitalistischen Wirtschaft": *ibid.*

70 *Schlachtflottenbau,* 447–448.

71 *Ibid.,* 7.

72 *Ibid.,* 263–264.

73 *Ibid.,* 7.

74 *Grosse Depression und Bismarckzeit* (Berlin, 1967).

75 *Ibid.,* 19.

76 Cf. the "Postscript" to *Bureaucracy, Aristocracy and Autocracy,* 231–232.

77 *Bismarck und der Imperialismus,* 19.

78 Cf. *ibid.,* 444.

79 *Ibid.,* 412.

80 Cf. Rosenberg, *Grosse Depression,* 264.

81 *Ibid.,*viii.

82 See Reinhard Spree, "Zur Kritik moderner bürgerlichen Krisen-

geschichtsschreibung," *Das Argument* 75 (1972), 77–103; see also Hans Schleier, "Der traditionelle Historismus und die Struktur-geschichte," *ibid.*, 56–76.

83 Reinhard Spree, "Zur Kritik," 91–92.

84 H.-U. Wehler, "Theorienprobleme der deutschen Wirtschafts-geschichte (1800–1945)" in *Entstehung und Wandel der modernen Gesellschaft. Festschrift für Hans Rosenberg zum 65, Geburtstag*, ed. G. A. Ritter (Berlin, 1970), 79.

85 Reinhard Spree, "Zur Kritik," 90.

86 *Ibid.*

87 "Einleitung" in H.-U. Wehler, *Krisenherde des Kaiserreichs 1871–1918* (Göttingen, 1970), 9.

88 "Probleme der modernen deutschen Wirtschaftsgeschichte," *ibid.*, 297; cf. *Bismarck und der Imperialismus*, 497.

89 These include *Probleme der Geschichtswissenschaft*, ed. Geza Alföldy, Ferdinand Seibt, Albrecht Timm (Düsseldorf, 1973); *Geschichte und Sozialwissenschaften*, ed. Peter Böhning (Göttingen, 1972); *Theorie der Geschichtswissenschaft und Praxis des Geschichtsunterrichts*, ed. Werner Conze (Stuttgart, 1972); K.-G. Faber, *Theorie der Geschichtswissenschaft*, 3rd ed. with new "Nach-wort" (Munich, 1974); Dieter Groh, *Kritische Geschichtswissen-schaft in emanzipatorischer Absicht* (Stuttgart, 1973); H.-W. Hed-inger, *Subjektivität und Geschichtswissenschaft. Grundzüge einer Historik* (Berlin, 1969); *Geschichte-Ereignis und Erzählung*, ed. Richard Koselleck and Wolf-Dieter Stempel (Munich, 1973); Rein-hart Koselleck, "Wozu noch Historie?", *Historische Zeitschrift* 212 (1971), 1–18; *Soziologie und Sozialgeschichte*, ed. Peter Chris-tian Ludz (Cologne, 1973); Friedrich Engel-Janosi, Grete Klin-genstein, Heinrich Lutz, *Denken über Geschichte* (Munich, 1974); Wolfgang Mommsen, *Geschichtswissenschaft jenseits des Histo-rismus* (Düsseldorf, 1971) and "Die Geschichtswissenschaft in der modernen Industriegesellschaft," *Vierteljahrshefte für Zeitge-schichte* 22 (1974), 1–17; Joachim Radkau and Orlinde Radkau, *Praxis der Geschichtswissenschaft* (Düsseldorf, 1972); *Ansichten einer künftigen Geschichtswissenschaft*, ed. I. Geiss and R. Tam-china, vols. 1 and 2 (Munich, 1974); Winfried Schulze, *Soziologie und Geschichtswissenschaft* (Munich, 1974). On critical discussions of German historical science, see Georg G. Iggers, *The German Conception of History* (Middletown, Conn., 1968) [German trans-lation: *Deutsche Geschichtswissenschaft*, 2nd ed. (Munich, 1972)];

H.-U. Wehler, *Deutsche Historiker* (cited n. 1); Imanuel Geiss, *Studien über Geschichte und Geschichtswissenschaft* (cited n. 33); *Geschichtswissenschaft in Deutschland*, ed. B. Faulenbach (Munich, 1974); from a "Left" perspective, "Kritik der bürgerlichen Geschichtswissenschaft," special issues Nos. 70 and 75 of *Das Argument*, 1972.

90 See, e.g., the joint statement of the Association of Historians of Germany and the Association of History Teachers of Germany in *Geschichte in Wissenschaft und Unterricht* 23 (1972), 1–13.

91 Faber, *Theorie der Geschichtswissenschaft* (see above n. 89).

92 Groh, *Kritische Geschichtswissenschaft* (see above, n. 89).

93 Geiss and Tamchina, *Ansichten* (see above, n. 89).

94 Cf. the volumes edited by Wehler, *Moderne deutsche Sozialgeschichte* (Cologne, 1966); *Geschichte und Psychoanalyse* (Cologne, 1971); *Geschichte und Soziologie* (Cologne, 1972); *Geschichte und Ökonomie* (Cologne, 1973); and his important collection of three theoretical essays, *Geschichte als Historische Sozialwissenschaft* (Frankfurt, 1973).

95 Wehler, *Geschichte als Historische Sozialwissenschaft*, 65.

96 *Ibid.*, 69.

97 *Ibid.*, 52.

98 *Ibid.*, 67–69.

99 *Ibid.*, 19.

100 *Ibid.*, 31.

101 *Ibid.*, 32.

102 *Kritische Studien zur Geschichtswissenschaft*, ed. Helmut Berding, Jürgen Kocka, Hans-Christoph Schröder, Hans-Ulrich Wehler.

103 James J. Sheehan, "Quantification in the Study of Modern German Social and Political History" in *The Dimensions of the Past*, ed. Val R. Lorwin and Jacob M. Price (New Haven, 1972), 301.

104 *Deutsche Agrargeschichte*, ed. Günther Franz, 5 vols. (Frankfurt, 1967–70).

105 "Innerbetrieblicher und sozialer Status der frühen Fabrikarbeiterschaft" in *Die soziale Frage. Neuere Studien zur Lage der Fabrikarbeiter in den Frühphasen der Industrialisierung*, ed. Wolfram Fischer and Georg Bajor (Stuttgart, 1967), 215–252.

106 See "Introduction," *ibid.*, 8.

107 Cf. Otto Büsch, *Industrialisierung und Gewerbe im Raum Berlin Brandenburg 1800–1850. Eine empirische Untersuching zur gewerb-*

lichen Wirtschaft einer hauptstadtgebundenen Wirtschaftsregion in frühindustrieller Zeit (Berlin, 1971).

108 Wolfgang Köllman, *Bevölkerung und Raum in neuerer und neuester Geschichte* (Würzburg, 1965); co-editor, *Bevölkerungsgeschichte* (Cologne, 1972).

109 Büsch, *Industrialisierung* (see above, n. 107), xi.

110 Cf. G. Ritter, "Leistungen, Probleme und Aufgaben der internationalen Geschichtsschreibung zur neueren Geschichte" in *Relazioni del X Congresso Internazionale degli Scienze Storiche,* vol. VI (Florence, 1955); D. Groh, "Strukturgeschichte als 'totale' Geschichte" in *Vierteljahrschrift für Sozial- und Wirtschaftsgeschichte* 58, (1971), 289–322: cf. Volker Rittner, "Ein Versuch systematischer Aneignung von Geschichte: Die 'Schule der Annales' " in I. Geiss and R. Tamchina, *Ansichten* (see above, n. 89), I, 153–172.

111 Theodor W. Adorno, *et al., Der Postitivismusstreit in der deutschen Soziologie* (Neuwied, 1969).

112 *Agrarkrisen und Agrarkonjunkturen in Mitteleuropa vom 13. bis zum 19. Jahrhundert* (Berlin, 1935); 2nd rev. ed. (Hamburg, 1966).

113 Cf. *Massenarmut und Hungerkrisen im vorindustriellen Europa. Versuch einer Synopsis* (Hamburg, 1974).

114 Cf. *Zur Sozialgeschichte deutscher Mittel- und Unterschichten* (Göttingen, 1973), "Kritische Studien zur Geschichtswissenschaft," vol. IV.

115 Walter Grab, *Norddeutsche Jakobiner* (Frankfurt, 1967); *Die revolutionären Demokraten. Eine Dokumentation,* ed. Walter Grab, 6 vols. (Stuttgart, 1971–).

116 *Preussen zwischen Reform und Revolution. Allgemeines Landrecht, Verwaltung und soziale Bewegung von 1791 bis 1848* (Stuttgart, 1967).

117 *Unternehmensverwaltung und Angestelltenschaft am Beispiel Siemens 1847–1914. Zum Verhältnis von Kapitalismus und Bürokratie in der deutschen Industrialisierung* (Stuttgart, 1969).

118 *Preussen zwischen Reform und Revolution,* 13.

119 *Ibid.,* 17.

120 Cf. *Geschichtliche Grundbegriffe. Historisches Lexikon zur politischen Sprache in Deutschland,* ed. Otto Brunner, Werner Conze, Reinhart Koselleck, 5 vols. (Stuttgart, 1973–), see especially Koselleck's introduction to vol. I and his "Begriffsgeschichte und

Sozialgeschichte" in *Soziologie und Sozialgeschichte*, ed. Peter Chr. Ludz (Opladen, 1972), 116–131.

121 *Unternehmensverwaltung und Angestelltenschaft am Beispiel Siemens 1847–1914. Zum Verhältnis von Kapitalismus und Bürokratie in der deutschen Industrialisierung* (Stuttgart, 1969).

122 See "Arbeitsbericht" of March 29, 1974 by P. Kriedte, H. Medick, and J. Schlumbohm; cf. also issues on research on industrialization, "Berichte und Kritik zu Der Prozess der kapitalistischen Industrialisierung" in *Sozialwissenschaftliche Information für Unterricht und Studium* 3 (1974), Heft 1 and 2.

123 Jürgen Kocka, *Klassengesellschaft und Krieg 1914–1918* (Göttingen, 1973), "Kritische Studien zur Geschichtswissenschaft," vol. VIII.

124 *Ibid.*, 1.

125 *Ibid.*, 138.

126 *Ibid.*, 136.

CHAPTER IV

1 Georg Lukács and Karl Korsch are undoubtedly right in stressing Marx's critical attitude toward the methods of the empirical natural sciences yet in my opinion go further than Marx intended when they categorically identify their methods with the "reification of all human relations" (Lukács) or speak of a "specifically bourgeois method of scientific research" (Korsch). See, Georg Lukács, *Geschichte und Klassenbewusstsein* (Neuwied, 1968), 64–71 [English translation: *History and Class Consciousness* (Cambridge, Mass., 1971), 5–10]; Karl Korsch, *Die materialistische Geschichtsauffassung und andere Schriften* (Frankfurt, 1971), 132.

2 Karl Marx, *Capital. A Critique of Political Economy*, Vol. I (New York, 1967), 10.

3 *Ibid.*, 316; Karl Marx, *Das Kapital*, Ullstein ed., I (Frankfurt, 1969), 279–280; cf. Roman Rosdolfsky, "Einige Bemerkungen über die Methode des Marxschen 'Kapital' und ihre Bedeutung für die heutige Marxforschung" in *Kritik der politischen Ökonomie. 100 Jahre Kapital*, ed. Walter Euchner and Alfred Schmidt (Frankfurt, 1968), 15–16.

4 Karl Marx and Friedrich Engels, "The German Ideology" in *Writings of the Young Marx on Philosophy and Society*, ed. Loyd Easton and Kurt H. Guddat (Garden City, N.Y., 1967), 441–442.

5 "Einleitung zur Kritik der Politischen Ökonomie" in Marx-Engels

Werke, vol. 13 (Berlin, G.D.R., 1971), 631–632 [English translation: *A Contribution to the Critique of Political Economy* (Chicago, n.d.), 292–293].

6 *Capital*, I, 372, n. 3.

7 "The Eighteenth Brumaire of Louis Bonaparte" in *The Marx-Engels Reader*, ed. Robert C. Tucker (New York, 1972), 437.

8 *Capital*, I, 10.

9 *Ibid.*, I, 18; cf. Marx's discussion of laws of population, *ibid.*, I, 632.

10 *Ibid.*, III, 232.

11 *Ibid.*, I, 20.

12 *Ibid.*, I, 19.

13 Preface to "A Contribution to the Critique of Political Economy" in Karl Marx and Frederick Engels, *Selected Works* (New York, 1968), 182.

14 *Capital*, I, 592.

15 *Ibid.*, I, 177.

16 "Economic and Philosophic Manuscripts" in *Writings of the Young Marx*, 293, 295.

17 *Capital*, I, 83; Marx's use of "nature" and "natural" in a normative sense are interesting: see *ibid.*, 169; see also the use of the term "irrational," *ibid.*, 552.

18 *Ibid.*, I, 80.

19 *Ibid.*, I, 81.

20 *Ibid.*, I, 73.

21 *Ibid.*, I, 310.

22 *Ibid.*, I, 539.

23 *Ibid.*, I, 645.

24 *Ibid.*, I, 488.

25 *Ibid.*, I, 763.

26 *Ibid.*; Marx speaks here of the "negation of negation"; cf. "Economic and Philosophic Manuscripts" in *Writings of the Young Marx*, 333.

27 *Capital*, I, 19.

28 "German Ideology," *Writings of the Young Marx*, 409.

29 See his explanation to N. K. Michailovski in a letter, end of 1877, in Karl Marx and Frederick Engels, *Selected Correspondence, 1846–1895* (New York, 1942), 352–355.

30 *Capital*, I, 625.

31 Letter to Michailovski, *Selected Correspondence*, 354.

32 *Capital*, I, 256–257.

33 *Ibid.*, I, 600.

34 Ibid., I, 299: cf. "Wages, Prices and Profit" in *Selected Works*, 224–229.

35 The theory of stages by which mankind developed was discussed in various places by Marx and Engels briefly and in very broad outlines, e.g., in the "German Ideology," the "Communist Manifesto," very succinctly in the Preface to a "Contribution to the Critique of Political Economy," most extensively in the brief section of the *Grundrisse* translated by Eric Hobsbawm as *Pre-Capitalist Economic Foundations* (New York, 1965), by Engels in "Socialism: Utopian and Scientific," "The Origins of Family, Private Property and the State," and elsewhere. A development of history by "stages" is implicit in much of Marx's and Engels' writings but the succession of states, e.g., the role of Asiatic, Slavonic, or Germanic modes of production, is conceived in varying form. Eric Hobsbawm is undoubtedy right that Marx nowhere sought to formulate a "general law" of historical development (*Pre-Capitalist Formation*, 43.) and that "the general theory of historical materialism requires only that there should be a succession of modes of production, though not necessarily any particular modes, and perhaps not in any particular predetermined order" (*ibid.*, 19–20).

36 Friedrich Engels, "The Peasant War in Germany" in *The German Revolutions*, ed. Leonard Krieger (Chicago, 1967), 7.

37 *Capital*, I, 9.

38 "The Eighteenth Brumaire," 459, 460.

39 Cf. *ibid.*, 445, 479.

40 "Germany: Revolution and Counter-Revolution" in *The German Revolutions*, 239.

41 Cf. Marx to Weydemeyer, March 5, 1852 in *Selected Correspondence*, 57.

42 For a concise survey of the organization of historical research in the German Democratic Republic, see *Einführung in das Studium der Geschichte*, ed. Walther Eckerman and Hubert Mohr (Berlin, G.D.R., 1966), 8–16; on the role of Party resolutions for historical studies, see 92–96; on the USSR, see Nancy Whittier Heer, *Politics and History in the Soviet Union* (Cambridge, Mass., 1971), 11–58.

43 For a discussion of the organization of the historical profession in Poland and on historiography in Poland since 1945, see *La Pologne au XIIIe Congrès International des Sciences Historiques à Moscou*, 2 vols. (Warsaw, 1970), particularly the essay by Jerzy Topolski,

"Développement des études historiques en Pologne 1945–1968," I, 7–76; also Jerzy Topolski, "Le Développement des recherches d'histoire économique en Pologne," *Studia Historiae Oeconomicae* I (1966), 3–42.

44 *Politics and History in the Soviet Union*, 58.

45 For an English discussion of the controversy, see J. M. H. Salmon, "Venality of Office and Popular Sedition in 17th-Century France. A Review of a Controversy," *Past and Present* 37 (1967), 21–43; a French translation of Boris Porchnev, *Les Soulèvements populaires en France de 1623 à 1648* (Paris, 1963) was published in the series "Oeuvres Etrangères" of the VIe Section.

46 *Einführung in das Studium der Geschichte*, 31; cf. Bollhagen's more extensive statement in *Soziologie und Geschichte* (Berlin, G.D.R., 1966). On law and causality in history, see Georg Klaus and Hans Schulze, *Sinn, Gesetz und Fortschritt in der Geschichte* (Berlin, G.D.R., 1967) and Gottfried Stiehler, *Geschichte und Verantwortung* (Berlin, G.D.R., 1972).

47 Heinrich Scheel *et al.*, "Forschungen zur deutschen Geschichte 1789–1848," *Historische Forschungen in der DDR 1960–1970*, Sonderband, *Zeitschrift für Geschichtswissenschaft* 18 (1970), 381.

48 Bollhagen, *Einführung*, 44–46; cf. *Soziologie und Geschichte*, 28–69.

49 Hans Schleier, "Der traditionelle Historismus und die Strukturgeschichte," *Das Argument* 75 (1972), 68.

50 Cf. Bollhagen and G. Brendler, *Einführung*, 81; for an application of the theory of periodization on a large scale, see the world history edited by I. M. Zhukov, *V semirnaia Istoria*, 10 vols. (Moscow, 1955–65).

51 *Pre-Capitalist Formations*, 43. See also Eric Hobsbawm, "Karl Marx's Contribution to Historiography" in *Ideology in Social Science*, ed. Robin Blackburn (New York, 1973), 265–283.

52 Institut für Marxismus-Leninismus beim Zentralkomitee der SED, *Geschichte der deutschen Arbeiterbewegung* (Berlin, G.D.R., 1966), I, 7; cf. Herbert Langer *et al.* in *Historische Forschungen*, 353.

53 (Berlin, G.D.R., 1959–69).

54 *Geschichte der deutschen Arbeiterbewegung*.

55 Cf. "Vorwort," *ibid.*, I, 1*–40*.

56 *Die Geschichte der Lage der Arbeiter unter dem Kapitalismus*, 38 vols. (Berlin, G.D.R., 1961–72).

57 *Historische Forschungen in der DDR 1960–1970.*
58 Cf. Hans Mottek, *Wirtschaftsgeschichte Deutschlands. Ein Grundriss*, 2 vols. (Berlin, G.D.R., 1957–64); also Mottek, *et al.*, *Studien zur Geschichte der industriellen Revolution* (Berlin, G.D.R., 1960).
59 Cf., e.g., Karl Obermann, "Die Arbeitermigrationen in Deutschland im Prozess der Industrialisierung und der Entstehung der Arbeiterklasse in der Zeit von der Gründung bis zur Auflösung des Deutschen Bundes (1815 bis 1867)," *Jahrbuch für Wirtschaftsgeschichte* (1972), Teil 1, 135–182, also "Zur Klassenstruktur und zur sozialen Lage der Bevölkerung in Preussen 1846–1849," *ibid.* (1973), Teil II, 79–120 and Teil III, 143–174.
60 Cf. H. Hanisch, "Über die Bedeutung der Bevölkerungsgeschichte als Teil der Wirtschafts- und Sozialgeschichte: Bemerkungen zu Karlheinz Blaschke, Bevölkerungsgeschichte in Sachsen bis zur industriellen Revolution," *ibid.* (1973), Teil IV, 205–220.
61 For a historiographical survey of historical research in the German Democratic Republic organized by topics, see the special volume of the *Zeitschrift für Geschichtswissenschaft*, Sonderband 18 (1970), *Historische Forschungen in der DDR 1960–1970*, and a similar volume published in 1960 for the preceding period.
62 Cf. Fritz Klein, W. Gutsche, *et al.*, *Deutschland im 1. Weltkrieg*, 3 vols. (Berlin, G.D.R., 1968).
63 Cf. Witold Kula, *Théorie économique du Système féodal, pour un modèle de l'économie polonaise 16e–18e siècles*, préface de Fernand Braudel (Paris and The Hague, 1970), 5.
64 *Ibid.*, 8–9.
65 Cf. *ibid.*, 2.
66 Jerzy Topolski, "The Model Method in Economic History," *The Journal of European Economic History* 1 (1972), 715; cf. Jerzy Topolski, "Zalozenia metodologiczne 'Kapitalu' Marksa," *Studia Filozoficzne* 54–55, no. 3–4 (1968), 3–33, with French résumé.
67 Topolski, "The Model Method," 714; for a word of caution from a Marxist perspective in regard to modern growth theory, see Claude Mazauric, *Sur la Revolution française. Contribution à l'histoire de la Revolution bourgeoise* (Paris, 1970), 13–14.
68 Witold Kula, "Histoire et économie: La longue durée," *Annales* 15e année (1960), 295.
69 Cf. Pierre Vilar, "Histoire Marxiste, histoire en construction. Essai de dialogue avec Althusser," *Annales* 28e année (1973), 165–198

[English translation: "Marxist History, a History in the Making: Towards a Dialogue with Althusser," *New Left Review* 80 (July–August, 1973), 64–106].

70 "The Model Method," 722–724; Topolski also includes Weber's ideal types in his critique of the instrumentalist approach.

71 "Histoire et économie," 312.

72 Kula, *Théorie économique du système féodal*, xi; cf. definition of "feudal" by Toulouse Colloquium, 1968, cited in Mazauric, *Sur la Revolution française*, 134.

73 *Théorie économique du système féodal*.

74 "Model gospodarczy Wielkopolski w XVIII wieku," *Studia i Materialy do Dziejow Wielkopolski i Polorza* 20 (1971), 57–71.

75 *Narodziny kapitalizmy w Europie XIV–XVII wieku* (Warsaw, 1965), French résumé.

76 E.g., *Studia nad folwarkiem szlacheckim w Polsce w latach 1500–1580* (Studies of the Gentry Farm in Poland in the Years 1500–1580) (Warsaw, 1960); "L'Économie du domaine nobiliaire moyen, 1500–1580," *Annales* 18e année (1963), 81–87; "Tentative Estimate of Polish Rye Trade in the Sixteenth Century," *Acta Polaniae Historica* 4 (1961), 119–131; "Là Campagne polonaise dans le cadre des transformation du marché des XVIe–XVIIe siècles. L'Économie de la Starostie de Korczyn," *Studiae Historiae Oeconomicae* 2 (1967), 57–81; "The Agricultural Production and Its Amount in XVIth Century Poland," *Studiae Historiae Oeconomicae* 4 (1969), 3–11; "Die Reallöhne und die Unterhaltskosten in Polen Ende des XVI. und erste Hälfte des XVII. Jh.," *Studiae Historiae Oeconomicae* 5 (1970), 117–128, "L'Alphabétisation en Pologne au XVIe siècle," *Annales* 29e année (1974), 705–713. See also the broadly conceived comparative essay on economic, social, and cultural conditions in sixteenth-century Europe, in his *Polska w Europie XVI stulecia* (Warsaw, 1973).

77 Witold Kula, *Miary i Ludzie* (Measures and Men) (Warsaw, 1970).

78 Henryk Łowmiański, *Począti Polski* (Warsaw, 1964–).

79 Polska Akademia Nauk, Institytut Historii, *Historia Polski* (Warsaw, 1960–).

80 David Caute, *Communism and the French Intellectuals 1914–1960* (New York, 1964), 276.

81 Cf. *ibid.*, 278; also *La Pensée*, November, 1953, 122.

82 Among important discussions Antoine Pelletier and Jean-Jacques

Goblot's critical discussion of the *Annales* in the *Pensée* should be mentioned, reprinted as *Matérialisme historique et histoire des civilisations* (Paris, 1969). Also of import is the colloquium sponsored by the Centre d'Études et de Recherches Marxistes, resulting in *Sur le Féodalisme* (Paris, 1971).

83 Cf. Vilar, "Marxist History: History in the Making," 66.

84 *Ibid.*, 76.

85 On Labrousse see Pierre Renouvin, "Ernest Labrousse" in *Historians of Modern Europe*, ed. Hans A. Schmitt (Baton Rouge, La., 1971), 235–254.

86 "1848-1830-1789-Comment naissent les revolutions?" in *Actes du Congrès historique du centenaire de la Revolution de 1848* (Paris, 1948), 1–21.

87 Cf. Roland Mousnier, "Problèmes de méthode dans l'étude des structures sociales des 16e, 17e et 18e siècles," in *Spiegel der Geschichte. Festgabe für Max Braubach*, ed. Konrad Repgen and Stephan Skalweit (Münster, 1964), 550–564; I. S. Kon, *Die Geschichtsphilosophie des 20. Jahrhunderts* (Berlin, GDR, 1964), II, 194–195.

88 *Histoire socialiste de la revolution française*, Édition revue par A. Mathiez, 8 vols. (Paris, 1922).

89 On Lefebvre see the memorial volume, Société des études robespierristes, *Hommage à Georges Lefebvre (1874–1959)* (Nancy, n.d.), including the article by Albert Soboul: "Georges Lefebvre, historien de la Revolution française, 1874–1959," 1–20; R. R. Palmer, "Georges Lefebvre: Peasants and the French Revolution," *Journal of Modern History* 31 (1959), 329–342; Beatrice F. Hyslop, "Georges Lefebvre, Historian," *French Historical Studies* 1 (1958–60), 265–282; Gordon H. McNeil, "Georges Lefebvre (1874– 1959)" in *Essays in Modern European Historiography*, ed. S. William Halperin, (Chicago, 1970), 160–174.

90 "La Revolution française et les paysans" in *Études sur la Revolution française*, 2nd ed. (Paris, 1963), 360.

91 Quoted in A. Soboul, *Paysans, Sans-culottes et Jacobins* (Paris, n. d.), 6.

92 *Les Paysans du Nord pendant la Revolution française* (Lille, 1924), self-published in a small edition; widely unavailable until republished by Albert Soboul in 1959.

93 This thesis is well developed in "La Revolution française et les paysans," 338–368; see also *Quatre-vingt-neuf* (Paris, 1939) [English

translation: *The Coming of the French Revolution* (Princeton, 1947)].

94 "Foules revolutionnaires" in *Études sur la Revolution française*, 374.

95 *La Grande Peur de 1789* (Paris, 1932) [English translation: *The Great Fear of 1789. Rural Panic in Revolutionary France*, introd. by George Rudé (New York, 1973)].

96 *Les Sans-culottes Parisiens en l'An II* (Paris, 1958); abridged edition (Paris, 1968) [English translation: *The Sans-Culottes* (New York, 1972)].

97 Cf. Alfred Cobban, *The Myth of the French Revolution* (London, 1955) and *The Social Interpretation of the French Revolution* (Cambridge, 1964); Elizabeth L. Eisenstein, "Who Intervened in 1788? A Commentary on *The Coming of the French Revolution*," *American Historical Review* 71 (1965) 77–103; Jeffrey Kaplow, Gilbert Shapiro, Elizabeth L. Eisenstein, "Class in the French Revolution: A Discussion," *ibid.* 72 (1966–67), 497–522; François Furet and Denis Richet, *La Revolution*, 2 vols. (Paris, 1965–66; Claude Mazauric's critique of Furet and Richet in *Sur la Revolution française. Contributions à l'histoire de la Revolution bourgeoise*, "avant-propos" by Albert Soboul, particularly 21–61; Furet's reply, "Le Catéchisme de la Revolution française," *Annales* 26e année (1971), 255–289.

98 *Les Sans-culottes* (1958 ed.) 3; *The Sans-Culottes*, xix–xx.

99 *Les Sans-culottes*, 1030–1031; *The Sans-Culottes*, 256–259.

100 Cf. *Les Sans-culottes*, 1025; cf. *The Sans-Culottes*, 251, 262.

101 *Les Sans-culottes*, 1031; *The Sans-Culottes*, 259. See the wording: "marche dialectique de l'histoire" in Georges Lefebvre, *La Revolution française* (Paris, 1951), 638, see also Lefebvre's general agreement with Soboul's conclusions in his review of *Les Sans-culottes* in *Annales historique de la Revolution française*, 1959, 173.

102 *La Lutte des classes sous la Première République, 1793–1797*, nouvelle ed. (Paris, 1968); see particularly the "Postface," II, 406–461 and Guérin's reply to his critics, including Soboul, II, 489–513.

103 *Paysans, Sans-culottes et Jacobins*, "Préface: A propos d'histoire sociale," 5–12; for a more extensive discussion of quantification and of Soboul's points of agreement with Braudel's conception of social structures, see Soboul, "Description et mesure en histoire sociale" in *L'Histoire sociale, sources et méthodes*, Colloques de l'École Normale Supérieure de Saint-Cloud (15–16 mai 1965), (Paris, 1967), 9–25.

104 Richard Cobb, *The Police and the People. French Popular Protest, 1789–1820* (Oxford, 1970).

105 (Oxford, 1959).

106 *Ibid.*, 5.

107 Charles Tilly, *The Vendée. A Sociological Analysis of the Counter-revolution of 1793* (New York, 1964).

108 Including George Rudé, *The Crowd in History, 1730–1848. A Study of Popular Disturbances in France and England 1730–1848* (New York, 1964).

109 See above, n. 97.

110 For a recent discussion of this tradition in relation to industrial leadership, see D. C. Coleman, "Gentlemen and Players," *Economic History Review* 26 (1973), 92–116.

111 In part, at least, this was reaction to some of the abandoned Whig generalizations or to over-simplified notions of a Marxist "scheme" of history.

112 In contrast to the traditional "men and manners" approach to social history.

113 Of whom Marx is the most notable.

114 James Phillip Kay, *The Moral and Physical Condition of the Working Classes employed in the Cotton Manufacture in Manchester* (London, 1832); P. Gaskell, *The Manufacturing Population of England* (London, 1833); John Fielden, *The Curse of the Factory System* (London, 1836); Edwin Chadwick, *Report on the Sanitary Conditions of the Labouring Population of Great Britain* (London, 1842).

115 W. E. H. Lecky, *History of England in the Eighteenth Century*, II (London, 1886).

116 Robert Owen, Engels, and Marx are the best known of such critics. Marx's own work, as discussed earlier in this chapter, was the ultimate product of the process described here. For discussion of the role and ideas of other critics, such as Thomas Hodgskin and James Morrison, *see* the final chapter of E. P. Thompson, *The Making of the English Working Class* (London, 1963; rev. ed. New York, 1968). Subsequent pagination refers to the 1968 edition. William Blake and some figures of the Romantic movement could also be regarded as playing a role in the development of this tradition.

117 Arnold Toynbee, *Lectures on the Industrial Revolution* (London, 1884), 93.

118 J. L. and B. Hammond, *The Village Labourer* (1911), *The Town Labourer* (London, 1917), *The Skilled Labourer* (London, 1919),

The Rise of Modern Industry (London, 1925), *The Age of the Chartists* (London, 1930); S. and B. Webb, *History of Trade Unionism* (London, 1894); G. D. H. Cole, *The Common People, 1746–1938* (with Raymond Postgate) (London, 1938); *A Short History of the British Working Class Movement, 1789–1925,* 3 vols. (London, 1925–27); *Chartist Portraits* (London, 1941).

119 There are still British universities where History and Economic History departments are not only separate but are units of different faculties or schools.

120 It is not without significance that one of the first attempts to present a more systematic analysis of industrialization as an economic process was made by a French scholar and was not translated into English until the late 1920s. Paul Mantoux, *The Industrial Revolution in the Eighteenth Century* (London, 1928).

121 John H. Clapham, *An Economic History of Modern Britain,* 3 vols. (Cambridge, 1926–28).

122 T. S. Ashton, *The Industrial Revolution* (Oxford, 1948), *An Economic History of England: The Eighteenth Century* (London, 1955), *Economic Fluctuations in England, 1700–1800* (Oxford, 1959).

123 For a few examples, see P. Mathias, *The Brewing Industry in England, 1700–1830* (London, 1959); A. H. John, *The Industrial Development of South Wales, 1750–1850* (Cardiff, 1950); W. H. B. Court, *The Rise of the Midland Industries, 1600–1838* (Oxford, 1938). Ashton himself had previously contributed with *Iron and Steel in the Industrial Revolution* (Manchester, 1924), and (with J. R. Sykes), *The English Coal Industry of the Eighteenth Century* (Manchester, 1929).

124 Any sense in which Tawney was initiating such a process must be qualified by recognition of Marx's own contribution.

125 While Tawney's work as an historian reflects the influence of Marx as well as Weber, he cannot be considered a Marxist for his response to capitalism was predominantly one of moral rejection. R. H. Tawney, *The Agrarian Problem in the 16th Century* (London, 1912), *Religion and the Rise of Capitalism* (London, 1926), "The Rise of the Gentry," *Economic History Review* 2 (1944), 1–38.

126 Christopher Hill, *The Century of Revolution, 1603–1714* (Edinburgh, 1961); *Reformation to Industrial Revolution* (London, 1967).

127 Hill, *Economic Problems of the Church* (Oxford, 1956).

128 Hill, *Society and Puritanism in Pre-Revolutionary England,* 2nd

ed. (London, 1964); *Intellectual Origins of the English Revolution* (Oxford, 1965); *God's Englishman; Oliver Cromwell and the English Revolution* (London, 1970); *The World Turned Upside Down; Radical Ideas during the English Revolution* (New York, 1972).

129 Hill, "The Norman Yoke" in *Democracy and The Labour Movement*, ed. J. Saville (London, 1954).

130 W. W. Rostow, *The Stages of Economic Growth: A Non-Communist Manifesto* (Cambridge, 1960). For earlier development of his theories, see "The Take-off into Self-Sustained Economic Growth," *Economic Journal* 66 (1956), 25–48.

131 A. Gerschenkron, *Economic Backwardness in Historical Perspective* (Cambridge, Mass., 1962); E. J. Hobsbawm, "From Social History to the History of Society" in *Historical Studies Today*, ed. Felix Gilbert and Stephen R. Graubard (New York, 1971), 5–7; A. Fishlow, "Empty Economic Stages," *Economic Journal* 85 (1965), 112–125.

132 *The Causes of the Industrial Revolution in England*, ed. R. M. Hartwell (London, 1967), 4, 9, 17.

133 E. J. Hobsbawm and R. M. Hartwell, "The Standard of Living in the Industrial Revolution: A Discussion," *Economic History Review* 16 (1963), 119–146.

134 These comments upon a structuralist position relate specifically to the context of British historiography and are not intended to encompass the *Annales* School.

135 Peter Laslett. *The World We Have Lost* (London, 1965), 26–70.

136 *Ibid.*, 151.

137 Hill, review of *The World We Have Lost*, *History and Theory* 7 (1967), 117–127.

138 *Times Literary Supplement* (May 5th, 1973), review of *Household and Family in Past Time* (Cambridge, 1972).

139 Historians of social structure, who assert the inadequacy of traditional political history in explanation of the past and claim that such history's one-time predominance was based on the accessibility of certain kinds of source material, may be unaware that they are themselves vulnerable to such criticism.

140 E. J. Hobsbawm, "Karl Marx's Contribution to Historiography" in *Ideology in Social Science*, ed. Robin Blackburn (New York, 1973), 265–283; E. P. Thompson, "An Open Letter to Leszek Kolakowski," *Socialist Register* (1974), 1–95.

141 Hobsbawm and Hartwell, *op cit.*

142 Thompson, *Working Class*, 231.

143 E. J. Hobsbawm, "The Crisis of the Seventeenth Century," *Past and Present* 5 (1954), 33–49 and 6 (1954), 44–63, reprinted with postscript, in *Crisis in Europe, 1563–1660*, ed. Trevor Aston (London, 1965), 5–58.

144 *Crisis*, ed. Aston, 5–6.

145 *Ibid.*, 57–58.

146 Hobsbawm, *Industry and Empire* (London, 1969), 49.

151 *Idem.*

152 *Idem.*

153 Thompson, "Time, Work-Discipline and Industrial Capitalism," *Past and Present* 38 (1967), 56–97.

154 Hobsbawm, *Primitive Rebels* (Glencoe, Ill., 1959).

155. *Ibid.*, 9.

156 Thompson, *Working Class*, 12.

157 *Idem.*

158 There also appears an obstacle based on attitudinal, merging into ideological refusal to accept the social groups which the new social history concentrates upon as the valid concern of professional study. See G. Kitson Clark, *The Making of Victorian England* (London, 1962), 166.

159 Thompson, *Working Class*, 10–11.

160 *Idem.*

161 For Thompson's own elaboration of this theme see his, *Open Letter*, 51–55.

162 Another example of the strength of Marxist influence in social history.

163 George Rudé, *The Crowd in History, 1730–1848* (London, 1964), 9.

164. *Ibid.*, 9–10.

165 Gareth Stedman-Jones, "History: The Poverty of Empiricism" in *Ideology in Social Science*, ed. Blackburn, 96–117.

166 Lawrence Stone, *The Crisis of the Aristocracy, 1558–1641* (Oxford, 1965); *Social Change and Revolution in England, 1540–1640*, editor (London, 1965); "Social Mobility in England, 1500–1700," *Past and Present* 33 (1966), 16–55. Asa Briggs, *Victorian Cities* (London, 1963). Harold Perkin, *Origins of Modern British Society, 1780–1880* (London, 1969). In his first lines, the author states his support of "the case for social history as a vertebrate discipline built around a central organizing theme, the history of society *qua* so-

ciety, of social structure in all its manifold and constantly changing ramifications."

167 Hobsbawm, "From Social History to the History of Society" in *Historical Studies Today*, 1–24.

Conclusion

1 Cf. Hayden White, *Metahistory*, 21, 12.

2 *Ibid.*, 4; cf. Claude Lévi-Strauss's discussion of the scientific character of history in *The Savage Mind* (New York, 1966), 257–262.

3 White, *Metahistory*, 2.

4 Cf. André Burguière, "Préface" to the special issue "Histoire et Structure," *Annales* 26e année (1971), iv; Emmanuel Le Roy Ladurie, "L'Histoire immobile," *ibid.* 29e année (1974), 673–692.

Bibliographical Note

THE FOLLOWING LIST is not intended as a complete or a comprehensive bibliography but rather as a guide for further readings.

There are no recent comprehensive histories of historiography. The most extensive and readable ones are Eduard Fueter, *Geschichte der neueren Historiographie,* 3rd ed. (Munich, 1936); George P. Gooch, *History and Historians in the Nineteenth Century* (London, 1914; reprinted Boston, 1959); James Westfall Thompson, *A History of Historical Writing,* 2 vols. (New York, 1942); and Harry Elmer Barnes, *A History of Historical Writing* (New York, 1937; reprinted 1962). Only Barnes and the encyclopedic Mathew A. Fitzsimons, *et al., The Development of Historiography* (Harrisburg, 1954) contain even brief treatments of twentieth-century historians. A helpful introduction to the development of historiography is the anthology of writings by major historians on history as a scholarly discipline edited by Fritz Stern, *The Varieties of History,* expanded edition (New York, 1973). Also useful is the volume by John Higham, Leonard Krieger, and Felix Gilbert, *History. The Development of Historical Studies in the United States* (Englewood Cliffs, N.J., 1965), which contains an extensive essay by Felix Gilbert on European historiography in the nineteenth and twentieth centuries. Interesting on the theoretical presupposition of historians in the first half of the twentieth century are the two volumes by the Soviet philosopher, I. S.

Kon, *Die Geschichtsphilosophie des 20. Jahrhunderts* (Berlin/ G.D.R., 1964). There are as yet few assessments of the status of historiography today. The most comprehensive is the collection of essays edited by Felix Gilbert and Stephen R. Graubard, *Historical Studies Today* (New York, 1971).

On the emergence of a sense of the past see Peter Burke, *The Renaissance Sense of the Past* (New York, 1970); on the beginnings of critical historical scholarship see George Huppert, *The Idea of Perfect History: Historical Erudition and Historical Philosophy in Renaissance France* (Urbana, Ill., 1970), and Donald R. Kelley, *Foundations of Modern Historical Scholarship: Language, Law, and History in the French Renaissance* (New York, 1970). On the eighteenth-century Enlightenment historians, particularly in Germany and Switzerland, see Peter Hanns Reill's study in press at the University of California Press; on the eighteenth-century forerunners of Ranke and nineteenth-century school of scientific historians, see Herbert Butterfield, *Man on His Past. The Study of the History Of Historical Scholarship* (London, 1955).

An important contribution to the sociology of knowledge of historical and other social scientific studies is Fritz Ringer, *The Decline of the German Mandarins. The German Academic Community, 1890–1933* (Cambridge, Mass., 1969); there is no study of comparable depth for other European countries. On the sociology of social scientific studies in France, see Terry Nichols Clark, *Prophets and Patrons: The French University and the Emergence of the Social Sciences* (Cambridge, Mass., 1973). A very factual account of the organization of historical studies in France, Great Britain, Western Germany, and the United States is contained in Boyd C. Shafer, *et al., Historical Study in West* (New York, 1968).

As for the development of historical studies on a national scale, three works may be mentioned for Germany: Georg G. Iggers, *The German Conception of History. The National Tradition of Historical Thought from Herder to the Present* (Middletown, Conn., 1968); the collection of historiographical biographies in *Deutsche Historiker,* ed. Hans-Ulrich Wehler,

5 vols. (Göttingen, 1971–72), which also treats various of the non-conformist historians not discussed by Iggers; and a small collection of essays edited by Bernd Faulenbach, *Geschichtswissenschaft in Deutschland* (Munich, 1974). Two slightly older studies, the first written from a conservative, idealistic perspective, the second from a Marxist-Leninist position are Heinrich von Srbik, *Geist und Geschichte vom deutschen Humanismus biz zur Gegenwart,* 2 vols. (Munich, 1950–51) and *Studien über die deutsche Geschichtswissenschaft,* ed. Joachim Streisand, 2 vols. (Berlin/G.D.R., 1963–65). A critical survey of nineteenth-century German historians is contained in Charles E. McClelland, *The German Historians and England. A Study in Nineteenth-Century Views* (Cambridge, 1971).

There are no recent comprehensive histories of French or British historiography in print. Useful for nineteenth-century France, but very brief, is Louis Halphen, *L'Histoire en France depuis cent ans* (Paris, 1914); on French historical studies since 1945, Jean Glénisson, "L'Historiographie française contemporaine: Tendances et réalisations" in *La Recherche historique en France de 1940 à 1965* issued by the Comité français des sciences historiques (Paris, 1965), pp. ix–lxiv. The two best studies of the development of French historical science of which I am aware are: Martin Siegel, "Science and the Historical Imagination in French Historiographical Thought, 1866–1914," a Columbia University Ph.D. dissertation, 1965; and William Keylor, *Academy and Community: The Foundation of the French Historical Profession* (Cambridge, Mass., 1975). Keylor emphasizes the social setting and the political function of French historiography, Siegel its theoretical presuppositions. On the *Annales,* see Maurice Aymard, "The *Annales* and French Historiography," *The Journal of European Economic History* 1 (1972), 491–511. On Bloch and Febvre in a historical context, see H. Stuart Hughes, *The Obstructed Path. French Social Thought in the Years of Desperation* (New York, 1966), ch. II.

To my best knowledge, no comparable study of historiography in Great Britain exists. For the nineteenth century, George P. Gooch, *History and Historians in the Nineteenth*

Century, mentioned above, remains useful. In the place of a history of historical writing, the anthology edited by J. R. Hale, *The Evolution of British Historiography from Bacon to Namier* (Cleveland, 1964) is particularly helpful. On recent British historiography, see *Changing Views of British History. Essays on Historical Writing Since 1939,* ed. E. C. Furber (Cambridge, Mass., 1966) and G. R. Elton, *Modern Historians on British History, 1485–1969. A Critical Bibliography 1945–1969* (London, 1970); more interpretative are the special issues of the *Times Literary Supplement,* "Historical Writing," January 6, 1956, and "New Ways in History," April 7, July 28, September 8, 1966.

No comprehensive study of Marxist historiography exists nor one of the historiography of the Eastern European socialist countries. Useful are the reports prepared for the International Congress of Historical Sciences meeting in 1970, such as the two volumes on Polish historical studies between 1945 and 1968, published by the Polish Academy of Sciences, The Committee on Historical Sciences and the Institute of History, *La Pologne au XIIIe Congrès International des Sciences Historiques à Moscou,* 2 vols. (Warsaw, 1970) and the extensive special issue of the *Zeitschrift für Geschichtswissenschaft* on historical studies in the G.D.R., *Historische Forschungen in der DDR, 1960–1970* (Berlin, 1970). For a discussion of the institutional and ideological background of Marxist studies in the social sciences and in history in France, see Pradeep Bandyopadhyay, "The Many Faces of French Marxism," *Science and Society* 36 (1972), 129–157.

There is a tremendous literature on the question whether and in what sense history is a science. Again the anthology by Fritz Stern, *The Varieties of History,* mentioned above, offers a useful survey of statements by historians. For a classical formulation of the problem, see Wilhelm von Humboldt, "On the Historian's Task," in Leopold von Ranke, *The Theory and Practice of History,* ed. Georg G. Iggers and Konrad von Moltke (Indianapolis, 1973), 3–23, also Ranke's own statements in the same volume. For an analysis of the German discussion

at the turn of the twentieth century on the question of histori-
cal knowledge see Maurice Mandelbaum, *The Problem of His-
torical Knowledge* (New York, 1938) and Carlo Antoni, *From
History to Sociology* (Detroit, 1960). Two standard guide
books to historical method at the end of the last century were
Ernst Bernheim, *Lehrbuch der historischen Methode,* 2nd ed.
(Leipzig, 1894) and C. V. Langlois and Charles Seignobos,
Introduction to the Study of History (London, 1898; reprinted
New York, 1966). In many ways a response to the latter is
found in Henri Berr, *La Synthèse en histoire,* nouvelle édition
(Paris, 1953), also Marc Bloch, *The Historian's Craft* (New
York, 1953), and Emmanuel Le Roy Ladurie, *Le Territoire
de l'historien* (Paris, 1973). See also H. S. Hughes, *History as
Art and As Science* (New York, 1964). Two important forums
for the current discussion of questions relating to the nature of
historical science are the journal, *History and Theory* (1960–   )
and the section "Débats et Combats" in the French journal *Annales: Économies, Sociétés, Civilisations.* A collection of significant essays from the early volumes of *History and Theory* is contained in *Philosophical Analysis and History,* ed. William H.
Dray (New York, 1966). A useful critical survey of both the
Anglo-American and the continental discussion is contained in
K.-G. Faber, *Theorie der Geschichtswissenschaft,* 3rd ed. (Munich, 1974). For a provocative argument against the concep-
tion of history as a science, see Hayden White, *Metahistory.
The Historical Imagination in Nineteenth-Century Europe*
(Baltimore, 1973). See also Peter Gay, *Style in History* (New
York, 1974).

Index